WOMAN'S MYSTERIES

The Hecaterion of Marienbad.

WOMAN'S
MYSTERIES

ANCIENT AND MODERN

A Psychological Interpretation
of the Feminine Principle as Portrayed
in Myth, Story, and Dreams

By M. ESTHER HARDING

Published by G. P. Putnam's Sons, New York,
for the C. G. Jung Foundation
for Analytical Psychology

Published on the same day in the Dominion of Canada
by Longmans Green Canada Limited, Toronto.
Printed in the United States of America.

Library of Congress Catalog Number 72-184527

SECOND PRINTING

Revised edition—1955—New York, Pantheon

First edition—1935—New York, Longmans Green

Library of Congress Catalog Number 72-184527

CONTENTS

LIST OF ILLUSTRATIONS

INTRODUCTION

by

Professor C. G. Jung

Esther Harding, the author of this book, is a physician and specialist in the treatment of psychogenic illness. She is a former pupil of mine and her endeavors have been concerned not only with the understanding of the modern psyche, but in addition, she has tried, as the present book shows, to explore its historical background. Preoccupation with historical subjects may at first glance seem to be merely a physician's personal hobby, but to the psychotherapist it is, in a certain sense, a necessary part of his mental equipment. Concern with the psychology of primitives, with folklore, mythology, and the comparative history of religions opens the eyes to the wide horizons of the human psyche and in addition it gives that indispensable aid we so urgently need for the understanding of unconscious processes. Only when we see in what shape and what guise dream symbols, which are apparently unique, appear on the historical and ethnic scene, can we really understand what they are pointing at. Also, once being equipped with this extensive comparative material, we can succeed in comprehending more nearly that factor which is so decisive for psychic life, namely the archetype. Of course this term is not meant to denote an inherited idea, but rather an inherited mode of psychic functioning, corresponding to that inborn *way* according to which the chick emerges from the egg; the bird builds its nest; a certain kind of wasp stings the motor ganglion of the caterpillar; and eels find their way to the Bermudas. In other words, it is a "pattern of behavior." This aspect of the archetype is the biological one—it is the concern of scientific psychology. But the picture changes at once when looked at from the inside, that is from within the realm of the subjective psyche. Here the archetype presents itself as numinous, that is, it appears as an experience of fundamental importance. Whenever it clothes itself with adequate symbols, which is not always the case, it takes hold of the individual in a startling way, creating a condition of "being deeply moved" the consequences of which may be immeasurable. It is for this reason that the archetype is so important for the psychology of religion. All religions and all metaphysical concepts rest upon archetypal foundations and, to the extent that we are able to explore them, we succeed in gaining at least a superficial glance behind the scenes of world history, and can lift a little the veil of mystery which hides the meaning of metaphysical ideas. For metaphysics is, as it were, a physics or physiology of the archetype, and its dogma (or teaching) formulates the knowledge of the essence of the dominants, that is, of the unconscious "leit-motives," of the psychic happenings predominating in that epoch. The archetype is metaphysical because it transcends consciousness.

Now, Dr. Harding's book represents an attempt to present certain archetypal foundations of feminine psychology. However, in order to understand the author's endeavor, one has to overcome the prejudice that psychology consists merely of what Mr. Smith and Mrs. Jones happen to know about it. The psyche consists not only of the contents of consciousness, which can be said to derive from sensory impressions, but also of ideas which seem to rest upon peculiarly altered sense perceptions—sense perceptions which are modified by a priori and unconscious pre-existing formative elements, i.e. by the archetypes. This insight leads us to the conclusion that one part of the psyche may be explained through recent causes, but that another part reaches back to the deepest layers of racial history.

If anything is certain concerning the nature of the neuroses, it is the fact that they are either based upon a primary disturbance of the instincts or at least affect the instincts to a considerable extent. The history of the evolution of human anatomy and of human instincts reaches back into geologic epochs. Our historical knowledge throws light upon but a few paces of this road, whose length may be counted in terms of hundreds of thousands of miles. However, even that little bit is of help when, as psychotherapists, we have to correct a state of disturbance of the instincts. In this connection it is the religions having myths of healing that teach us the most. They might indeed be considered as psychotherapeutic systems which support our understanding of instinctual disturbances, for these are evidently not just of recent date but have existed since the most ancient beginnings of time. Although certain types of illness, notably those of infectious character, as for instance *typhus antiquorum,* may disappear while others may rise anew, there is still little probability that tuberculosis, for instance, might have been an entirely different illness five or ten thousand years ago. The same is true of psychic processes. Therefore, in the descriptions of abnormal psychic states furnished by antiquity, we are able to recognize features and connections which are familiar to us; and when it comes to the phantasies underlying certain psychoses and neuroses, then it is we find the most illuminating parallels in ancient and classical literature.

It has been established for some time by experience that a certain one-sidedness of the conscious, in other words a disturbance of balance, brings about a compensation from the side of the unconscious. This compensation is accomplished by means of the constellation and stressing of material which is not infrequently simply complementary and which assumes archetypal forms of expression to the extent to which the *fonction du réel,* i.e. the correct relation to the surrounding world, is disturbed. When, for instance, a woman develops a too masculine orientation—something that may very easily happen owing to the social emancipation of women in the present day world—the unconscious compensates this relative one-sidedness by a symptomatic accentuation of certain feminine tendencies. This process of compensation takes place within the personal sphere as long as the vital interests of the personality have not been harmed. When, however, more profound disturbances occur, as, for instance, when a loss of contact with the masculine partner has occurred, owing to the compulsion to be always in the right, then archetypal figures appear on the inner scene. Such difficulties are quite frequent and they can only be removed by psychotherapeutic methods, once they have reached a pathological degree. Therefore, analytical psychology has striven for a long time to acquire as wide a knowledge as possible of the archetypal concepts and connections which are stirred up by the unconscious, in order to be able to comprehend the nature of the archetypal compensation in each case.

That Dr. Harding, in addition to her professional work, has

devoted herself to the considerable and even self-sacrificing effort of compiling, clearly and systematically, the archetypal material of the feminine compensation, brings a most welcome contribution to these endeavors. This investigation is valuable and important, not only for the specialist, but also for the educated layman, who is interested in a psychology founded on experience of life and the understanding of people. Our times, which are characterized by an unusual philosophical disorientation in respect to basic concepts of life, stands in need, above everything else, of a vast amount of psychological insight, in order to give a new definition to the *ens humanum.*

C. G. Jung

Küsnacht-Zurich

PREFACE

The symbolism of the moon is a fascinating subject for research, leading into many unexpected fields rich in significance for the spiritual life of our times. In the present volume only a few outstanding features have been selected in order to emphasize the meaning of the initiation to Eros, which in the past represented an essential phase of development, but is almost entirely neglected in our day.

We live in an age of executives and scientists, and our leaders are chosen from those ranks. Little attention is paid to the achievement of an inner development in the emotional realm. Indeed it is generally taken for granted that an individual's emotions are what they are and that they are not subject to development—certainly not to education.

But to be childishly immature in one's relationships implies that one has only an undeveloped personality with which to meet all the intricacies which make up the problems of the world. Our modern difficulties, whether social, political, or economic, are in the final analysis human problems. Any fundamental discussion of these matters always reveals the same basic difficulty: "If only human beings were different"—more honest, more conscious of the effects of what they do, if they would trust each other more, if only they were convinced of the trustworthiness of others and incidentally of themselves, if only no one was trying to get ahead by undercutting another—then we could deal readily enough with material supplies and their distribution, which form the chief question of social, economic, and international controversy. But human beings are selfish and egotistic. Their love and consideration are shallow and unreliable, and pitifully narrow in their range.

Being practical-minded people we accept these characteristics

of human nature as inevitable. Only the dreamer and the un-
practical person talk of a Utopia, where everyone shall be honest and shall love his neighbor as himself. True, human nature
will never be changed overnight or in the mass. We have to deal
with the world as it is, but that does not mean that nothing can
be done about the emotional immaturity which underlies so
many of our difficulties.

Emotional development cannot be reached by thinking about
the emotions, nor by a system of education rationally applied.
The mind is developed by making the student think and the
body by making him exercise. Yet these statements, though true
in one sense, are quite false in another. For no one can *make* a
student think or exercise himself. It is only when the student
voluntarily applies his mind to the problems presented to him,
or disciplines his body to overcome the difficulties of his exercises or athletics, that development results. In a similar way no
prescribed course of emotional exercises can produce emotional
development.

The ancient religions of the moon goddess represent the education of the emotional life as taking place, not through a course
of study, not even as the result of a system of discipline, though
both these things doubtless entered in, but through an initiation. The interpretation of the moon mysteries suggested in the
following chapters links our modern life problems to those of
the ancient peoples who recognized that in their day, as in ours,
the world at times became sterile and was laid waste, not by war
or pestilence, but because some essential fertilizing spirit had
been withdrawn. Everything became dry and dusty and infertile. If there was food it did not serve to nourish; we also have
found that farm products in excess in one place do not nourish
the hungry in another. If there was energy it did not enable a
man to support his family or build a life of dignity and culture
for himself; a similar situation exists today, for promising young
men and women are entering a world which lies under threat
of annihilation; their good gifts and high hopes may well be
doomed to decay unused. But while we cling rather desperately
to the hope that better arrangements, better man-made regulations, may overcome these tragic discrepancies, and while the
cynical remind us that war is the only occupation which is never
oversupplied with the young and the strong, the ancients said,
in symbolic language, that the moon goddess, goddess of love

and fertility, was absent in the land of No-Return, and our modern poets dimly voice the same idea.

Perhaps if more attention were directed to reinstating the goddess in the individual life, through psychological experiences, the modern equivalent to the initiations of the moon goddess, a way out of this impasse might open before us.

One hesitates to dogmatize in these matters. Each human being is so blind and can only see that which is before his eyes, but the wisdom of the ages, represented in myths and religious symbols, has without doubt a larger vision, a longer range, than that of any individual. If we can understand its teachings aright they can be taken with a certain justification as a guide, in the sense of a signpost, which might point the way for us as for our predecessors.

I present these thoughts about the meaning of the ancient moon initiations entirely undogmatically. They cannot be proved by any rational argument. But confirmation of the interpretation is accessible to the practicing analytical psychologist and to those who have been analyzed by the method Dr. Jung has evolved. Whenever such an analysis reaches a certain level the psychological development growing out of the exploration of the unconscious leads through experiences similar to the initiations we are about to discuss. Often the symbols which arise in the dreams and phantasies are strikingly similar to those of the old mystery religions, and the outcome in psychological development for the individual corresponds to the change which the initiation was said to produce.

Naturally this is evidence which cannot be evaluated except through actual experience, for when it is merely reported it is always exceedingly unconvincing. When, however, it is met with, not occasionally only, but repeatedly, it forms a very powerful corroboration for the interpretations outlined in the following chapters, which point out a usable if somewhat overgrown and unrecognizable path. I offer these reflections of a psychologist hoping that they may make clearer the intimations of a way through the darkness, which guides the traveller when conscious knowledge of his goal is lacking.

I have written this book as a follower of Prof. C. G. Jung of Zürich. His teaching permeates it from beginning to end, for it is to his genius that we owe the ability to understand the constructive meaning of the products of the unconscious. If these same symbols and rituals had been interpreted reductively, as for instance by the Freudian method, interesting points in regard to their constitution would have been found, but the whole meaning of the initiation would have escaped observation. For it was Dr. Jung who first discovered the key to those hidden treasures of the unconscious, and in making use of that key to unlock a new deposit of the world's treasure house, I want to reassert my allegiance to his method and my personal appreciation of his gift to his fellow human beings.

I also want to express my thanks to the workers in another field. The psychologist is dependent on the anthropologist whenever he needs to discuss general products of the psychical activity of man. In compiling the anthropological data for this book I am indebted first and foremost to Mr. Robert Briffault for his monumental work *The Mothers*. Frazer's *The Golden Bough* and Hastings' *Encyclopaedia of Religion and Ethics* have also been invaluable and I wish to express my appreciation to their authors and to the many other authorities whom I have consulted.

In addition I want to express my thanks to the following publishers who have most kindly permitted me to quote from copyright material: The Abingdon Press, New York; The American Numismatic Society, New York; The Cambridge University Press; The Clarendon Press, Oxford; The Constable Company, London; The D. Appleton-Century Company, New York; Faber and Faber, London; George Allen and Unwin, Ltd., London; Harcourt, Brace and Company, New York; Jonathan Cape, London; John Watkins, London; The Journal of the Polynesian Society, New Plymouth, New Zealand; Luzac and Company, London; The Macmillan Company, London and New York; The Methuen Company, London; Putnam's Sons, New York; and to Professor T. S. Eliot and Sir E. A. Wallis Budge for permission to quote from copyright material.

My thanks are also due to Dr. Edward Whitmont for his translation of Dr. Jung's introduction.

WOMAN'S MYSTERIES

1

MYTH AND THE MODERN MIND

Not so many years ago the title of this chapter would have evoked a smile, for while myths might be studied as part of the strange world of the primitive, they could have no place in relation to the mind of modern man. During the nineteenth century and the early part of the twentieth, when the most advanced thought was concerned in exploring the external world, and attention was directed almost exclusively to the objective realm, all subjective factors were considered only a hindrance to the search for truth. Scientists, with few exceptions, paid attention to the inner psychical realm only that they might be sure to exclude it from their observations. They differentiated science from imagination and objective observations from subjective guesses. In this way chemistry evolved from alchemy, astronomy from astrology, and geography from the dim foreshadowings of the picture maps, which made up a sort of pregeography. The geologist with his instruments of exact measurement replaced the waterfinder with his witch hazel, the physician with his laboratory tests replaced not only the medicine man but the old family physician as well, whose skill rested more on a curious sixth sense than on exact knowledge.

Occasionally the searcher for objective truth had to admit, however, that the guess of earlier centuries came extraordinarily near the truth. When this happened he usually dismissed the matter as due to coincidence, never suspecting that the subjective guess might have a meaning in a different realm from the one he was considering.

Today, however, we begin to realize that these things must be looked at a little differently. It is as if the impressions of the world, which crowd in upon human consciousness, were a matrix, an ore, from which man has gradually extracted his organized knowledge. Objective science is such an extract. All those factors which do not contribute directly to objective knowledge and were excluded by the older scientific attitude, form a residue, discarded in the hundred and fifty years just past, being accounted only as slag. But another distillation process has already been initiated by a new kind of scientist, whose concern is not solely with the material world. From the "slag" discarded by the last century these workers are seeking treasures of another character. Their search is also for truth, but now their definition of truth includes the subjective, the nonmaterial.

The strange ideas of alchemy or astrology, the superstitions of the witch hazel or the magic philter, as well as the "personal equation," which haunts the most exact observer—these all need explanation. Psychologists are asking whence do superstitions arise. They can hardly be explained by spontaneous generation, and the physical scientists assert that they are not a part of the objective material. Astrological myths, for instance, have nothing to do with the sun, moon, and stars as physical objects. Yet these myths are universal among primitive peoples and the ancients. They even persist among ourselves, but here they show themselves no longer as direct superstitions or myths, but rather as inner states or attitudes of mind which can be observed in inexplicable changes of feeling and mood not to be accounted for by the external situation, but which are often, nonetheless, referred to the state of the weather or to some other external "variable" as though there were a direct relation of cause and effect between the two. While if we turn to the background of consciousness we find that ideas, not unlike the primitive's myth, underlie the feelings and moods of modern man. In his musing and dreams, in his poetry and phantasies these ancient thought-feelings hold unquestioned sway. Who has not at some time been profoundly affected by the sight of the full moon rising over the sea?—affected, that is, in a way which cannot be explained simply along aesthetic lines. Though even if his emotion were merely due to the aesthetic combination of light and shade the argument would still stand. For there is more in such an experience than just the objective material fact, there is also a subjective experience which in a man's life is perhaps more important and more powerful than the scientific knowledge of the nature of moonlight. For the sentient human being, with thousands of years of evolution behind him, may be touched by

4

the scene so that dim memories of ancient nights awake within him enabling him, perhaps, to act on an emotion which transcends his little, everyday self, resulting, it may be, in a poem he could not have conceived in the hard light of day, or, perhaps, giving him courage to yield to a but half-realized love whose acceptance can change the whole course of his life.

This inner or subjective aspect of experience is not nonsense nor is it only superstition. Material science, it is true, has disregarded it, but it remains a potent factor in human life. Indeed the discarded element contains that subjective or psychical factor which constitutes spirit. The scientist of the nineteenth century as sceptic or agnostic denied the existence of spirit. This is hardly to be wondered at for, as we have seen, he eliminated as irrelevant all evidences of its presence. But men in a more naïve state of culture made no such distinction between objective "fact" and subjective "superstition." The subjective or psychical factor was perceived by them as though it were a part of the object. There was no realization that these added facts were a part of the observer, indeed there was no differentiation between objective and subjective. The qualities which the object possessed per se, and those which were assumed to exist on account of its effect on the observer, were not differentiated. The subjective element was *projected* into the object.

An example may make this distinction clearer. If a man is color-blind and matches a piece of red cloth with a piece of green we do not say this is nonsense, we make instead a judgment about his powers of perception, namely, that he suffers from red-green color blindness. What he sees in the external world gives information about himself, which is correct even while his observation of the object is false, as judged by the consensus of people with normal sight. But we should also realize that this observation gives information about those people who see red and green as different. If color-blind people were in the majority, the tables would be turned and the ability to differentiate red and green would be considered an abnormality, which would in turn be used as a test of the subject, not of the object. It is our unconsciousness which makes us say "but the cloth *is* red," that is to say, it is our superstition.

H. G. Wells took this problem as the theme of "The Country of the Blind," which depicts a country where the general limitation, in this case blindness, is taken as the basis of morality.

There the greatest crime was to see. Sight was hedged about with the strictest and most dread taboo. To know that which others did *not* know was impious, a crime of the deepest dye. This story is not without special significance at the beginning of a book which attempts to pierce the veil of unconsciousness surrounding a subject protected, until recently, from all inquiry by the most passionate fanaticism.

On investigating any superstition, two similar factors will always be found: one in the object; in the illustration used above this is the red factor, having to do with the power of the object to reflect certain waves of light; and the other in the subject, in this case the capacity of the retina to respond in a particular way to waves of a certain wave length and not to respond in this same way to any other waves. The naïve observer naturally is not aware of these two factors. He takes himself and his subjective capacities for granted and instead of realizing them endows the object with qualities which are only partly objective, that is, he creates a superstition about the object which arises from a confusion between what is objective and what subjective. Whenever the subjective factor is inadequately recognized, this is the inevitable result; for the unrealized subjective element is projected to the object and is interpreted by the observer as external fact.

For instance, the astrologers and alchemists made most careful observations of the external world but they interpreted their findings without differentiating the subjective factor which came from the unconscious, and which contains just that part of man's psyche of which he is unaware.

In much the same way we also fail to take account of our psychological peculiarities and characteristics. We are ordinarily entirely ignorant about them, unconscious even that they exist. Or if a dim awareness of our psychological lack comes to us we turn away from fuller knowledge. For as in Wells' "Country of the Blind" it is taboo to see more than other people. These subjective factors, however, are potent psychical entities, they belong to the totality of our being, they cannot be destroyed. We may ignore them, repress them, but they continue to exist. So long as they are unrecognized outcasts from our conscious life, they will come between us and all the objects we view, and our whole world will be either distorted or illuminated by the superadded subjective factor. Thus the object is

6

altered so that what we perceive is never really the object itself but always our view of the object. The scientific method deals with this dilemma by eliminating the subjective and psychological factors as far as possible and then concerning itself with the objective or relatively objective data which remain.

Such a process excludes the human element and results necessarily in a mechanical concept of life. Indeed it produced the machine age where value was largely measured in terms of available physical energy. Yet if this is so it is strange to recall how satisfied our predecessors were with this mechanistic view of life, for we in the present generation are increasingly dissatisfied with it. Those men of the nineteenth century had an enthusiasm for science, for objective or factual truth which was religious in its intensity. There was nothing mechanistic about them, in spite of their own theories. Their concern with scientific truth was like a new faith. The explanation for this lies in the fact that during the phase of mechanical expansion their living spirit was occupied with devising ever more and more ingenious methods of conquering ever wider fields, in which their scientific ingenuity could find scope. In other words, the enterprise they were really concerned with was the expansion of their own powers and the increase of conscious control of the objective world. Their aim was, unknown to themselves, a psychological one. They were really concerned with the subjective factor, though this they did not realize. For that which they thought they had eliminated so carefully had escaped their observation and once again motivated their enthusiasm.

Our dissatisfaction has been emphasized by the world problems of the past few years, during which it has become more and more evident that happiness and the fullness of life are not to be found through mass production and the discovery of new sources of energy supply. This dissatisfaction shows itself not only in general anxiety but also in neurosis and unhappiness, and in a sense of frustration, a lack of any real enthusiasm. In particular, are we dissatisfied with the character and quality of our human relationships. Our fathers were either able to make more satisfactory relationships than we are, or they were less sensitive to disharmony and ennui. Whatever the reason, there is no doubt about the large part unhappiness and neurosis, dependent on unsatisfactory human relationships, plays in the dissatisfaction with life from which so many people suffer. The

7

life of today is empty and sterile and we look for renewal, whether we want to or not, from that source of spiritual awakening which lies within. For our science has proved itself strangely impotent in face of a threatened breakdown in our culture.

In order to gain a new vantage point from which a fresh world philosophy may, perhaps, be built up, a renewed contact with the deeper levels of human nature is needed, so that a really vital relation may be established with the laws or principles which activate humanity. Only through such a renewing experience can we hope to be able to bridge the chasm which has opened up before our Western civilization.

In the past when a breakdown of morality and economics— of world philosophy—confronted a civilization it seemed that nothing could be done except to reinforce the ideals on which the culture was built, whether these were materialistic, or spiritual. But in most cases recovery was impossible, the ideals had carried the civilization as far as they could, further expansion along those lines was impossible, and the culture crumbled. Barbarians surged in. The dark ages supervened until through the succeeding centuries a new culture was evolved, not, however, from the remnants of the old, but arising spontaneously from the new soil, from the inferior people who invaded and destroyed their civilized and cultured predecessors.

Some believe that this fate is about to overtake our Western civilization and that those things which we and our ancestors have built up are about to be destroyed, while our values will go into the discard, replaced by others which are not values to us but represent those powers and impulses which we have most strenuously repressed and denied.

Perhaps this is the fate that is in store for us. But perhaps another solution of the problem may be available. The highly developed is always replaced by the undeveloped, the civilized by the barbarian. This is the inevitable course of history. Today, however, a new factor has come into play. Through the study of the unconscious we have found a way to be reconciled with the barbarian within ourselves. The world drama can be and indeed not infrequently is played out within the individual. Power and prestige abstracted from the highly developed parts of the psyche are applied to the more lowly parts so that they may be educated, may be raised from their position of barbarism and degradation. By this process the individual can pass from an exclusively intellectual and rational attitude to one where the forces latent in the unconscious are given due recognition and are thus no longer in stark opposition to the conscious attitude. If this peaceful revolution within the individual could be accomplished in a sufficient number of people, might it not be that a renewal of life, even in the whole of Western civilization, could take place without the necessity of passing through a phase of destruction and barbarism? For the revolution would take place *within,* in individuals, it would be a psychological happening and would make unnecessary the overthrow of a one-sided civilization by a people representing the excluded elements.

For this reason it is essential that we study the unconscious in order to reconstruct our attitudes in accordance with the neglected forces which still manifest themselves there. Foremost among these neglected values is the subjective factor, which is deliberately eliminated in the attempt to differentiate the object as a thing in itself.

The neglect of the inner or subjective aspect of life has led, particularly for women, to a certain falsification of her living values. For example, in the conventional judgment of the past a woman had one prime adaptation to make, the adaptation of wife and mother. If she married well she succeeded, if she failed to marry she was all too likely to be considered a failure. The success or defeat of her whole life, even, might be measured in the general estimation of the world, by this external or objective standard alone. And, indeed, being married, the success or failure of her marriage itself was judged also by external standards. If any difficulty arose in her relation to her husband her tendency was, and still often is, to seek for an external remedy. It is not uncommon, for instance, to hear that a woman has tried to heal an emotional breach with her husband by taking a trip or redecorating the home. The subjective side of the problem is, in such cases, discounted and allowed to vent itself only in moods or bad temper, or in some neurotic disturbance.

In homes where the external standard rules and the subjective side of life is ignored, these neurotic manifestations are not taken seriously into account. For the most part they are even disregarded as mere emotionality, nervousness, or little weaknesses of temperament. In more recent times a woman faced

9

with home problems of this character, perhaps a badly maladjusted child, would learn something of modern psychology and child training and try by applying what she had learned, objectively, to accomplish by an external technique what would really follow naturally if she did but know how to apply her own feminine feelings and reactions to the situation. But in so far as her own subjective life is disregarded, this natural effect of her being is nullified and she is left with no resource but a mechanical technique, at best a poor substitute for a living reality.

Today, the success or failure of a woman's life is not judged to anything like the same extent on the exclusive criterion of marriage. Her adaptation to life may now be made in various ways, each of which offers some opportunity for solving the problems of work, of social relations, and of her emotional needs. If, however, in order to gain discipline and development on all sides of her personality she seeks to make an adjustment to life which is not one-sided but is as many faceted as her own nature, her task is a most complex one. For while the stirrings within, which require a field of activity in the outer objective world, are accepted by herself and others as legitimate, other longings, which also have their origin deep within her being and which seek for a spiritual and subjective fulfillment, are not so generally acknowledged. The manifestation of these needs is frequently considered to be little more than moods, whims, emotionality, superstition, and so forth.

So pressing have these subjective problems become, however, in many instances, that the psychological factor which the older physical scientist eliminated is now being eagerly sought out and analyzed. Once again the stone which the builders rejected is becoming the headstone of the corner. For every human being has not only impulses and instincts which need a life lived collectively in the social group for their satisfaction but other instincts and impulses also which urge him to find himself as a unique individual. Each one has a nature which seeks for love and relationship, and also there is imbedded in everyone the necessity to strive for impersonal truth. These opposing tendencies are expressions of the duality of human nature which is both objective and subjective. In all human beings such an opposition is at work and leads inevitably to conflict. In the Western world of today this conflict is most severe and bears hardest upon women because Western civilization lays especial emphasis on the value of the outer, and this fits in more nearly with man's nature than with woman's. The feminine spirit is more subjective, more concerned with feelings and relationships than with the laws and principles of the outer world. And so it happens that the conflict between outer and inner is usually more devastating for women than for men.

There is another reason why this problem is a particularly urgent one for women today. This is related to the recent development of the masculine side of woman's nature which has been so marked a feature of recent years.[1] This masculine development is definitely related to her life in the world of affairs; in the majority of cases it is even sought as a prerequisite for earning a living in the world, practicing a profession, or following a trade. The change of character, which has accompanied this evolution, does not stop at the professional part of a woman's life but affects her whole personality and has caused profound changes in her relation to herself and to others.

So long as the masculine side of woman's nature was allowed to remain, as it was in the past, undeveloped and unconscious, it either slept unrecognized or it functioned in a purely instinctive fashion. The recent awakening of woman from her long apathy has brought to the fore latent powers which, naturally enough, she is eager to develop and apply in life, both for her own satisfaction and advantage and to increase her contribution to the life of the group. This step forward in conscious development is not without its difficulties and drawbacks. Woman has moved away from the old, well-established, woman's way of conduct and psychological adaptation and finds herself today beset by problems which neither she herself, nor the pioneer women who initiated the movement for woman's emancipation, foresaw. These changes have produced for woman an unavoidable inner conflict between the urge to express herself through work, as a man does, and the inner necessity to live in accordance with her own ancient feminine nature. This conflict seems to condition the whole experience of life for all those modern women who are at all aware of themselves as conscious individuals. For them a one-sided life is not sufficient; the conflict between the opposing tendencies of masculine and femi-

[1] For a fuller discussion of this subject see M. E. Harding, *The Way of All Women* (New York: Longmans, Green & Co., 1933).

nine within them has to be faced. They cannot resume the feminine values in the old instinctive and unconscious way. Through acquiring a new degree of consciousness they have cut themselves off from the easy road of nature. If they are to get in touch with their lost feminine side it must be by the hard road of a conscious adaptation.

The problems of adaptation, arising from woman's newly acquired consciousness of duality, have necessarily to be dealt with in their *modern* aspect. Yet the need for the reconciliation of these two parts of the woman's nature is an age-old problem, it is only in its application to practical life that the modern note is struck. We have but to look below the veneer of modern life to find the same problem on a deeper level. There it is not a question of how a woman may adapt in the world of work and of love in such a way as to give due weight to both sides of her nature, but it is rather a matter of how she may adapt to the masculine and feminine *principles* which rule her being from within. Here she has to turn to that discarded subjective material which to the objective scientists of the nineteenth century was only superstition or moodiness.

In these terms the problem is no longer one of the twentieth century alone. It is one which has concerned women from the most primitive times. I do not mean to imply, however, that women of the past have been consciously occupied with this problem as an intellectual question; psychological consciousness of that kind is a phenomenon peculiar, perhaps, to today. For those who were, or still are, less advanced in psychological evolution such questioning is not at all necessary. Only for advanced "moderns" has it become a necessity of life to question everything and to seek to understand. Nevertheless this problem has dominated much of the inner activity and thought of men and women throughout the ages, as the mass of myth and legend dealing with the subject bears witness. For the experience of life which the centuries brought to primitive and antique man was consolidated into conventions and customs, which formed and still form the basis for external conduct. Another kind of wisdom brought by this same experience was embodied by the intuitive insight of the race in myths and religions, particularly in religious mysteries and rituals, which do not formulate a consciously held intellectual knowledge or opinion but instead shadow forth an unconscious sense of "how things are."

The myths and rituals of ancient religions represent the naïve projection of psychological realities. They are undistorted by rationalization, for in matters which deal with the spirit realm, that is, the psychological realm, primitive people and the people of antiquity did not *think*; they *perceived* by an inner or intuitive sense, as indeed we still do today. Hence these products of the unconscious contain psychological material which is uncensored and from which a store of knowledge may be gleaned of an inner reality underlying the life of the group, which would otherwise be inaccessible to us.

Jung has pointed out that myths and rituals represent the phantasy of the group and that this material may be interpreted psychologically by a method similar to that employed in the study of the unconscious products of individual men and women, when it will yield information relating to the hidden psychological realities on which the group life is founded. Therefore, by an analysis of the dreams and phantasies of an individual, we can discover what psychological attitudes really underly his conscious façade, what are his genuine motives, what is the true nature of his relations. This reality may not correspond at all to the idea of his inner state which he himself holds. His conscious ego may distort the facts and be self-deceived by desires and instincts for self-preservation, self-esteem, and the like. But in the unconscious, truth cannot be dissembled in this way. The unconscious can only *mirror* the actual facts and therefore cannot lie. For this reason a dream or phantasy may tell the expert more about a man's real character than anything he himself can say. His dreams and phantasies show without bias his relation to his personal problem. In certain instances they show much more than this, for, inasmuch as he is the child of his age and culture, his "personal problem" may well be but an individual version of a general or collective one. To the extent that this is so, his unconscious material will show the relations of psychological forces and tendencies in a general form, which would be applicable to many people, all situated as he is. But in dealing with dreams and phantasies we have always to bear in mind that we are studying a single individual whose personal circumstances will color the presentation of what may yet be a collective or general problem, hence we cannot unhesitatingly say that the dream or phantasy of an individual shows *how things are* in any general way, but only how they are in *this* case.

Myths and rituals, however, represent the unconscious processes of whole tribes or races. They have been adapted to the common needs of countless generations by a process of conventionalization, through which the personal elements have been eliminated. There remain the general themes which are common to all the individuals of the group. The fact that equivalent myths and rituals are strikingly similar, even as to detail, in the cultures of widely separated peoples, indicates that they represent general psychological themes which are true of humanity no matter where. And indeed the dreams and phantasies of modern people occasionally show a similar generalized character resembling ancient or primitive myths. This resemblance between the dream and some ancient myth may occur in cases where there is no knowledge of the existence of such a myth so that the dream cannot be explained as "borrowing." It is a spontaneous creation of the unconscious. Jung first elaborated this theory in his *Psychology of the Unconscious* [2] and has since added much to that first attempt to understand the personal problem of an individual by means of the collective images in his dreams. But he has done more than this for he has shown how these collective images occur in people whose personal problem depends on an unsolved collective adaptation.

Practical experience of the unconscious of many people of very different caliber teaches that the dreams and phantasies tend to have this generalized or mythlike character in two classes of individuals. First, those people whose personal life has never yet emerged fully from its unconscious beginnings or has been swamped by collective material surging up from the depths of the unconscious; and second, the mythlike character may show itself also in the dreams of another class of people, namely those whose personal problems have already been largely dealt with either by the experience of life itself or through analysis. This generalized character of dreams is thus found in people at the two extremes of development— those who have not yet achieved an individual life apart from the collective stream of inner images and those who have

[2] To appear in the Collected Works of C. G. Jung, vol. 5, in a revised version as *Symbols of Transformation* (New York: Pantheon Books [Bollingen Series XX] and London: Routledge and Kegan Paul).

largely assimilated their personal problems and worked their way through to a wider viewpoint.

In the case of those individuals who have not yet achieved a satisfactory personal life, but are still "trailing clouds of glory," as it were, the object of analysis must first be to establish that which is lacking, namely a personal relation to the world. This situation and problem I shall not consider further here, but turn instead to those cases where an adequate personal life has been built up, and yet collective material breaks through into the dreams, while at the same time there is serious dissatisfaction with the life which has been achieved. In such cases the individual's problem cannot be understood if it is viewed only from the personal angle. For no human life consists only in the personal. To earn one's living, marry, and beget children, and take one's place in the social group is not enough. Beyond this, each man and woman must acquire a broader understanding of life if he is not to be suffocated in the childishly personal. As civilized beings it is necessary, as Jung has pointed out, to find for ourselves a *Weltanschauung* [3] or world outlook, which implies a more fundamental adaptation to the world, both in its outer and inner aspects, than is usually necessary to steer one's way through a small or provincial life, where an almost completely unconscious and instinctive functioning suffices. Many people, it is true, live and die on this plane, hardly more aware of the stirrings of the spirit than animals or peasants. But those individuals whose dreams contain a preponderance of collective images are faced with the necessity of building for themselves a better *Weltanschauung* and of concerning themselves with these general questions, whether they come in terms of outer problems, such as social and economic or international relations, or in the need for inner philosophical or religious formulations. If the dream material is reduced by analysis back to the personal life and is interpreted as having to do merely with the satisfaction of the personal side of instinct, the individual will suffer serious maiming of his psyche.

If, on the other hand, it is recognized that when the personal factors cease to hold the predominating place, the problem is

---

[3] Jung, *Contributions to Analytical Psychology*, trans. by H. G. and C. F. Baynes (New York and London, 1928), p. 141 *et seq.*, to appear in the Collected Works, vol. 8, in a revised version as *On Psychic Energy* (New York: Pantheon Books [Bollingen Series XX] and London: Routledge and Kegan Paul).

being presented as *one* instance of a universal human problem, the individual can be released from the bondage of the personal to find a solution along larger lines. Through an understanding of the universal, and archetypal, meaning of the dreams and phantasies a solution of the individual's life problem may often be reached both on the personal side and also, with a larger significance, in its relation to modern culture and civilization. For unless an individual plays his part adequately on this world stage, he will reach only half his development. His task in life is to fulfill his personal obligations and care for his personal needs and *also* to bear his share of the cultural burden of mankind. This latter task means that he must find his due relation to those impersonal forces which determine racial and national movements, both in the realm of external achievements and in the inner world where principles and philosophic and religious ideas are the objects to be attained.

Perhaps the most important of these inner laws, which need fresh exploration today, are the masculine and feminine principles. These terms do not readily convey to the average reader any very definite idea. By "principle" I mean an essence, or inner law, not as a law that is imposed by a legal authority but rather using the term as it is used in science, where we speak of the law of gravity, the laws of mathematics, or the law of evolution. These laws or principles are inherent in the nature of things and function unerringly and inevitably.

Even in man, who has rebelled against the gods, defying many a natural law, these things still work. But by his godlike capacity to harness nature he has in part lost sight of these laws or principles. In the physical realm he knows that he overcomes nature only by obeying her laws, but in his own person he has, in not a few cases, become so entranced by his power to stand against nature that he has forgotten her laws. In the Western world this is so in regard to the essence or principle of masculine and feminine. Not infrequently we hear it affirmed that there is no essential difference between men and women, except the biological one. Many women have accepted this standpoint and have themselves done much to foster it. They have been content to be men in petticoats and so have lost touch with the feminine principle within themselves. This is perhaps the main cause of the unhappiness and emotional instability of today. For if woman is out of touch with the feminine principle, which dictates the laws of related-ness, she cannot take the lead in what is after all the feminine realm, that of human relationships. Until she does so there cannot be much hope of order in this aspect of life.

Many women suffer seriously in their personal lives on account of this neglect of the feminine principle. They may be unable to make satisfactory relationships or may even fall into neurosis and ill-health on account of the inadequacy of their development in this most essential direction. For this reason, a woman's relation to the feminine principle within herself is undoubtedly of great personal importance to herself, yet it is not only a personal problem but also a general, even a universal problem for all women. It is a problem of womanhood, and beyond that a problem of mankind.

In the following pages an attempt has been made to clear the way for a new understanding of this principle of woman. For unless it can be apprehended anew no further step can be taken either in the psychological development of woman herself, nor in the nature of the relationship which is possible between men and women. Indeed we can go a step further than that, for men also need a relation to the feminine principle, not only that they may the better understand women, but also because their contact with the inner or spiritual world is governed not by masculine but by feminine laws as Jung has pointed out in his *Two Essays on Analytical Psychology* and elsewhere in his writings. So that a new relation to this woman principle is urgently needed today to counteract the one-sidedness of the prevailing masculine mode of Western civilization.

But important though it is, the feminine principle or essence cannot be understood through an intellectual or academic study. For the inner essence of the feminine principle will not yield itself to such an attack, the real meaning of femininity always evades the direct interrogator. This is one reason why women are so mysterious to men—to the man, that is, who persists in trying to understand a woman intellectually.

Take for instance the case of a man who has elicited by direct questions all he can of his wife's reasons for a certain attitude or action and finds that there still remains an intangible something to which she clings as though it were of the greatest significance to her. Yet he cannot guess its nature or value for it always eludes him. Naturally he feels baffled. When this

inexplicable *something* has been touched upon in a discussion
between them the man is likely to lose patience and brush it
aside, carrying his point by the weight of his personality. But
the woman "convinced against her will is of the same opinion
still," for considerations which are of supreme importance to
her are in this way completely disregarded. The man under
such circumstances feels her to be elusive and unreliable, for
from his point of view the discussion had ended in a way that
was perfectly convincing, while she persisted in acting as though
entirely unconvinced.

In a situation such as this the man does not realize that the
discarded values form the very essence of the feminine approach
to life, constituting a part of the feminine principle or Eros.
For to him these things seem to be but the outcome of moods
or whims, impalpable nothings which are best treated with a
tolerant disregard.

This woman was unable to express the values which were yet
of great importance to her because she did not understand them
herself. She was only aware that she was dissatisfied with the
outcome of the discussion. For she was held by unknown considerations in an unconscious and compulsive way. Such a
situation is not a unique one but is quite typical. Women in
general find themselves, when discussing any vital problem with
a man, held by factors which they can rarely explain. The
woman's relation to her own feminine principle is something
which controls her from deep within her own nature but she is
often supremely unaware of what it is that holds her. She has
no conscious understanding of herself, and is for that reason
totally unable to explain herself to a man and, even if she could
put her feeling into words, he would not know what she was
talking about unless he also had had experience of the deeper
functioning of the human being which would allow him to
comprehend her.

In seeking to understand the nature of these hidden reactions
we must renounce our superior intellectual attitude which considers them only errors, mistakes, or dross and attempt to understand them in their own terms. For they are so impalpable
that the intellect and rational analysis cannot grasp them. Even
women themselves are at a loss to define or explain them, because they are almost universally separated from the very prin-

ciple by which they are controlled within, albeit unknown to themselves.

When intellectual acumen fails us in this way we have to turn to unconscious products for enlightenment and see whether a study of symbols and instinctive ways of acting may not throw some light on the obscurity. For unconscious factors of the psyche are first sensed, not in concepts, but are perceived in the outer world, projected into inanimate nature. So that when man sees human qualities and characteristics as belonging to inanimate objects these are not just arbitrary imaginings but are reflections of his own unconscious qualities. When he regards natural phenomena naïvely, personifying them as in myths and folk tales or in the poetic language of art, he is interpreting Nature in accordance with his *own* nature. His unconscious is projected to the outer world.

In the ancient half-forgotten folk myths of a people we find relics of archaic, primitive ways of thinking which have been largely displaced in the Western world and in modern times by the more developed cultures superimposed upon them. But they are not for that reason extinct nor are they without meaning, as is shown by the fact that they reappear, today, from the unconscious in dreams and phantasies. Through a study of them something may be learned of those unrecognized laws which rule in the unconscious where our modern rational and scientific ways of thought are powerless to penetrate.

And so in taking up the question of the woman's relation to the feminine principle which is her mainspring, no attempt has been made to discuss the matter from a purely intellectual standpoint, but instead it is presented in the form in which it is actually experienced by modern woman, as well as by her more primitive and less rationally developed sisters. The material taken for consideration and psychological interpretation has been gleaned from ancient and primitive sources and from the dreams and phantasies of modern people and portrays its subject as parable or allegory, not as rationally established fact. From a consideration of this widely disseminated material certain characteristics of the feminine principle emerge, together with the laws which govern the woman's inner relation to it. These principles and laws are generally valid. An understanding of them brings out clearly the difference between masculine and feminine—a difference which surely needs restating today when so many men are womanish and so many women mannish.

The symbol which above all others has stood throughout the ages for woman, not in her likeness to man, one aspect of *homo sapiens,* but in her difference from man, distinctively feminine in contrast to his masculinity, is the Moon. In poetry, both modern and classical, and, from time immemorial in myth and legend the moon has represented the woman's deity, the feminine principle, much as the sun, with its heroes, symbolized the masculine principle. To primitive man and to the poet and dreamer of today the Sun is masculine and the Moon feminine.

The moon, first as an influence of fertility and later as a deity, has been considered throughout the ages to be in a peculiar relation to women. It is source and origin of their power to bear children, the goddess who keeps watch over them and all matters that primarily concern them. These beliefs are very widespread. They are to be found almost all the world over and persisting from remote times up to the present. They occur among the Indians of both North and South America, among the negroes of Africa, among the primitive tribes of Australia and Polynesia, among the aboriginal peoples of Asia, and the exceedingly primitive people of Greenland. The peasants of Europe have similar legends which also permeate folk tales everywhere, while the people of India, of China and Mongolia, of Arabia and Syria, of ancient Greece and Rome, and the Celtic peoples of Northern and Western Europe incorporate these beliefs about the moon into the very center of their religious structure.

It would therefore seem that a study of moon symbolism might give us some understanding of the nature of this *principle of woman* which has fallen upon such evil days of neglect and decay in our modern life.

And so we turn again to the ancient differentiation of male and female, arising from the depths of the unconscious in the form of symbols whose eternal reality is still exemplified to us in our everyday experience of the Great Light which rules the day of reason and intellect, and the Lesser Light which rules the night of instinct and the shadowy perceptions of the inner intuitive world.

2

THE MOON AS GIVER OF FERTILITY [1]

According to the beliefs of the most primitive peoples, the moon is a kind of beneficent presence whose light is considered, not only favorable, but even indispensable for growth. The moon is a fertilizing force of quite general efficacy. It causes the seeds to germinate and the plants to grow, but its power does not end here, for without its aid animals could not bear young, and women could not have children. In a temperate climate the sun's power is thought of as causing things to grow, but in hot countries the sun seems hostile to life, scorching the young green things and destroying them. To those primitive peoples who live in southern climates the sun appears as a force hostile to vegetation and reproduction. To them the moon is the the fertilizing power. But strangely enough the belief that the power of growth resides in the moon is not confined to hot climates. As we shall see, the people of Greenland, for instance, hold the same views. To these peoples it is not that the moon *represents*, or is an emblem of, the power of fertility; that is an altogether modern concept. We know, for instance, that the germ of life is in the seed and the warmth of the sun does but foster that germ. But to the primitive, the seed is an inert mass, like a stone, entirely lacking in any power to grow. To him, that power has to be bestowed on the seed by a fertilizing force, or, perhaps, by a deity of fertility. When he speaks of the moon as possessing and bestowing the power of fertility he means exactly *that*. It is no *façon de parler* for him. Plants and seeds would not grow without the influence of the moon. Animals and

[1] The reader who wishes for further data on the myths of the moon is referred to Robert Briffault's monumental work, *The Mothers*, in three volumes, published by Macmillan and Co., New York, 1927. Briffault's bibliography and collection of material have proven invaluable in making the present study.

women cannot bear young without the energizing power of the moon.

The welfare of a small tribe depends first on its numbers and second on its food supply. The number of babies born into the tribe is a matter of great tribal importance. The population can be, and generally is, prevented from increasing too rapidly in relation to the food supply by "direct action." Primitive people are as a rule entirely cold-blooded about disposing of unwanted infants and usually have some quite efficient, if not altogether harmless, method of procuring abortion. But control in the opposite direction is beyond man's power. An influence stronger than any he possesses has to intervene to increase the numbers of the tribe or to increase the yield of the cleared lands. As we have seen, it is almost universally felt by primitive peoples that this power resides in the moon. It is not surprising therefore to find that a worship, or placation of the moon as giver of fertility and as guardian of the food supply is to be found in tribes who have as yet hardly any ordered or organized religion. It is recorded that tribes who seem to take no account of the sun, certainly not worshipping it, do worship the moon as a great deity. Tylor in his *Primitive Culture* [2] reports that the primitives of Brazil, who are in a very rude state of savagery, worship and respect the moon, and that the Botocudos are said to give the highest rank among the heavenly bodies to the moon. An old account of the Caribs describes them as esteeming the moon more than the sun.

In tribes who have advanced in culture beyond these rude savages, religious ideas become clearer and more definite. The Ahts and Greenlanders, who are, however, still very primitive, believe that the moon is even able to impregnate women. For this reason their women will not look at the moon and will not sleep on their backs without first rubbing spittle on their stomachs to prevent them swelling, that is to prevent themselves becoming pregnant by the moon. The Nigerians also believe that no husband is needed for procreation, as the women become pregnant by the moon. In this case, however, the moon does not impregnate the woman directly but, as they believe, the Great Moon Mother, who sits above in the sky, sends the Moon Bird to earth to bring babies to the women who want them.

[2] E. B. Tylor, *Primitive Culture* (New York, 1924), II, 299.

This idea is not unlike our own myth of the stork. The Buriats of Western Mongolia also believe that the moon may be the cause of a woman's pregnancy without the intervention of a man. E. Best in an article on "The Lore of the Whare-Kohanga"[3] states that the Maori believe that the moon is the permanent husband of all women. To them the marriage of man and woman is of no particular account because the true husband is the moon. As evidence for this conviction they state that women menstruate when the new moon appears.

Many other peoples have similar beliefs. For primitive people are by no means all convinced that the man plays any very important part in reproduction. Some think that his function is merely to rupture the hymen or to dilate the passage so as to open a way for the moonbeam to enter, for the moon is the real fertilizing agent. Other tribes do not even make as close a connection as this. They think that the moon alone and un-aided can get a woman with child. Other people think that while the most usual way for a woman to become pregnant is now through intercourse, yet this was not the case in earlier times. Then the moon alone had this power and even today, they say, certain babies are begotten by the moon, not by any mortal father. Such children are usually royal babies or are marked out for some great destiny, as befits their celestial parentage.

To the people who hold these beliefs it follows that as pregnancy does not depend on any human act of intercourse the woman herself is in no way responsible. If she becomes pregnant it is the moon's doing and has no relation to sexuality. In tribes as primitive as these we are considering, there is usually no restriction on sexual intercourse before marriage, so that the connection between pregnancy and any particular act of intercourse is naturally not realized. And as the duration of pregnancy is not known until a much higher stage of culture has been reached, the failure to connect the two is not so surprising as it seems at first sight.

In most primitive tribes it is believed that the moon not only causes the pregnancy but also watches over the birth of the child. When a woman is about to give birth to a baby she calls to the moon for help. Often the chief duty of the midwife is

[3] E. Best, "The Lore of the Whare-Kohanga," *Journal of the Polynesian Society*, XIV (New Plymouth, New Zealand, 1905), p. 211.

to make suitable prayers and offerings to the moon so as to secure the woman an easy delivery.

In primitive communities the moon is frequently called The Lord of the Women. For the moon is regarded, not only as the source of woman's ability to bear children, but also as the protector and guardian of women in all their special activities. In such tribes the women have charge of all matters concerned with the food supply except the hunting and killing of game. It is the women who must search for wild roots and fruits and prepare them for eating. And when the tribe becomes more settled and begins some primitive agriculture it is the women's task to care for the fields as soon as the men have done the preliminary clearing. Planting, cultivating, and harvesting are all women's tasks. For it is generally thought that only women can make things grow, because they alone are under the direct guardianship of the moon whose power to make things grow and increase is delegated in some measure to them. For primitive peoples consider that women must be of the same nature as the moon, not only on account of their tendency to "swell up" as the moon does, but also because of their monthly cycle which is of the same duration as the moon's. The word for menstruation and the word for moon, are either the same or are closely related in many languages, a fact which shows the close connection that is felt to exist between women and the moon. Her monthly cycle is of the moon, a direct evidence of her essential a-tone-ness with the heavenly body. The strange beliefs and customs that relate to this moon cycle and the taboos that cling to menstruation will be taken up in detail in a later chapter. Here it is sufficient to state that this correspondence beween woman and the moon is taken to be absolute proof of the "fact" that they are of like nature.

These beliefs are exceedingly primitive and naïve. In their original form they seem so remote from us as to be utterly incomprehensible. They suggest a way of thinking that is quite foreign to our own mentality with its scientific outlook and emphasis on rigid causality. Yet many of these ideas have survived today in customs, proverbs, and folk ways whose significance is realized only dimly if at all.

It is difficult for us, however, to understand the rationale for these beliefs about the moon. The complete absence of any causal relation between sleeping in the moonlight and becoming pregnant makes them seem unthinkable to us. But primitive man knows nothing of what we call logic. In this case he would argue in some such way as this. The moon when it first appears as new moon is small, it then grows to a round fullness. Woman is of like nature with the moon, so exposure to its influence produces a similar effect in her. If a woman with a flat stomach is exposed to the light of the young moon her stomach also will grow large and full. In fact a sort of mimetic effect takes place. In cases where a woman does not want a child she takes precautions against pregnancy by avoiding exposure to moonlight, or she uses an apotropaic ritual, as the Aht woman does when she rubs spittle on her stomach to prevent its swelling. This is perhaps the most primitive form of contraceptive we know of. When, however, a childless woman wants a baby she exposes herself to the light of the new moon or makes offerings to the moon and invokes its aid. The waxing moon is "patron" of all things that grow, or should grow. Only, this word patron represents a much later idea than these we are considering. For patron would mean one who watches over or cares for the things that grow, but to the primitive the moon is the cause of all growth and increase. It is literally the *power* of growth.

Similar ideas are held by peoples far more advanced than the Nigerians and the Ahts, only then they lurk in a sort of twilight. It is half-belief, which is not looked at any too closely, perhaps for fear that the intellect would reject what the less conscious feelings cannot help but accept. The crescent moon, for instance, has been used throughout the ages as a charm to bring increase, increase of flocks and herds and corn, and more especially increase in the family, a blessing desired, perhaps more than any other, by primitives and peasants whose only insurance against poverty and destitution in old age is the blessing of stalwart sons and daughters. All Western Asia once wore the crescent for this purpose, just as the women of southern Italy still wear it as a charm or amulet to secure the Moon Mother's help in childbirth. Today the Catholic women of Italy would tell you that the Mother who is "Moon of our Church" is Mother Mary. But as they say it they will as likely as not look up to the moon in the sky and make a gesture of reverence.

Among ourselves it is felt to be lucky to see the new moon. We say to each other "There's a new moon tonight" with a little more pleasure and sense of satisfaction than the mere fact would seem to warrant. Perhaps this is all that remains in our consciousness of the old attitude. Or, perhaps, we amusedly go through the old ritual, look at the moon over the left shoulder, curtsy, take out money and turn it over, for the moon "the Increaser" will multiply it for us, and so, go without looking back. These are simple folk rituals and seemingly silly, but they are all to be found in the worship of Hecate, the Greek moon goddess, where they are parts of elaborate ceremonials. The growing phase of the moon, its waxing, represented to all these primitive peoples the generative aspect of the heavenly power. But this period of increase in strength is short-lived. The power of the moon is soon spent and a period of decrease follows. The moon gradually wanes and finally disappears entirely and the nights are again dark. Primitives felt very differently about this second half of the moon month. They thought that the moon was being overcome, eaten up, by a dark and destructive power. The waning moon thus represented to them the powers of destruction and of death. Under the waning moon it is said that "all things are minished and brought low." The time of the waning moon, by a natural deduction, was considered unlucky for any enterprise, such as sowing grain, that needed growth. When there was no moon, or as we should say, in the dark of the moon, the destructive powers were at their height. Floods and storms, or destructive pests, were to be expected, and ghosts walked or flitted shrilling through the air. This was the time when the powers of sorcery and black magic could be evoked to work their mischief unchecked, for the dark moon was captain of the hordes of ghosts and Mistress of Black Magic.

These beliefs about the phases of the moon were not just formulas to the people who held them. They were accepted quite simply as having to do with matters of fact, consequently, the everyday life of whole communities was regulated in accordance with the phases of the moon. For instance all agricultural proceedings had to be timed with the moon's changes, and it was a matter of great importance for the public welfare that the people should know exactly when a new moon was to be expected. In the absence of calendars it became one of the chief functions of the headman or king to keep watch for the new moon and then to call all the people together and tell them that now is the time to sow their seed or to harvest their crops. In China the new moon was formerly proclaimed by heralds sent out by the royal astronomer.

During the waxing moon all those things that need to grow had to be attended to. This meant that the ground must be prepared ahead so that the seed could be sown during the first quarter of the moon, otherwise it would rot in the ground. Sheep must be sheared under the waxing moon so that the wool may grow again quickly; but trees must be felled under the waning moon or the wood will not mature well, hay and grain must be cut under the waning moon or they will ferment and the grain will sprout.

All these regulations were felt to be essential if man was to succeed in his attempts to increase the food supply of nature. He had to work with her laws, not against them, and he believed that her laws were controlled by the moon.

Many superstitions related to the moon are still to be found among country people both in the British Isles and on the continent of Europe, but they are perhaps most common among the negroes of the southern United States. On one plantation a necklace of "birth beads" is still treasured. It was brought over from Africa by the slaves and has been carefully guarded ever since. It is not often that a white person is allowed a glimpse of the precious talisman which is brought into use whenever a woman is in childbed. The roughly carved beads bear symbols of power, chief among them being the crescent moon.

Another highly valued charm among the negroes is a rabbit's foot. This charm is most powerful if the rabbit was caught in a graveyard at the full of the moon. Under these circumstances the amulet is indeed invincible. The graveyard of course refers to the magic power of the ghosts, but, we ask, why a rabbit? The full moon gives the clue. The markings to be seen on its face are called The Mark of the Hare in Thibet, China, and Ceylon, as well as in Africa and North America. Indeed the Hare in the Moon is as well known as our own Man in the Moon. The rabbit or hare represents, to the negro as well as to the American Indian, the animal incarnation of the hero. We recall the stories of Brer Rabbit among the negroes of the United States which correspond exactly to myths of a rabbit hero in West Africa. In North American Indian mythology

Hare plays a similar role. For instance, among the Iroquois, Great Hare is one form of Great Manitu, the Great Spirit, who is either himself the moon or his grandmother is the moon. This hare incarnation corresponds roughly to the Christian symbolism of Christ as Hero, who is the Lamb that was slain. The Easter Bunny contains a symbolism that lies close to these ideas. Easter, as we shall see later, was originally a moon festival and was connected with the resurrection of the moonman or moon hero, long before the dawn of Christianity.

When we come to discuss the beliefs of the moon religions it will be found that these same powers and characteristics are ascribed to the moon deity and are there elaborated into a complete system.

In writing about the beliefs of his own day Plutarch wrote that the waxing moon causes growth and increase and is "of good intent." It is strange to us to think of the moon as having "intention" either good or bad; it implies a personification of the moon which is foreign to us. The Greeks of Plutarch's time were far from primitive, so that it is not only primitive people who can be swayed by such an idea. In the last chapter it was shown that personifications of this kind have their origin in the unconscious. For the unrealized parts of the human psyche are projected onto the outer world and give rise to myths and superstitions. In former days, as we have seen, the reproductive, or creative, power of the female was not recognized as such and so was projected to the moon as representative of the feminine principle. For those early people were entirely unaware that it is part of the feminine essence to reproduce. They thought of that power as resident in the moon and only lent to females, whether of the plant or animal kingdom, on account of a certain similarity in the nature of female on earth and moon in heaven. It is helpful to realize this, for in the unconscious we still feel and act much as primitive man does.

3

THE MOON IN MODERN LIFE

To ancient and primitive man, the moon was the visible representative of womanhood. The ancients naturally did not understand the nature of the power which they revered in the moon, but we realize that to them it stood as a symbol of the very essence of woman in its contrast to the essence of man.

In the myths and customs outlined in the following chapters, are set forth in shadowy form the feeling, the reaction, which men and women had, not towards a particular woman, not even towards women in general, but to feminineness itself, to the *feminine principle* which was and is, in spite of the feminist movement and the masculinization of modern women, the mainspring of woman, controlling both her physical life and her inner psychological being.

The same feminine principle, or Eros,[1] functions in man as well as in woman. But while in woman her conscious personality is under the guidance of this principle, in man it is not his conscious but his unconscious that is related to the Eros. His conscious personality, being masculine, is under the masculine rule of Logos. In the unconscious, however, he is given over to the

[1] Throughout this book the term Eros is used in its philosophical sense, where it represents the principle of psychic relatedness. This term has been elaborated by Jung in many of his writings. He correlates this Eros principle with the feminine law, contrasting it with the Logos Principle which is characteristically masculine. [Jung, "Woman in Europe," *Contributions to Analytical Psychology* (New York and London, 1928), p. 176.] So that when the term Eros is used no reference is intended to the Greek god of that name. The little winged god is, like his own arrows, a thought or impulse of love which strikes from a distance, which flies into you. Such an ocurrence is naturally connected with the principle of Eros, for when such a missile strikes anyone he is compelled to seek closer relationship with the human source of that impulse. In the same way the whole realm of the erotic is closely connected with the Eros, but is not identical with it. The erotic is one field in which the Eros manifests itself, but not the only one.

"other side." There his soul,[2] which mankind has consistently regarded as feminine, rules. This feminine soul of man is the anima. The nature of his anima, and his relation to her determine the nature of his relations to women and also his own inner relations to that spiritual realm over which his anima rules.

A discussion of the nature of the feminine principle and the laws which govern it is of vital importance to both men and women today, for, as we have seen, in our Western, twentieth-century culture this principle has been neglected and its requirements have been met only by a stereotyped and mechanical observance of conventional customs, while the care and tendence of the life-giving springs, which lie hidden in the depths of nature, have been disregarded. For these sources of spiritual or psychological energy can only be reached, or so the myths and ancient religions say, through a right approach to the feminine essence of nature, whether this functions in inanimate form or in women themselves. It is therefore of the greatest importance that we seek to establish once more a better relation to the feminine principle.

In facing this subject we have to disabuse ourselves of all preconceived ideas of what woman is like or of what is the "truly womanly," and approach it with an open mind. Our civilization has been patriarchal for so long, the masculine element predominating, that our conception of what feminine is, in itself, is likely to be prejudiced. For instance, it has become an established "fact" among us that masculine is strong and superior and feminine weak and inferior. Only in recent times has this dogma been challenged by the revolt of women who have not only questioned the theory but have also demonstrated in practice that it does not hold water. But the preconception still persists that men are in some peculiar way, not dependent on personal achievement, or character, or strength, superior to women—that man *qua man* is superior to woman as such. In matriarchal societies the reverse of this assumption is held to be true.

Pure matriarchal societies are very rare today, but there are

2 Soul is used here not in the theological sense of an immortal part of man which shall replace him at death, but in the psychological sense of an unseen figure which represents the unconscious, or relatively unconscious part of his psyche.

still in existence a good many societies where the underlying "mother rule" still persists although men have risen to an apparent power. Among the Dobus of Melanesia, for instance, the clan is formed by relationship through the mother, it is a clan of women and their related males. The husband has no place in it. His presence in the village is tolerated during his wife's lifetime, but if she should die he has to return to his mother's village, where he comes under the rule, not of his father, but of his mother's brother.

The rise of masculine power and of patriarchal society probably started when man began to accumulate personal, as over against communal, property and found that his personal strength and prowess could increase his personal possessions. This change in secular power coincided with the rise of sun worship under a male priesthood, which began to supersede the much earlier moon cults, which, however, remained in the hands of the women. Sun worship was usually introduced and established by an edict of a military dictator, as happened in Babylon and Egypt, and probably in other countries as well.

The results of this change in emphasis between masculine and feminine were far-reaching. Perhaps one of the most important was that the concept of what constituted religious, or spiritual, values, which had been symbolized by the moon, was transferred to the sun and came under masculine control.

In the days of moon worship, religion was concerned with the unseen powers of the spirit world, and even when the state religion was transferred to the sun, a god of war, of personal aggrandizement, and of the things of this world, the spiritual qualities remained with the moon deities. For the worship of the moon is the worship of the creative and fecund powers of nature and of the wisdom that lies inherent in instinct and in the at-one-ness with natural law. But the worship of the sun is the worship of that which overcomes nature, which orders her chaotic fullness and harnesses her powers to the fulfilling of man's ends. The masculine principle, or Logos, thus came to be revered in the person of the Sun God, and the godlike qualities inherent in man, his capacity to achieve and to order, to formulate, discriminate, and generalize, were venerated in a sun hero, who undertook his twelve labors and slew the dragons of ignorance and sloth, thus acquiring consciousness, a spiritual value of a different order.

Our modern, twentieth-century attitude is the result of this shift in emphasis from the values symbolized by the moon to those represented by the sun. It has resulted in a conviction that intellect is the greatest spiritual power and that everything could be ordered rightly if only people would use their intelligence. The majority of people even believe that the difficulties of our present-day world could be solved simply by the right application of economic laws, or by some other rational system, and that people can be made good by some educational technique. We hold, in fact, that God is intelligence and that he is incarnate in man's rational intellect. Needless to say, this concept has left out of count the nonhuman creative power of the masculine principle, the Logos, which is its truly divine aspect, but such are the sterile days upon which our concept of the divine has fallen.

Yet to many thinking men and women doubts have occurred. If intellect is the supreme power, why are things in the world apparently so much worse than they were a while ago? Why does the millennium recede ever further into the distance as man increasingly seeks to control natural phenomena? There are not wanting critics who say that conditions are too complex for man's intelligence to cope with and that less misery and unfairness occurred under nature's ruthless yea and nay than under any humanly devised code.

Side by side with the optimism of those who pin their faith to an increased rational control of nature, is to be seen a profound disbelief in the very principles on which our system rests. The revolt from the ordered and rational is evident, not only in political and social movements, but more significantly still, in the realm of art. In literature as well as in the plastic arts, the established laws of aesthetics are often discarded in order that the images which rise spontaneously from the unconscious may be allowed to express themselves freely. The art products, which result, may be bizarre or incomprehensible, and, judged from the standpoint of the rational intellect, meaningless or even pathological or debased; but that they are living, energized, replete with unknown meaning is proved by the fascination they have for such large numbers of people. In his essays on Picasso and the *Ulysses* of Joyce, Jung has discussed two such art creations, and has shown how these works also follow a law, but not the law of reason, the masculine Logos. Instead they turn aside from the rational and the consciously controlled and go by the path of the left, which leads down to darkness, into the primordial slime from which life first emerged. In these depths are the dark, sinister, feminine beginnings, in a region ruled over, not by the bright Logos of intellect, but by the dark Eros of the feelings.

The chaotic strivings of these modern artists were hampered by the struggle against the medieval orderedness which has continued to envelop us, to use Jung's expression, up to the ears. The laws of the new realm which they were seeking to explore did not manifest themselves in their works in any free or undistorted fashion, because they are still fighting against the authority of the old. Yet if we are to profit by the turn in the tide of events, whose movement has gained such rapid speed during the last half-century, it is essential that we should learn the nature of these laws.

In the religions of the moon deity this was the spirit that was recognized as the supreme power and worshipped as such. Here the laws of the feminine principle were formulated and rituals were prescribed which aimed to put man into a right relation to a power recognized as beyond human control.

The material of the myths and religions whose interpretation we are about to consider is religious material. It has to do, not with adaptations to outer objects and circumstances, but with inner, spiritual, or psychic attitudes. Spiritual attitudes naturally show themselves in the kind of adaptation which an individual makes in his ordinary life, but that is a secondary effect and not the primary object of a religious ritual or observance. So, when we consider the feminine principle or Eros and the demands which an adequate relation to it make upon the individual, we shall not expect to find a rule of etiquette or of conventional good behavior. Indeed, one effect of the prestige in which the masculine order has been held among us is that the feminine side of life has come to be regarded in a sentimental way, while the rules of feeling have been entirely routinized into a conventional form which has further stifled the already repressed feminine. The characteristics which are generally considered womanly: the undiscriminating kindliness, the general or even universal charm, the yea-saying are by no means necessarily evidences of a developed relation to the Eros. The Eros is a spiritual or psychological principle, or, in the older term, it is a divinity. To be related to this principle means to be orientated to that which transcends personal aims and ambitions, it means gaining a relation to a nonpersonal value, just as to become related to the Logos means acquiring a relation to nonpersonal truth. Submission to either principle, in fact, implies that one is redeemed from a personal or ego orientation and from the desire for personal power and gives one's allegiance to that which is beyond the personal. It is this that is the religious attitude.

In nature the feminine principle, or as naïve man would say, the feminine *goddess*, shows itself as blind force, fecund and cruel, creating, cherishing, and destroying. It is the "female of the species, more deadly than the male," fierce in its loves as in its hate. This is the feminine principle in its daemonic form. The Chinese call it Yin, the shadowy power of the female. Just as in Babylon, Arabia, and the Near East every earth goddess is also a moon goddess, so to the Chinese yin is both earth and moon. Wilhelm writes: "The yin principle is everything dark, shady, cool, feminine, and this power commences its power in the autumn." [3] The power which begins in the autumn to overcome the sun is the cold and the dark of winter. This it is which the Chinese consider the essence of the female principle, the great Yin, symbolized by the tiger gliding stealthily through the grass, waiting to leap upon its prey with claws and fangs, yet looking all the while sleek, gentle, and catlike, making one almost forget its ferocity. This feminine power was named Eros, by the Greeks, it signifies *relatedness,* rather than love, for in the idea of Eros, negative, or hate, is comprised as well as positive, or love.

The ambivalent and potent character of the feminine principle is an ever-present psychological reality to men. To them women, seemingly, partake of its daemonic power, though many men are unaware of this fact. But the almost universal fear that men have of falling under the power or fascination of a woman and the attraction that this same bondage has for them are evidences that the effect a woman produces on a man is not infrequently daemonic in character. The depreciatory attitude which many a man takes towards women is an unconscious attempt to control a situation in which he feels himself at a disadvantage, or he seeks to undercut the dreaded power of the

3 Richard Wilhelm, *The Soul of China* (New York and London, 1928), p. 318.

woman by inducing her to act towards him as a mother. In this way he is released in large measure from his fear, for in his relation to his mother nearly every man has experienced the positive aspect of woman's love. Even so, he is not entirely free from apprehension, because in making the woman mother he, at the same time, makes himself child, and is thus in danger of falling into his own childishness. If this happens he may be overcome by his own weakness, which once more leaves the woman all-powerful in the situation. Consequently, for the most part a man approaches a woman with fear, albeit unconscious fear, or with hostility born of fear, or perhaps with a dominant attitude that is intended to overcome her at a stroke.

The image of woman as daemonic is not due as a rule to any experience the man has had with a particular woman; although his experience may confirm his unconscious presupposition, it depends rather on a universal assumption which rests on the nature of the man's own anima, or feminine soul, his inner image of *the feminine*. For the anima is not a woman but a feminine nature-spirit, which reflects the characteristics of the daemonic, nonhuman moon goddess, and gives to man a direct experience of the nonhuman Eros in all its power, both glorious and terrible. In ordinary life a man does not contact the hard, predatory, implacable masculine principle directly, but meets it in human guise, mediated by his superior function, disciplined thinking, or trained physical strength. But the feminine within himself is not mediated through a cultured and developed human personality. The feminine principle, the moon goddess, acts upon him directly from the unconscious, approaching him intimately, like a traitor from within. Small wonder if he dreads and distrusts it.

With the woman the situation is somewhat different. She usually does not experience the feminine principle directly in this daemonic form. For it is mediated to her through her own womanhood and her own developed feeling approach to life. But if she will stop long enough to look within, she also may become aware of impulses and thoughts which are not in accord with her conscious attitudes but are the direct outcome of the crude and untamed feminine being within her. For the most part, however, a woman will not look at these dark secrets of her own nature. It is too painful, too undermining of the conscious character which she has built up for herself; she prefers to think that she really is as she appears to be. And indeed it is her task to stand between the Eros which is within her, and the world without, and through her own womanly adaptation to the world to make human, as it were, the daemoniac power of the nonhuman feminine principle. In our Western civilization we have separated ourselves so far from the more instinctive aspects of the Eros, and have domesticated the superficial part of it so highly, that in her Eros attitude to the world—in her social and domestic relations, that is—the woman's way has become completely organized and conventionalized, with the result that, not only are these social and domestic relationships frequently rendered stale and infertile, but the woman herself suffers from being cut off from the springs of life in the depths of her own being.

When a man and woman seek to form a relationship, more intimate than a merely conventional acquaintance, great differences in their points of view and in the relative values which they assign to life become apparent. These discrepancies in their attitudes are dependent on the fact that the psychic constitution of men and women are essentially different; they are the mirror opposites the one of the other. That which to the man is spiritual, good, to be sought after, is to the woman daemonic, powerful, and destructive, and vice versa. So that their essential nature and values are diametrically opposed.

Yet, because their natures are complementary, men and women have an inescapable need of each other and are compelled to attempt to make mutual relationships. So great, however, is the divergence of their aims that conflict between them inevitably arises whenever they come into close association. This conflict may at times seem utterly irreconcilable, and the burden which their need for each other imposes may become intolerable.

The conventional way of handling this agelong problem is to remain as unconscious as possible of the deeper subjective effects of contact with the other sex, allowing nature and instinct to care for the intimate side of the association, while masking the real nature of the psychological relationship with a veneer of politeness. In recent years, as the authority of this conventional way of handling the problem of the man-woman relationship has been gradually undermined, the real conflict between them has blazed up into a social conflagration of no small extent, and now it is almost as common for a marriage to end disastrously as for it to go its way on the conventional path of the so-called happy marriage, where all too often tolerance and unconsciousness act as soporifics deadening more active discontent.

This external conflict between men and women is, however, but a picture of a subjective conflict of even greater prevalence, which is pursued within each individual, although, perhaps, without his conscious awareness. For no individual is entirely male or entirely female. Each is made up of a composite of both elements, and these two constituents are not infrequently in constant conflict within the psyche. Until this personal aspect of the problem is resolved the individual man or woman will not be able to find a solution of the external difficulty in his relationships, for he will inevitably project the less conscious, less disciplined part of his own psyche upon his partner. The man, for instance, will encounter his own undomesticated feminine elements in his relation to his wife and will see all that she is and all she does through the mists of his own unredeemed and daemonic anima. Her motives will be distorted, in his view, and her actions misunderstood. Sometimes the distortion may make her seem cruel, hostile, or crafty, at others on account of the same distortion he may impute to her kindness, understanding, and tolerance which are no less untrue and deceptive. He is, indeed, incapable of seeing her clearly because he does not see himself, either fully or truly. Until he does so and can come to terms with the "other side" of himself he cannot have any true or genuine relation with a woman. But to do this means facing an inner conflict which may well prove to be a very painful experience. Yet the problem is not solved, either by being ignored, or by projecting the unacceptable factor to the other sex. If man is to be whole he must face his unwholeness squarely. His inner conflict will only be resolved when he has found a relation to both aspects of himself and is reconciled with those ruling powers of the psyche, the masculine and feminine principles, which are inherent in the very nature of every individual.

In the symbolism we are about to consider and which seems to be practically universal, the feminine principle or Eros is represented by the moon and the masculine principle or Logos by the sun. As the creation myth in Genesis states: God created two lights, the greater light to rule the day and the lesser light to rule the night. The sun as masculine principle is ruler of the day, of consciousness, of work and achievement and of conscious understanding and discrimination, the Logos. The moon, the feminine principle, is ruler of the night, of the unconscious. She is goddess of love, controller of those mysterious forces beyond human understanding, which attract certain human beings irresistibly to each other, or as unaccountably force them apart. She is the Eros, powerful and fateful, and incomprehensible.

In the myths and religions relating to the moon is to be found a mine of information about the nature of the Eros and the laws which govern its functioning. These accumulations represent the wisdom of antique and primitive men who were nearer to nature than ourselves. They may hold treasures of understanding for us, or, on the other hand, they may be merely archaeological curiosities. We cannot take them uncritically as representing a wisdom appropriate for us, as well as for the ancients, but neither can we discard them as valueless merely because they are old. The fact that the symbolisms of the moon which were evolved by widely separated peoples in so many ages correspond so closely with each other is evidence that they sprang from the depths of the human psyche where truths slumber that are of universal validity. Images, that arise in this way from the depths of man's unconscious psyche in the form of symbols, are apt to have a truth which transcends human wisdom or intelligence. But we might still say these things were true and valid for the people who produced them, but why should we take them into serious consideration? The answer is that similar images arise today in the unconscious products of modern men and women. They are to be seen in artistic creations—pictures, poetry, drama—and also they are present in the dreams and phantasies of the ordinary individual who has no claim to artistic capacities.

The sensible attitude would seem to be neither to credit nor to discredit the wisdom of the ancients but instead to examine these myths with an open mind. If they do not appeal to us directly they will convey no truth to us and we may as well waste no further time upon them. But if they do speak to us, their strange nonrational logic will carry its own conviction and no rational proof of their truth will be necessary.

4

EARLY REPRESENTATIONS OF THE
MOON DEITY

Symbols and forms appearing in the dreams of modern people
are often strikingly similar to some ancient carving or primitive
picture. Unless one is familiar with these crude archetypal
images one may be at a loss how to interpret them in the modern dream; their meaning escapes one, yet the feeling the
dreamer has in regard to such symbols indicates that they are
of importance and carry a significance which yet remains unconscious. An individual having such a dream may feel the urge
to draw the symbol or represent it in some other objective
way.

The ancients evidently had a similar reaction to their inner
experiences. If these had power, mana, they were conceived of
as gods, and the urge to represent them in some concrete form
was evidently a very powerful motive indeed. When we consider the amount of work necessary, with the tools at their
disposal, to engrave the pictograms and carve the stone images
which have come down to us, we marvel at the intensity of the
emotion which could have motivated such a concentrated effort.
The gods must, indeed, have been forces of the greatest moment
to antique man and to the primitives of a later date, to have
inspired the undertaking whose results are still extant.

The earliest representation of the moon deity, and perhaps
the most universal, was a cone or pillar of stone. (Figure 1.)
This stone was peculiarly sacred. Sometimes it was of meteoric
origin, a fabulous thing which fell upon the earth out of the
sky. The miraculous origin of these stones must have greatly
increased the awe and veneration with which they were regarded. In other cases the stone was not left in its natural form
but was worked. In Melanesia, for instance, a crescent-shaped

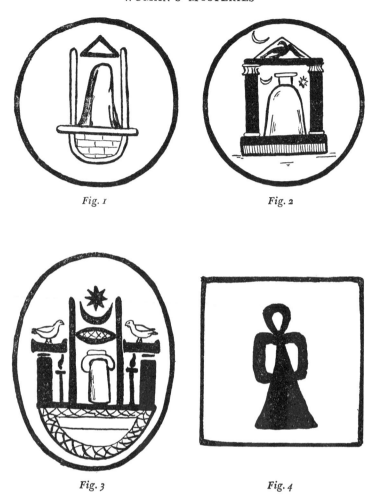

Fig. 1   Fig. 2

Fig. 3   Fig. 4

Fig. 1. The Sacred Stone of the Moon Goddess, enshrined in her temple. The image is shown as a simple cone or ompholos. (From *Religions de l'antiquité,* Georg Frederic Creuzer, 1825.)

Fig. 2. The Sacred Stone of the Moon Goddess. (From *Sur le Culte de Vénus,* Felix Lajard, 1837.)

Fig. 3. The Gateway of the Shrine of Venus at Paphos. Here the stone resembles the Emblem of Isis. (From *Symbolical Language of Ancient Art and Religion,* R. Payne Knight, 1892.)

Fig. 4. Emblem of Isis.

stone is worshipped as one aspect of the moon. It is usually to be found in company with a circular stone representing the full moon.[1]

The color of the stones varied, too; sometimes they were white, sometimes black, corresponding to the bright and dark aspects of the lunar deity, of which mention has already been made. At Paphos in Cyprus, the Baaleth or Astarte was represented by a white cone or pyramid. A similar cone represented Astarte at Byblus and Artemis at Perga in Pamphylia, while a black meteoric stone was worshipped as Cybele at Pessinus in Galatia. Cones of sandstone came to light at the shrine of The Mistress of Turquoise among the precipices of Mount Sinai, which suggests that the Great Moon Goddess was worshipped on this Mountain of the Moon in the form of a cone, before Moses received the Tables of the Law there.

In Chaldea the Great Goddess, Magna Dea, who was goddess of the Moon, was worshipped in the form of a sacred black stone which is believed to be the very stone still venerated at Mecca. Al-Kindy tells us in his *The Apology,* that Al-Uzza, one aspect of the threefold Great Goddess of Arabia, was enshrined in the Ka'aba at Mecca, where she was served by ancient priestesses. She was the special deity and protector of women. Today the Ka'aba still survives and is the most holy place of Islam.[2]

On this black stone is a mark called the Impression of Aphrodite. The Greek form of the name has for some reason come to be associated with this mark, which is an oval depression, signifying the "yoni"[3] or female genitalia. It is the sign of Artemis the goddess of Untrammelled Sexual Love, and clearly indicates that the Black Stone at Mecca belonged originally to the Great Mother.

The stone is covered with a black stuff pall called "the shirt of the Ka'aba," and it is served by men who have replaced the "ancient priestesses." These male servitors are called Beni Shaybah which means the Sons of the Old Woman. The Old Woman is a very general title for the moon, so that the men who now serve the Black Stone are the linear descendants of the old women who performed the same duties in ancient times.

1 Robert Briffault, *The Mothers* (New York and London, 1927), II, 681.
2 R. F. Burton, *Personal Narrative of a Pilgrimage to Al-Madinah and Meccah* (London, 1855–6), II, 161.
3 John O'Neill, *The Night of the Gods* (London, 1893), I, 117.

The stone, which represents the Moon, does not always appear in exactly the same form. Sometimes it is a mere rounded mound, resembling the "Omphalos," which is probably the earliest representation of the earth mother, but more often it is elongated, forming a cone or pillar, while in many cases it is worked or carved. A few of the characteristic forms of the sacred stone are collected in figures 1–5.

Goblet d'Alviella in his *Migration of Symbols*, has arranged pictures of these stones in a series, culminating in the statue of Artemis which in her characteristic hieratic attitude completes the series without departing from the general form. He suggests that the form of the statue has grown out of the stone, as it were. The stone was the original representation of the moon goddess which gradually took on human characteristics. This transition can be readily appreciated by comparing the stones in the accompanying figures with the very archaic statue of Artemis in figure 24 and the much later statues reproduced in figure 25.

Such a comparison makes it clear that these columns are not phallic, as has often been supposed. They have an entirely different history from the "Herms" with which they are sometimes confused, and which were usually marked with a phallic symbol, an arrow or acute-angled triangle, such as is commonly found on other phallic pillars, representing the masculine efficiency or potency of the great man in whose honor they were erected. It corresponds to the feminine symbol often found on the sacred stones of the Moon Mother, which is a symbol of the generative power of woman and of her sexual attraction for men, having a slightly different connotation from the cup, the chalice, and the grail, which are womb symbols and represent the maternal qualities of woman rather than her sexual attraction, but the two ideas are not far apart and often merge into each other. Thus in these stone figures it is evident that an attempt was made to represent woman, her form, her sexuality, her feminine essence.

In addition to the cone or pillar of stone, a wooden pillar or a tree is frequently found as an emblem of the moon. The sacred Moon Tree is of very ancient date, and appears over and over again in religious art. It is especially frequent in Assyrian pictures. (See figures 6–13.) Figure 13 is a very beautiful picture of the sacred moon tree, which is covered with fruits.

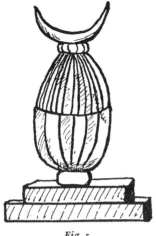

Fig. 5

Fig. 5. Deus Lunus. (From *A New System or Analysis of Ancient Mythology,* Jacob Bryant, 1774.)

Fig. 6. The Sacred Moon Tree of Babylon. The lower branches bear torches, symbolizing the light of the moon.

Fig. 7. The Sacred Moon Tree of Chaldea with fruits.

Fig. 8. The Sacred Moon Tree with trellis and torches.

Fig. 9. Three forms of the Sacred Moon Tree of Assyria, showing the gradual conventionalization till it is a mere stump or pillar. (All from *Sur le Culte de Mithra,* Felix Lajard, 1847.)

Fig. 6   Fig. 7

Fig. 8   Fig. 9

43

Fig. 10

Fig. 11

Fig. 12

Fig. 13

Fig. 10. The Sacred Phœnician Moon Tree, guarded by Winged Lions. (From *The Migration of Symbols,* Goblet d'Alviella, 1894. By permission of Constable & Co., London.)

Fig. 11. Assyrian Moon Tree guarded by Unicorns.

Fig. 12. Assyrian Moon Tree in the form of a stump or pillar, guarded by Winged Monsters.

Fig. 13. Assyrian Moon Tree with Unicorn and Winged Lion. The Hero is about to fight the Monster. (Figs. 11, 12, and 13 from *Sur le Culte de Mithra,* Felix Lajard, 1847.)

Two animals, a winged lion and a unicorn, attend the tree; one is going and one coming; they doubtless, with the tree itself, indicate the three aspects of the moon, Sinn Triune. The human figure which stands by, knife in hand, may be Sinn himself, or it may be the hero who fights the devouring monsters.

Sometimes the sacred moon tree is pictured as an actual tree, or plant, with the crescent moon or the moon god in its branches. (Compare figure 20 with figure 6.) At other times it is conventionalized in some measure. It may even appear as a mere truncated pole; occasionally it is so changed and simplified that it resembles the stone pillars which have already been discussed. The truncated tree figures in myths relating to several of the moon deities. In some moon religions the cutting down of the tree became an important part of the ritual reenactment of the death or passion of the god; the coffin containing the body of Osiris was enclosed in the trunk of the tree, whose branches were lopped off so that it could form the roof-tree for the king's palace; Diana, the Great Goddess, was brought from Greece to Italy hid in a bundle of faggots. And most instructive of all, at the festival of the mourning for Attis, a pine tree was cut down, the branches of this tree were lopped off, and the dead god Attis was tied to the trunk. The whole ritual portrayed his castration and death before the mother, the tree being here, as elsewhere, both a symbol for the mother who embraces and encloses the son, and also for the son himself, who by that embrace is castrated and killed.

A similar theme is found in the Wak-Wak tree of Persia, Arabia, Turkey, and India. This was a sacred tree on which dead bodies hung and on which, also, human heads bloomed. It is a tree of death and a tree of life. The word *Wak-Wak* closely resembles the term *wakan,* which like *taboo* means spiritual, consecrated, wonderful, and is used also of women at the menstrual period.

The Ashera which is so frequently mentioned in the Old Testament, was a conventionalized tree and was treated as though it were the goddess Ashtarte, herself. The prophets condemned the worship of the Ashera and the New Moons and Sabbaths on which its service was carried out. These and the groves where the Ashera were set up are all parts of the ritual of the moon goddesses. So it was against the Moon Mother, who had reigned in Sinai before Jehovah's coming, that the monotheism of the Jews had its greatest struggle.

The moon tree is often shown in pictures, covered with fruits or lights, like our Christmas tree. In one Assyrian picture it has ribbons like our Maypole. Perhaps a dance may have taken place around the tree in those faraway days, like the dance which is still performed round the Maypole on May Day. In such a dance the ribbons would be interwoven, as in our own dance, to represent the decking of the bare tree with bright-colored leaves and flowers and fruits, all gifts of the moon goddess, giver of fertility. Sometimes the tree is shown enclosed in a sort of shrine or sanctuary or around it is a trellis, making a miniature garden. (Figure 7.) It will be recalled that the Moon Goddess was worshipped in a grotto or a natural grove or a garden. In poems and religious texts it is not infrequently stated that the "Tree grows in the midst of the garden." The sacred stone at Paphos which is represented in figure 3 is also usually shown inside a trellis which makes a garden of the shrine.

In certain Mycaenian pictures the sacred olive tree is seen growing in such a shrine, the one reproduced in figure 17 comes from a Cretan gem of the Minoan days. Here the moon is not in the branches of the tree but is hidden in the secret place in the midst of the altar, as it is also in an ancient Italian carving from the Barberini Palace in Rome. (Figure 14.) In the first of these a worshipper approaches the altar, perhaps to ask for an oracle from the moon, whose tree is the source of inspiration and secret wisdom.

A cross or pole, standing upright in a crescent, has been found in certain Greek churches. This is of pre-Christian origin and the cross or pole probably represents a truncated tree (figure 15).

In still other pictures we find the tree modified so that it resembles a lotus or a fleur-de-lys. This modification occurs both in Assyrian and in Egyptian representations. In the pictures reproduced the crescent moon crowns the tree in figures 6 and 7 and in figure 20 the god Sinn, himself, sits enthroned on the crescent. The god and his throne together form the fruit of the tree. This fruit is the source of that drink of immortality, of secret knowledge, and of inspiration so highly prized by the gods and so jealously guarded by them. Belief in the wonderful powers of this tree long predated the Genesis story of the trees "in the midst of the garden," but we cannot fail to be struck by the similarity of the powers ascribed to them and of their surroundings. In the garden of Eden the fruit of knowledge and the fruit of immortality grew on separate trees. More often both these gifts are thought of as the fruit of the one tree which grows in the "central place of the earth," as an ancient hymn has it.

This hymn, known as the Hymn of Eridu, is one of the very earliest religious poems which have come down to us from the remote past. Eridu was the center of an ancient civilization on the borders of the Persian Gulf. Probably the peoples afterwards called Chaldeans originated there and subsequently

Fig. 14

Fig. 15

Fig. 16

Fig. 17

Fig. 14. Shrine of the Sacred Moon Tree from an ancient Italian carving found in the Barberini Palace, Rome. (From *Ancient Pagan and Modern Christian Symbolism*, Thomas Inman, 1876.)

Fig. 15. Pre-Christian symbol found in Greek churches.

Fig. 16. Assyrian Winged Moon, from an Assyrian cylinder, probably eighteenth dynasty. (From *Symbolism on Greek Coins,* Agnes Baldwin Brett, 1916. By permission of American Numismatic Society.)

Fig. 17. Shrine of the Sacred Moon Tree from a Cretan gem of the Minoan period. (From *Themis,* Jane Harrison, 1912. By permission of the Cambridge University Press and The Macmillan Company.)

migrated to the Euphrates where they founded the city of Ur. The hymn commemorates the moon tree and its fruit, and is as follows:

Its root (or fruit) of white crystal stretched toward the deep.
Its seat was the central place of the earth;
Its foliage was the couch of Zikum, the (primeval) mother.
Into the heart of the holy house which spreads its shade like a
    forest
hath no man entered,
There (is the house of) the mighty mother, who passes across the
    sky
(In) the midst of it was Tammuz.

This sacred tree is the "house of the mighty mother who passes across the sky," a beautiful description of the moon. In the midst of it is Tammuz, the Green One, son of the Moon Mother, Ishtar, who is himself also the Young Moon, successor to Sinn, who is represented in figure 20 as the divine fruit of the sacred moon tree.

"Its root stretched toward the deep" proclaims that the power of the moon extends even into the underworld. In figure 22 Sinn, in his black aspect, is judging the dead. It is a picture of the underworld life of the moon god and here also we find the moon tree has its place. The line "into the heart of its holy house . . . hath no man entered" proclaims the fact that the meaning of the Moon Goddess and her moon tree is a mystery, indeed it might be called the Mother of Mysteries.

The moon tree is frequently represented as guarded or attacked by animals or monsters. In the Assyrian and Phoenician pictures the animals are lions, unicorns, goats or winged monsters. (Figures 10–13.) They correspond to Typhon or Set of the Egyptian story, and to the earlier Devil of Darkness, who, in the myths, attacked the Moon God and slew him. But the animals in the shrine of the moon have another significance, for the moon god was later replaced by a moon goddess, mother of all living creatures, a representation of fecund feminine nature. This goddess is usually represented as many-breasted, not only in very archaic statues, but later ones as well, whose beauty and refinement bespeak a high level of culture in the artist. (Figures 23 and 25.) Her many breasts witness to her universal maternal and fostering instinct, while also suggesting her own animal origin. In her arms and all over her robes are grouped her animal children.

The farther back we go in our search for the origins and meaning of the Moon Goddess the nearer do we come to the animal concept. Hecate was once, in the dim past, the three-headed Hound of the Moon; Artemis was a Bear; Isis was Hathor the Cow-Goddess; Cybele was once a Lioness or a lion-headed goddess. She sits on a lion throne and rides in a chariot drawn by lions; and Atargatis, Queen of Heaven, is shown riding a lion, her head surrounded by rays. In the later centuries of the Egyptian worship of Osiris it was said that Apis, the Bull, was the *spirit* of Osiris. This saying gives a direct clue to the evolution of the religious thought.

First the moon deity was an animal, then the spirit of the god is an animal. Later the god or goddess is attended by animals. Later still these animal attendants were replaced by human beings who wore animal masks, performed animal dances, and were called by animal names. We are told, for instance, that little Athenian girls danced as bears to Artemis of Brauronia, the Bear-Goddess, while Bear-men attended the Celtic moon goddess, who was once manifested in bear form.

The bear, indeed, represents the fierce and terrible aspect of the Goddess herself, which not only creates but also destroys life. Later the two aspects of the Goddess become partially differentiated and separated, so that in the famous sculpture of "The Mourning Aphrodite of Lebanon," the animal, in this case a boar instead of a bear, is killing the youthful Adonis, while Aphrodite laments in deepest grief. Yet the boar is also Aphrodite, herself.[4]

The animal attendants and animal emblems surrounding the goddess in her shrines must have constantly reminded the worshippers of later days, of those wilder aspects of her nature from which she had in part evolved. Her animals she still kept near her, for she could not be comprehended except in the light of her past.

The psychological meaning of this gradual change in form is clear. In extremely early days, before civilization had progressed very far, feminine instinct was perceived as entirely

4 See Chapter 7.

animal. Then the fierceness of the mother's care for her young and the voracity of her lust for the male in the mating season were the most obvious and dominant characteristics of beast and woman alike. As civilization progressed, however, women began to develop something nearer akin to the emotion which we call love, and the goddess of women rose gradually above her animal nature. She was represented now as woman but with the fierceness of her feminine instinct not far away. She rides her lion, gives birth to her animals, wears her headdress of cow horns and is attended by her beasts, while she herself transcends in some measure the fierce animal passions which these things represent.

This situation is not far removed from the condition of our own civilization today. Our women have learned human manners and emotions—pity, consideration, love; but not far beneath the surface, slumbering in unconsciousness, the old primitive form of feminine instinct lurks, ready to spring up again and perhaps even to reassert its power over consciousness in any really critical situation. If a woman's babe is starving to death, no one is surprised if she should revert to primitive ways of satisfying its needs, or if this seems impossible she may even destroy it in face of dire necessity. The frequent occurrence of crimes of passion bears witness to the pantherlike qualities which feminine instinct may develop when frustrated. These things we recognize as manifestations of human nature, deplorable perhaps, but, because we feel them to be inevitable, the outcome of forces beyond the personal control of the individuals concerned, we condone them even if we do not actually accept or admire them.

This rapacious aspect of the Moon Goddess is represented by the lion or panther; her maternal and nurturing aspect is more frequently represented by the cow, whose horns naturally suggest the "hornéd moon." In her human form the goddess is often attended by a goat, a cow, or a bull. In the picture reproduced in figure 42 two playful goats are harnessed to the chariot which bears the moon across the sky on its nightly journey, and, in an exactly similar goat chariot, Cybele, crowned with a rayed headdress, is carried on the same journey. The Moon Goddess is often shown wearing little horns as a headdress, a device which was common in Babylonian as in Greek art.

The Moon Goddess is thus the heavenly cow and her child.

the young moon, is the Bull Child. Pasiphae, the Minoan Moon Queen, She who Shines for All, was mother of the holy Bull Child. In a medieval Latin hymn Christ is described as the "Wild wild Unicorn whom the Virgin caught and tamed."

The Bull Child, son of the Moon Mother, is the hero who comes to earth and shows men the way to salvation. He stands between earth and heaven, for he is a man, subject to death as man is, but he is also Son of the Virgin Moon Mother, the Eternal and Unborn. He partakes of the nature both of man and of the gods. The initiate of Osiris was taught a word of power to use as introduction to the world of the gods when he sought entrance there after death. He was to proclaim himself "Child of Earth and Starry Heaven." Christ himself, in his mythological aspect, was such a divine son, the holy unicorn tamed by the Virgin and so, perhaps, transformed into Aries, the goat or, as he is more commonly called, the Lamb. In this aspect his non-warlike qualities are the ones that are emphasized. He is entirely docile and accepting. For the Son of the Moon Mother always accepted his fate and never resisted it although he was condemned to death annually. This mildness is frequently the chief characteristic of the moon hero, as, for instance, where the hare carries this role. Just because of his docility and lack of belligerence the hare is often able to find a way, where a more headstrong or direct attack would lead to disaster. The hare thus becomes the leader or guide. This quality of gentleness corresponds also with an aspect of feminine nature which is the exact opposite of the cruel or fierce impulses represented by the lions and panthers of the Goddess. For feminine nature, like the moon, is light as well as dark; and the light, unlike that of the sun, is mild and cool, aptly represented by gentle and timid animals such as the hare.

Two other elements of feminine nature remain to be considered. These are represented in myth and religious pictures by winged creatures and the serpent. Birds, especially doves, are shown in the shrine of the moon goddess and her animal attendants are also frequently winged (figure 3). The horns of the crescent itself are sometimes replaced by wings as though the moon were flying across the sky. Such a winged moon, containing the Moon God, Sinn, is shown in figure 16. In this picture streams of water, which may be rain, or more probably nectar, or the moon drink, soma, are pouring down to earth, where they are caught in a vase or chalice.

Sometimes the Moon Goddess herself has the wings of the moon. On an arc, or box, of Cypselus, Diana is represented as winged, and Artemis, too, frequently has high, curved wings, or again she may be represented with a bird's head. Doves and pigeons are prominent in the shrines of Aphrodite; and Ishtar, at the flood, chose a dove as her messenger, a detail of the story which appears also in the Hebrew version of Noah and his ark. The dove, sent out to see whether the waters were receding, flew to the olive tree and plucked a green leaf. In Greece and perhaps also in Mesopotamia, the olive represented the moon tree. (Figure 17).

The light of the moon which shines from heaven above and brings enlightenment and wisdom to the earth is frequently personified and represented by a bird, usually a dove. The Sophia, the Holy Wisdom of the Gnostics, is, in fact, the light of the Heavenly Mother and is equated to the Holy Dove of the Spirit. For to the Gnostics the Holy Spirit is feminine, is indeed *the* feminine essence, the Eros. This is the latest and most evolved form of the moon goddess, only dimly foreshadowed by the myths which we are considering here. The writings of the Catholic Fathers, of which we shall speak later, prepare us to expect that the same symbolism which originated in the ancient cults of the moon goddess will still be preserved in the forms which have been hallowed for us through Christian teaching. These correspondences are even clearer in the writings of the Gnostics than in orthodox Christianity, where for the most part they have been concealed or entirely removed. But the Holy Dove, still to be found in Christian churches, and venerated in Christian teaching as the Messenger of God, Bringer of Wisdom, was known to ages long since past, as the messenger and incarnation of the Magna Mater, She who Shines for All.

The animals already considered in connection with the Moon Goddess are "yin" animals, to use the Chinese word, and represent the various aspects of feminine instinct, but in addition to these yin animals a close association has always been made between serpents and the moon, and this on more than one account. In the first place the serpent was credited with the power of self-renewal because of his ability to change or renew his skin. This power was felt to be akin to the power of the moon which renewed itself month by month, after its apparent death. The ever-changing, ever-renewing character of both moon and snake have given rise to beliefs which ascribe the power of immortality sometimes to the moon and sometimes to the serpent. Primitive and ancient myths also relate that the gift of immortality was brought to men sometimes by the moon and sometimes by a serpent, in other cases the serpent reveals to men the virtue that is concealed in the fruit of the moon tree or in the soma drink which can be brewed from it.

The serpent, however, is associated with the moon for another reason. Snakes live in dark holes and go down through cracks in the earth and in rocks. They live in a subterranean region which to the ancients was the underworld. Their movement is secret and mysterious, they are cold-blooded and inaccessible to human feeling. For these reasons they have always been considered to be related to the underworld and to the shades of the dead. In its dark phase the moon, also, has to do with the underworld and with chthonic powers, and in this aspect the divinities of the moon can appear, as can all underworld deities, in the form of snakes. For instance, Hecate, the dark moon goddess, was herself partly snake in form, or was shown with snakes in her hair, and Ishtar was said to be covered with scales like a snake.

There is a third role which the snake played in the worship of the Moon Goddess, namely as a representation of the Phallus. Pallas or Priapus was worshipped in the temple of Vesta, where he was sometimes represented as a snake; while Pan had a place in the temple of Selene. In nearly every place where she was worshipped the Moon Goddess was attended by women priestesses and usually her guardians were virgins, often hierodules, or sacred prostitutes. As the snake has to do with her worship it is not surprising that this creature also is tended by maidens. On certain Ophite jewels Cybele, the great Moon Goddess, is seen offering a cup to a snake, and at Spireus, in the shrine of Apollo, himself a latecomer among the gods, a sacred snake was kept, perhaps reminiscent of an older worship that the Olympian had usurped. This snake was fed by a virgin, who significantly enough had to be naked when she performed her service. The great earth mother, Demeter, was attended in her temple at Eleusis, by a snake, called Kychreus, and a mystical

union with a snake probably formed the central ritual of the
Eleusinian mysteries of the Great Mother. The Snake theme
turns up in another rather unexpected place. The God of
Mount Sinai, the name of which means Mountain of the Moon,
was served by attendants called Levites. These Levites wore the
lunar crescent as a headdress. Hommel states that the word
Levi, meaning *to wreathe* or *be devoted,* is used in Minoan
inscriptions in connection with the god Wadd who was God of
Love and God of the Moon.

In myths and also in primitive beliefs it is very commonly
stated that snakes hold congress with women and that women
may become pregnant by them. It is also thought in some places
that the bite of a snake is responsible for a girl's first menstruation, and that women are particularly liable to attract "serpent
love" when menstruating. For this reason the women of some
tribes will not go into the bush, or to a spring, when menstruating for fear of becoming pregnant by a snake, or in other cases,
they may make pilgrimages for this very purpose to a spring believed to be inhabited by a sacred snake. Sometimes the snake
in these beliefs is replaced by a fish, which is then surrounded
by the same fears and taboos which are so characteristic in relation to the snake.[5] The Moon Goddess herself was sometimes
represented as half fish, in which form she is perhaps the forerunner of our own mermaids. Ishtar, for instance, in the form
of Derketo, was a sort of fish leviathan (figure 30). She was
the great whale dragon who made the disastrous flood and lamented that her children were made like the fishes of the sea.
The king's child, who fell out of the boat of Isis and was
drowned, was called the Fisher,[6] a title which orthodox Christianity, as well as the Gnostics, applied to Christ, though sometimes, with a change of metaphor which is very common in
mythology, he is called *Ichthyos,* the Fish. A medieval hymn
calls him the "Little Fish which the Virgin caught in the foun-
tain." Thus he is fisher and fish, a dual role which has to do
with the hero function of the god, who, by partaking of the
nature of both man and god can, through his passion, in some
measure assimilate the human to the divine.

5 J. A. MacCulloch, "Serpent Worship," Hastings' *Encyclopaedia of Religion
and Ethics* (New York and Edinburgh, 1920), XI, 399.
6 See Chapter 13, p. 174.

5

THE MOON CYCLE OF WOMEN

As we have seen, the belief that there is a peculiar connection between woman and the moon has been universally held from the earliest times. Her power to bear children, surely a most mysterious thing, was thought to be the gift of the moon, while the activities which were her particular charge, agriculture, making things grow, tending the fire, and cooking the food, depended for their success on the good offices of the moon. To primitive man, her monthly rhythm, corresponding as it does with the moon's cycle, must have seemed the obvious result of some mysterious bond between them.

Some of the North American Indians, for example, hold the moon to be really a woman, the First Woman; at her waning the moon has her "sickness," the word used for menstruation. Peasants in some parts of Europe are reported to believe that the moon menstruates and that she is "sickening" during the period of waning, while the red rain or heavenly blood, which old folklore asserts often falls from the skies, is "moon-blood."

In other languages, too, words for menstruation and for moon are either the same or are closely related. Our word menstruation signifies "moon change," *mens* being "moon." German peasants call the menstrual period simply "the moon"; in France it is called *le moment de la lune.* Briffault[1] has collected many other examples of this verbal connection. For instance, the Mandingo use the word *carro* for both moon and menstruation; in the Congo *njonde* has a similar double meaning. In the Torres Straits and in India the same word is used for menstrual blood and for moon. The Maori call menstruation *mata marama* which means moon sickness and they believe that a girl's first menstruation is due to the moon's having had connection with her during her sleep.

[1] Robert Briffault, *The Mothers* (New York and London, 1927), II, 430–32.

During menstruation women are almost universally put under certain restrictions which seem strange to us with our rational attitude in relation to physical occurrences. An examination of social customs reveals the fact, however, that in all parts of the world and among all peoples, with the single exception of the more highly educated white races—and even this exception needs some modification—women during menstruation are considered to be taboo. Taboo is a curious word. It means, variously, unclean, holy, or set apart, and we find that during the period of their sickness, women of many tribes are considered to be in a state so peculiar that any object they touch is defiled or loses its efficacy.[2] For this reason when a woman is menstruating she cannot remain with other people nor go about her usual occupations. She must isolate herself and remain alone. Sometimes she merely retires for those few days to a room set apart for the purpose. This room is usually dark and airless, for the light of the moon must not fall on a menstruating woman. In other cases a special house called the menstrual lodge is provided on the outskirts of the village where the women can retire, but sometimes even that amount of care is not granted to them and they must go to the bush and protect themselves as best they can from heat, storm, or cold in whatever rude shelters they can construct. In many tribes similar taboos surround women in childbirth, and often when their time draws near the women have to go away from the village, entirely unassisted, into the bush and fend for themselves. Food may be brought to them and left at a distance but in some cases the woman is not allowed to touch her own food but must either be fed with morsels passed to her on a stick or if she feeds herself she must wrap her hand in a cloth before touching the food. Sometimes it is even prohibited for her to touch her own person, in such cases she is provided with a stick for scratching her head. A remnant of this old taboo was still to be found in rural places in England at the beginning of the twentieth century where a woman in childbed was not supposed to comb her own hair lest some evil result. And at the end of her lying-in period, which was considered to be one month in duration, she needed to be released from her *taboo* condition by a religious ritual. A special service of the Churching of Women

[2] For a general consideration of this subject see J. G. Frazer, "Balder the Beautiful," *The Golden Bough,* Part VII; I, 22–100, and Briffault, *op. cit.,* II, 365–412.

is provided for this purpose in the Anglican and Roman rituals, a survival of the old belief that a woman who has borne a child needs to be disinfected, not surgically, but religiously. This custom is related to the old superstition that until a woman has been to church to be purified of her "confinement," it is unlucky for her to go out of doors. As for the old menstrual taboo, traces of it can still be found in Europe where a menstruating woman may be forbidden to touch butter, wine, or meat, lest these foods be rendered quite unfit for human consumption, while the taboo against washing at such times remains in certain sections of society almost to the present day.

Among primitive peoples, however, the taboo extends to much greater lengths than this. When a woman is under a menstrual taboo she may not be approached by any man. Even her shadow is polluting so that if she walks abroad she may not use the ordinary trails, and anything that she touches is immediately destroyed. There is also a very widespread scruple among primitives against passing under an overhanging bough, for fear a woman may have climbed over or sat upon it and contaminated the spot with menstrual blood. Briffault suggests that a similar idea may underlie our own superstition against walking under a ladder. The usual reason given for the wisdom of observing this "taboo" is that something might be dropped upon you from above. In England I have repeatedly heard it said that a drop of *red* paint might fall upon you. I have never heard that there is any danger of green paint or white, it is always red. Now red paint is everywhere considered to be a substitute for blood. A red cross means taboo all the world over; it is the sign of *the* taboo, the blood of the woman. For the taboo on the menstruating woman is probably the first observed by man and the type and pattern of all taboos.

The uncleanness of the menstruating woman is considered amongst primitive peoples to be of the nature of an actual infection or contamination, a positive evil which may be conveyed to everything she comes in contact with. In many places not only is the food she has actually touched considered to be contaminated, but all food of the same kind is also rendered unfit for food. In some tribes, for instance, a woman may not eat fish during her periods, nor touch an ear of corn, lest the entire supply perish.

The evil effects of her touch reach beyond the realm of food:

sickness and disaster of all kinds may be caused by a chance encounter with her. For these reasons women are required to seclude themselves most strictly during their "dangerous" periods and to exercise the greatest caution in their contact with the outside world. The penalties imposed for carelessly exposing themselves at such times are naturally exceedingly severe. For it is believed that if a man "looks upon a menstruating woman his bones will soften, he will lose his manhood," will even die, while his weapons and implements will become useless, his nets will no longer catch fish, and his arrows will not kill deer. And, in addition, the power of the "war-bundle," which represents the warrior's commitment to the warlike undertaking and at the same time is a charm or amulet for its success, will be destroyed by such a contact, so fatal was the power of instinctive desire aroused by the woman's condition believed to be.

It was also believed that a menstruating woman had a polluting effect on fire. If by any chance she should come near it, it is extinguished, the ashes carried out, and a new fire kindled, notwithstanding the fact that to kindle a fire is a long and arduous task. Among the primitive peoples of the Malay Peninsula young girls who are, as it were, Vestal Virgins, are charged with the carrying and tending of the fire when the group is on the march. But if a girl should be menstruating she is excluded from this office.

Similar ideas regarding the pollution of fires prevail among the fire worshippers of the Orient; neither the Zoroastrians of Persia nor the Parsees of India will allow a menstruating woman to come near the sacred fire. The great lawgivers of ancient times, Zoroaster, Manu, and Moses, each incorporated prohibitions relating to menstruation into their systems. In the laws of Manu, the Hindu lawgiver, it is stated: "The wisdom, the energy, the strength, the might, and the vitality of a man who approaches a woman covered with menstrual excretions, utterly perish. If he avoids her while she is in that condition his wisdom, energy, strength, sight, and vitality will all increase." [3]

The regulations regarding menstruation seem to represent the first taboo imposed by primitive man, or should one not

[3] G. Buhler, "The Laws of Manu," *Sacred Books of the East* (Oxford, 1879–1910), XXV, 135.

rather say they form the first taboo which "the gods" imposed on primitive man? For menstruation is a perfectly natural function and one cannot but wonder why it was placed under a taboo when other natural functions are accepted quite openly and naïvely. Various reasons have been assigned in explanation. They include a supposed horror of blood, as such, on the part of primitive man, a supposition which can be discarded, for primitive man knows no such general horror although it is true that he surrounds blood with great precautions. But no taboo attaches to the person who bleeds if the bleeding is caused by a wound. The customs relating to a menstruating woman are in an entirely different category. They can perhaps be best understood when it is realized that to the primitive mind menstruation is due to a kind of infection, or to the result of possession by an evil spirit.

Where it is believed that an evil spirit has entered into the woman, the measures taken to expel it are very similar to those which we ourselves practice when we have been *infected* or possessed by some evil thing. Primitives attempt to drive out the evil spirit by purging and fasting; by flagellation and fumigation with smoke; by washing the body and the clothes of the afflicted individual; in some cases even her hair is pulled out or she is shaved. These well-meant efforts to drive out the evil are carried to such lengths at the first menstruation, that the girl may be almost killed. We, too, drive out or dispel a physical evil, such as a disease germ, a toxin, or a fever, by identical methods; while if the evil is psychological, that is spiritual, again we use these same methods, metaphorically, or indeed concretely as well. "Spare the rod and spoil the child" refers to one method of exorcising an evil temper. "Purge me with hyssop and I shall be clean" refers not to physical autointoxication but to moral evils. Fasting and castigation are the most usual penances prescribed to purify from sin, while the incense used in churches is not far in its significance from the fumigation of a sickroom, even though it has other meanings as well. Whenever primitive man senses and dreads a supernatural force, there we must look for a psychological factor, unknown to him and therefore perceived *in the object* to which it has been projected.

The question we must ask, however, is what is this "evil"

which has entered into the woman and how does it work? Amongst animals and in those human societies where the primitive course of nature still regulates the affairs of the tribe, the congress of the sexes is regulated by the needs and desires of the female, not by the desire of the male. Only at the time of heat will the female animal permit the male to have access to her. From the physiological standpoint menstruation in women must be considered as being equivalent to heat in animals and it might be expected that in line with the animal practice, this would be *the* time when no taboo would be imposed. But the contrary is the case. The female *animal,* far from rejecting the advances of the male at the season of heat, desires and seeks his company. No taboo restrains her in the exercise of her charms. All the males of the species from far and wide are attracted to her and are unable to attend to any other interest so long as she is in that condition. Whoever has kept a female dog will know how powerful is the "evil spirit" with which she is possessed. The males who seek her out forego sleep and food and neglect their "duties" in their own homes. They are indeed bewitched!

In human societies the whole tribal organization would be broken up if instinct were allowed to run riot in this way; the situation obviously had to be controlled before any advance in culture could be made. The will of primitive man is, even under the most favorable circumstances, unstable; if tribal undertakings are ever to be put through, women in the dangerous condition of menstruation must be kept out of their way. For the men of the tribe might dance all night to concentrate their attention on the coming hunt but if the party met a menstruating woman as they started out, weapons and determination would be thrown aside together. Anything which could so arouse their untamed desire must be considered an "evil." The men of the tribe would be compelled to protect themselves by segregating the dangerous female, and in this way protect themselves also from the devastating effect of their own sexuality. The welfare of the whole tribe thus demanded that women must remain in seclusion during their sickness.

According to the Talmud, if a woman at the beginning of her period passes between two men she thereby kills one of them; if she passes between them towards the end of her period she only causes them to quarrel violently.[4] This warning is put into almost psychological terms!

This untamed desire on the part of the men naturally constituted a menace for the women. Certain primitive myths suggest that in self-defense against the excessive demands of the men, women imposed abstinence upon themselves, in spite of the fact that the period of greatest sexual desire, with them as with animals, is either immediately before or immediately after menstruation. This is the point of view expressed in an Australian myth reported by Spencer and Gillen in *The Northern Tribes of Central Australia*. "The Mara Tribe," they state, "has a legend according to which the menstrual period was brought on, in the first instance, because in the Alcheringa (the heroic age) a number of bandicoot men who were making ceremonies had too frequent intercourse with a lubra.[5] This brought on a great discharge and the woman said, 'I think I will not walk about a lubra any more, but a bandicoot,' and so she stuck grass all over herself, and went away and hid in a hole, so that the men could not find her, and ever since then women have had monthly periods," [6] and, one might add, have secluded themselves during the time of the flow.

In certain instances women, even in primitive tribes, have been known to make use of the taboo deliberately, to exclude an unwanted husband, a trick which could easily be played in communities where the count of time is very inexact. And in the beginning it is altogether possible that women may have segregated themselves during menstruation of their own accord, for their physical condition gives them an acknowledged right to isolate themselves without consulting the men, and that in societies where otherwise they may be practically slaves and are always liable to sexual demands.

The development of a menstrual taboo was, indeed, an absolute necessity for primitive peoples if their cultural evolution were to proceed. Without such a safeguard, it would seem well-nigh impossible for either men or women to have developed any specifically human value, or to have released themselves from

---

[4] J. Meyel, *Die Medizin der Talmudisten,* p. 15.

[5] "Bandicoot" and "lubra" are the totem names of intermarrying clans, but men of the bandicoot totem may not marry a bandicoot woman.

[6] W. B. Spencer and F. J. Gillen, *The Northern Tribes of Central Australia* (London, 1904), p. 602.

the complete domination of animal instinct. Today, a more objective and scientific understanding has freed us from the taboos and fears which for primitive man surrounded menstruation. But it is well to remember that these ancient customs were instituted, however gropingly and however unconsciously, to combat a real psychological danger; namely that at certain times the feminine instinctive nature of woman was liable to prove the undoing of men. If we are not to be precipitated again into the chaos from which primitive man extricated himself by his superstitions and taboos, we must become more conscious of the emotional factors concerned, a consciousness which can only be gained through a greater psychological understanding.

In the instances quoted above the taboos were mostly intended to protect the community from the destructive effect of the woman's mana, but on certain occasions the magic power of menstrual blood was used for other purposes. There are many records of its being used as a potent healing charm resorted to in extreme illness. In other cases the destructive effect of the menstruating woman may be used in a positive way, as, for instance, when a girl in that condition is made to run naked round a harvest field infested with caterpillars, which, it is firmly believed, will all be killed and the harvest saved. In these cases the destructive power is turned against the evil, while the crops are protected from harm.

The ancient Hindus considered menstruation to be an evidence that a woman was peculiarly under the influence of the moon. There is a Vedic text to this effect which reads: "The blood of the woman is a form of Agni and therefore no one should despise it." Menstruation is here connected with fire, for Agni is the fire-god and is closely related to the light of the moon. In this text the menstrual blood is definitely stated to be sacred, because it is a manifestation of him.

In India, the Mother Goddess is thought to menstruate regularly; during these times the statues of the Goddess are secluded and bloodstained cloths are displayed as evidence that she has had her sickness. These cloths are very highly prized as "medicine" for most illnesses. In the same way Ishtar, the moon goddess of Babylon, was thought to be menstruating at the full moon, when the sabattu, or evil day, of Ishtar was observed. The word *sabattu* comes from Sa-bat and means

Heart-rest; it is the day of rest which the moon takes when full, for at that time it is neither increasing nor decreasing. On this day, which is the direct forerunner of the Sabbath, it was considered unlucky to do any work or to eat cooked food or to go on a journey. These are the things that are prohibited to the menstruating woman. On the day of the moon's menstruation everyone, whether man or woman, was subject to similar restrictions, for the taboo of the menstruating woman was on all. The Sabbath was at first observed only once a month, later it was kept at each quarter of the moon's phases.

In the Fourth Dynasty of Ur (the third millennium B.C.) it is recorded that taboo days were observed at the new and the full moon, when no cooked food could be eaten (that is, anything which had been touched by fire was prohibited), no journey could be taken and no work could be done. Similar directions were given for the observance of the four "evil days" in the Babylonian calendar. They run as follows: "An evil day. The Shepherd of the Great People shall not eat flesh cooked upon coals, or bread from the oven [or 'anything touched by fire']. He shall not change his garment, nor put on clean raiment, nor offer sacrifice. The king shall not ride in his chariot. He shall not deliver judgment. The priest shall not give oracles in the secret place. The physician shall not lay his hands upon the sick. The day is inauspicious for all affairs whatsoever. At night the king shall bring his offering before Marduk and Ishtar." [7] The Babylonian "sabattu" was the "evil day" of the moon goddess Ishtar, when it is not unlikely that she was thought to be actually menstruating.

The sabbaths of the Jews were closely related, in their origin, to the Babylonian sabbaths, and the Christian weekly day of rest is directly connected with the Jewish sabbath, even though it is observed on a different day of the week. This historical fact all can readily concede, but it is strange to us to think that the prohibitions connected with "sabbath observance" are, in their far-off origins, menstrual taboos connected with the belief that the moon is herself a woman having a monthly period and sickness.

[7] A. H. Sayce, "A Babylonian Saints' Calendar," *Records of the Past* (London, 1876), VII, 157.

6

THE INNER MEANING OF THE
MOON CYCLE

We can readily understand how it was that to naïve people the
sun should be god of the men and the moon of the women, because of their characteristics, which seem to correspond to male
and female and so justify the choice of these symbols. A symbol, however, is not just a sign or token, a "chosen" image, it is
something far more significant. Primitive man did not choose
his gods in any conscious or comprehending way. The process
of god-choosing, to coin a word, takes place entirely otherwise.
The volition seems to be in the symbol which obtrudes itself
upon man's consciousness. It has fascination for him, *mana*,
it demands attention or worship. He cannot forget it or get rid
of it, it has a peculiar power which insists that he do certain
things in regard to it. The history of religion is the history of
the power of such symbols. We now know that this power
comes from the unconscious and that this is the secret of its
fascination for the human being. When the value represented
by the symbol has been entirely explored and made conscious
its power leaves it, and the object which held the meaning of the
symbol becomes only a natural object once more. But while
its power lasts the symbol is the representative of an unknown
truth. It rises spontaneously from the depths of the unconscious
and expresses or manifests the hidden fact in an image whose
meaning can only partly be grasped by consciousness.[1] Of a
symbol we can never say "this is this," or "that is that," trans-
lating each factor into equivalent terms of the known. For the
symbolic creations of the unconscious contain layer after layer
of meaning which cannot be exhausted in a word.

The fact that the sun seems to mankind to be a symbol of

[1] Jung, *Psychological Types* (New York and London, 1923), p. 601.

male, while the moon symbolizes female is easily appreciated. To begin with—the sun is the constant and reliable source of light and heat, but the moon is changeable. The sun is either present in the heavens or absent from them. It shines during the day, then it disappears on its long night journey, but in the morning it always reappears in the East. The moon follows a different order. She does not shine in the day but is ruler of the night. It might well be expected that she would shine during the night as the sun shines in the day. Sometimes it is true, she shines, as at full moon, but at other seasons her light is withdrawn and the night is left completely dark. Furthermore in her time of rising she seems to be dependent only on her own whim. The darkness falls at the setting of the sun. Surely the moon should then rise and give us light throughout the dark hours, but she is not to be relied on. When the sun sets the moon also may be about to set. On other nights she does not rise until the hours of darkness are almost past. And more anomalous than all else besides, at certain times her pale face may be visible hanging in the sky, at midday, her ghostly presence seeming almost a protest at the obvious and blatant light of the sun.

Once I questioned a group of men and women on their feeling about the moon. One man said: "The moon seems to me an especially feminine being. This impression is produced by its soft light and the fact that it is to be seen only in the night, that is, in mystical circumstances." This is a strange remark, for "feminine beings," women, are to be seen in the day just as much as men are. Yet what he meant is obvious. The quality which is characteristically feminine does shine only in the night, after the light of the sun is removed and the masculine activities of the workaday world are laid aside. For this reason it is difficult to talk about the significance of moon symbolism. Lao Tse, the Chinese sage, said in regard to Tao: "The Tao which is talked about is not the true Tao." It might as justly be said: "The feminine essence, when it is talked about, is no longer the true feminine essence"; or, as Dr. Jung once expressed it in poetical terms, "Yin is like a mother-of-pearl image hidden in the deepest recesses of the house."

In these unaccountable qualities of the moon, man has seen a symbol of woman's nature which to him appears erratic, changeable, fickle, not to be relied on. But the symbolism can be carried further; just as, in the case of the moon, an order or rule underlies her conduct, so with woman also a rule or law underlies her apparent fickleness. Yet this law ruling woman is no more obvious or simple than the law ruling the moon, which to the average layman is by and large incomprehensible. So also the feminine principle, which underlies so great a part of woman's conduct, is not to be easily understood.

The moonlike character of the woman's nature appears to man to be dependent only on her whim. If she changes her mind, he may concede that by general accord it is her privilege to do so; it never occurs to him that she changes it because of changed conditions within her own psyche, as little under her control, perhaps, as changes in the weather. The man always assumes that she has changed her mind on account of a caprice, or even perhaps from reasons of selfish expediency. He expects that when she says she will do a thing, then she should do it. In a sense, of course, it is true that she should, but inasmuch as the woman's nature depends on a changing, cyclic life-principle it may well be that when the time comes for her to fulfill her promise the conditions have really changed. This is very difficult for a man to understand because his inner principle is the Logos; and by this principle if a thing is right today, it will still be right tomorrow. Consequently if a man decides a problem in the affirmative today he expects, if external conditions have not changed, to be able on the morrow to follow the course of action decided on. For the woman, the external circumstances have naturally to be taken into account, but in addition to this, because of the ever-changing character of her moon-principle, the inner circumstances must also be constantly reconsidered.

To man her dependence on an inner principle whose chief characteristic is *change* must make her appear fickle and unreliable, just as the moon is called "the fickle planet." Certain women no doubt do exploit the prerogatives which have been accorded them by society and arbitrarily change their minds to suit their own convenience. But this abuse of their privileges by some women does not alter the fact that woman's nature is cyclic in itself, and this quite apart from her personal or egotistic desires. The *nature* of woman is nonpersonal and has nothing to do with her own wishes, it is something inherent in her as a feminine being and must not be regarded merely as something

66

personal. Indeed the very fact that woman has been accorded these prerogatives and is not judged exclusively by masculine standards is evidence enough that humanity recognizes she is ruled by inner laws which are different from those governing men. To understand woman, then, it is necessary to take into account her moonlike character and to gain some insight into the law of change which governs her.

The cyclic character of her life is the most natural thing in the world to a woman, even while it remains a complete mystery to men. Every woman will bear me out when I say that life *is* cyclic. If this statement is to be put psychologically we must say, not that life is cyclic, but that woman experiences life through the medium of her own ever-changing nature, hence to a woman the *experience* of life is cyclic. A subjective perception of this kind is, however, naturally projected, because no one, as a rule, stops to question what part of his perceptions rightly belongs to the object and what part depends on his own qualities as observer. In this case, obviously, if a woman is up one day and down another it will seem to her as if objects or conditions change rhythmically, so that work is easy today and the same task is hard tomorrow; things go well this week but will probably be obstinate and refractory next week. Even more marked changes take place in her feeling tone, everything is hopeful and rosy now but in a short while it will be gloomy and depressing. In this way her subjective perception of life is projected to the external world and she feels as though the cyclic change were a quality of life itself.

Men, who experience life primarily through their rational Logos nature, are unable to appreciate the quality of the woman's perception as being equally valid with their own. It is a truism that we have no exact knowledge of things as they are; while we all have the prejudice that they are as we see them. Even our science, product of the masculine point of view, may well be biased and one-sided. So that, naturally, we have no means of knowing whether men may not be as much deceived by their masculine nature as women are, obviously, by their feminine nature.

Certain men, however, seem to be dependent, almost like women, on the changes of their inner feelings. A curious inversion of the masculine and feminine parts of the psyche has taken place in such men. The rational, Logos, functions have been relegated to the background, while the feminine part of the psyche, which is usually concealed, comes to the fore and forces their changing moods into undue prominence. This change results from domination by the anima,[2] the feminine spirit in man, which, however, should not rule the conscious but the unconscious. Consequently the domination by the feminine spirit has a peculiarly unpleasant quality. For such men are not ruled by changes in the nonpersonal Eros, but by moods and whims which have as their chief characteristic that they are exceedingly personal. Domination by the anima produces a curious womanish quality, a dependence on personal likes and dislikes, on moods and feeling tones to the exclusion of all capacity to react with adequate feeling in accordance with any judgment of fact or the validity of an impersonal truth. This situation is a travesty of the woman's submission to her inner law of change.

For to women, life itself *is* cyclic. The life force ebbs and flows in her actual experience, not only in nightly and daily rhythm as it does for a man but also in moon cycles, quarter phase, half phase, full moon, decline, and so round to dark moon. These two changes together produce a rhythm which is like the moon's changes and also like the tides whose larger monthly cycle works itself out concurrently with the diurnal changes, sometimes increasing the swing of the tides and at others working against the tidal movement, the whole producing a complex rhythm hard to understand. In the course of one complete cycle, which most strangely corresponds to the moon's revolution, the woman's energy waxes, shines full and wanes again. These energy changes affect her, not only in her physical and sexual life but in her psychic life as well. Life in her ebbs and flows, so that she is dependent on her inner rhythm.[3]

2 Anima is the term Jung uses to denote the feminine part of a man's nature, which is unconscious to him and therefore usually projected. The term animus is similarly used to denote the masculine part of a woman's nature. See Jung, *Two Essays on Analytical Psychology* (New York and London, 1953), and for a practical discussion see M. E. Harding, *The Way of All Women* (New York, 1933).

3 By this I do not mean to suggest that during the ebb tide of her energy cycle, woman is seriously incapacitated. I only wish to emphasize the fact that her energy is not constant but comes in spurts as it were. It has been amply demonstrated that women are entirely capable of living adequately at all periods of their moon cycle, and carrying on their work, whether it be in the home or in the office, regardless of what phase they may be at. The menstrual cycle of women has

To men these cyclic changes are most incomprehensible, and in their endeavor to escape from the dominance of the male, inherent in our patriarchal civilization, women themselves disregarded the effects of their own rhythm and tried to resemble men as closely as possible. Thus they fell once more under the dominance of the male. This time it was not under the male without, that is under men, but under the rule of the male within. They lost touch with their own feminine instinct and began to function consciously, through the masculine qualities of the animus.

In societies where the simple facts of nature are less controlled and distorted by personal or ego desires, the lives of women are arranged in a pattern dictated by their moon cycle. The social customs which prevail in so many parts of the world in relation to the woman's cycle were developed in part on account of man's fear of that in woman which he did not understand. His fear doubtless contributed its share also to the development of the taboos controlling this aspect of feminine nature. For her sexual cycle had an uncanny power over him, arousing at once his own instinct and his dread of its power. This was naturally projected to the woman whose condition made him aware of his helplessness in face of his own instinctive desire. The connection between menstruation and childbearing added its quota of supernatural dread, for the birth of children is a perpetual marvel to men. "How do I know," said one primitive, "that my wife will bring forth a human child? Why should it not be a calf, or a wolf?" What he does not understand, the primitive fears and what he fears that he seeks to control by taboo regulations and restrictions.

Women themselves cannot have been entirely under compulsion in this matter, however, but must have co-operated in developing a social custom which depended so largely for its observance on the individual woman's submission to the law of her own nature. And, indeed, as the myth of the Bandicoots shows, in some cases the customs were initiated by the women themselves, as a protection from the insistent sexual demands of the men, and to preserve their own woman's values.

---

been adduced as an argument against their ability to carry a job, in an absurd and arbitrary fashion. Except in certain abnormal cases where the period constitutes an illness it does not and should not hamper a woman unduly in carrying her usual load.

In primitive communities a woman's whole life is focussed around the regular changes of her physiological cycle. Periods of work at home and in the community, of social life with her neighbors and of marital relationship with her husband, alternate with periods of seclusion. At regular intervals she is obliged to go away alone: she may not live in her own home with husband and children; she may not cook, nor tend the cultivated patch, nor walk abroad; she is precluded from performing any of her customary tasks; she is compelled to be alone, to go down into herself, to introvert. Anthropologists, who, as a rule, are more interested in the customs of a tribe than in the psychology of individuals, have not asked what effect these customs have on the women themselves. Yet, this periodic seclusion must inevitably have had a profound effect on the women's relation to life.

The days spent alone, in the menstrual lodge, fasting and performing other purificatory rites is, perhaps, equivalent to the initiation ceremonies which are so generally practiced by the men and boys at puberty. Corresponding rites do exist for girls in some communities but they are far less common. Initiation ceremonies usually include isolation, fasting, and purification. Circumcision and the endurance of some ordeal are also necessary parts of most initiations, and during the weeks or months of preparation, the boys are usually placed under certain taboos. These ceremonies bear a striking resemblance to the rites performed by women at their monthly periods, which as we have already seen include isolation, fasting, and purification. The similarity is so consistent that it can hardly be accidental.

Before their initiation, for instance, young boys, among the American Indians, spend a long period alone in the woods devoting themselves to fasting, purging, and the sweat bath. This discipline is undertaken with the hope and intention of obtaining a vision or initiatory dream. The ordeal is designed to bring the initiant into direct touch with the deeper layers of the unconscious. Through this he experiences the authority of that divine "something" which is the voice of his own true nature whereby he is released from childish dependence on the authority of the parents.

The dream which the youth has at this time becomes the guide for his whole life; he chooses his vocation and his guardian spirit from its indications; and in every crisis of his life he goes back for guidance to his initiatory dream. The women do not go into a similar seclusion for a single initiation experience, but every month they must go apart for a few days and remain alone, in close touch with that instinctual force which dominates them from within, from the depths of their own physical nature. It is probable that the contact which women obtain with the deeper trends of the unconscious at this monthly retreat is less formulated, less articulate, than is the case with the men. The men seek a dream or vision, which is then subjected to conscious thought and work; it is interpreted either by the medicine man or by the council of elders. In this way each youth translates his piece of wisdom or inspiration into an ideational form, as a picture, even if not as an intellectual concept. The way in which the initiatory dream influences the whole life course of the American Indian is most clearly brought out in the biographies of Plenty-Coups, a Crow Indian,[4] and of Black Elk, a Sioux.[5]

But the women, so far as we know, do not formulate, either in picture or in idea, the message which they gain from the unconscious during their seclusion. This is perhaps understandable since woman is, in a sense, closer to nature than man. The voice of nature speaks to her so closely *in* her own person, that a higher state of consciousness is necessary before a woman even asks herself *what* it is that she has learned.

In modern times we have released ourselves from the superstition that a menstruating woman is unclean or particularly dangerous. We have also come to realize that menstruation is not a "sickness" in the sense of its being an illness. And yet in spite of the increasing acceptance of this common-sense attitude, most women would agree that at or about the time of the period they do feel certain difficulties either physical or psychological or more commonly both. They tend to be irritable and out of temper, disinclined for exertion, physical or mental; while the even balance of their normal attitude to life is disturbed.

The tendency of our day is for women to go about their business, disregarding entirely these changes of mood, and suppressing or overriding by a conscious effort of will the indications of cyclic changes within themselves which are de-

---

[4] F. B. Linderman, *American* (New York, 1930).
[5] J. G. Neidhardt, *Black Elk Speaks* (New York, 1932).

pendent on a hidden moonlike aspect of their nature. Certain
women, however, unable to repress the evidence completely, become aware of their own fundamental rhythm, not in the form
of psychological changes, but as physical disabilities which may
be so severe as to demand that they go home from work for a
few hours to recover.

In primitive communities seclusion was prescribed for all
women, who did not have to be ill in order to participate in the
advantages to be gained from a period of solitude each month.
When in modern times the superstitious character of the taboos
was realized, the practices based upon them were discarded,
but it does not necessarily follow that we are ready to throw
the whole custom overboard, merely because we understand
the superstitious character of the taboo. Superstitions are based
on psychical contents which have been projected to the object.
If we are to be released from their dominance we need to comprehend the categorical imperative of the unconscious which
they represent. In Western civilization, when the practices
based on menstrual taboos were discarded without any such
understanding, the unconscious took its revenge. Physical ills
associated with the period became a conspicuous characteristic
of all women of the leisured classes. The seclusion and isolation of women formerly required by custom for taboo reasons
was, during many centuries, obtained through physical dis-
ability. It almost seems as though the unconscious said: "If
you will not do this thing for the gods, you shall be compelled
to for the body."

Today it is recognized that normal menstruation should not
cause illness. Thus in our day there is a general understanding
that the taboos and restrictions which ancient and primitive
peoples imposed on the menstruating woman were superstitious and also that the physical disabilities of the Victorians
were often neurotic in origin, but we do not seek any further
for the cause of these widespread illusions. Instead we discard
both attitudes, basing our position on a rational consideration
of physical facts, saying that these customs of our forefathers
were *nothing but* superstition or *nothing but* neurosis, that in
either case they had no basis in objective fact. We fail to take
into account, however, that psychological contents are always
perceived, first, as outside ourselves, projected into the external
world. The ancient taboos were a reaction to man's own over-

powering instinct which he perceived as a dangerous quality of the woman in relation to whom his instinct was aroused. And we must admit that the very obvious and mysterious change which took place in her excused and justified his mistake. So he hedged her about with prohibitions. In a similar way woman perceived her own need for withdrawal from the man as a dangerous quality inherent in her own condition. Her need to withdraw, whether due to her preoccupation with the dark powers of her own feminine instinct stirring within her, or to a reaction against his overpressing attentions, was projected. To her it seemed that her presence or touch would call down a curse upon him, she was unclean and must therefore withdraw.

If a need for solitude exists which remains unconscious, not recognized as a psychological necessity, it will be projected to the external world and may show itself as a sense of being unclean, or unacceptable, perhaps dangerous, to others. The unrecognized or unconscious psychological need produces symptoms of guilt or uncleanness, or even of persecution. The menstrual taboo represents such a state of affairs but in a general form. The taboo is, as it were, a general symptom which has its origin in a general psychological attitude of withdrawal on the part of women at this time, of whose significance the race is still, for the most part, unaware.

Today, symptoms whether of physical illness or of emotional disturbance are dismissed as neurotic or imaginary, while their meaning is overlooked. It would be more intelligent to take as symbols these indications from the unconscious, which show themselves as taboos or as the physical symptoms of illness and to interpret them into psychological terms where they are indeed realities. The effort to overcome nature by undermining the factual basis of the superstition or the symptom would then take its rightful place. For the difficulty may well be an indication of some disturbance in the unconscious, emotional or moral, of which the sufferer is unaware. To consider menstruation merely as "the curse," I borrow the college girls' slang, to be submitted to or tolerated for the one and only reason that it cannot be avoided, means to lose the deeper experience of an essential part of feminine nature, to lose, what Keyserling would call, "one aspect of consciousness." For if a woman is in resistance to any part of her own nature she cannot garner its values, but experiences only its negative aspect, in this case the physical and psychological disabilities which menstruation undoubtedly carries with it and which, indeed, on account of her own resistant attitude, are almost inevitably enhanced. The realization that her symptoms indicate that her conscious attitude is not in harmony with the deeper needs of her own nature would enable her to approach the problem in a more intelligent and constructive way. The significance of the old taboo customs is to be sought along two avenues of approach. First, the question of what is the meaning to the woman herself of her seclusion and second, what is the meaning of her exclusion from the life of the group.

We have already suggested that her monthly isolation had for the woman herself something of the same significance that the puberty rites had for the men and boys. During that time of enforced solitude the women gained, perhaps, a closer contact with the instinctive forces within them. The modern woman has lost touch with this value and it is possible that her menstrual disabilities may be related to this loss. At the time of the period, instinctive feminine nature stirs in her and like a rising tide engulfs at least a part of her consciousness. This is not necessarily only a negative experience, it can also be a positive one, just as sleep can hardly be considered as only waste of time, however inevitable. For during sleep the physical resources are replenished, and it is also a means of getting into touch with the deeper layers of nature, ordinarily lost in the inaccessible regions of the unconscious. It is generally recognized, for instance, that something of value can come out of "sleeping on" a difficult problem. The greater wisdom which comes to us out of the dark and blind period of the night is evidence that the spirit of man, his "I" travels in realms where greater understanding dwells and can bring back to this world a value which he may not be able to see clearly or to formulate either in word or picture. So the woman also has an opportunity at the dark of the moon to get into touch with a deeper and more fundamental layer of her own psychic life. Symptoms of physical or emotional disturbance at that time, indicate that there is a conflict between her conscious attitude and the demands of her own nature, and if she recognizes them as an indication of her need to be by herself, because an inner necessity is calling to her to introvert, to withdraw psychologically from the demands of her external life and live for a little while in the secret places of her own heart, she may be able to re-establish her contact with the deeper part of her own nature.

To withdraw in this way and give attention to that other side, so commonly sacrificed in the struggle to achieve an adequate and conventionally correct adaptation, produces a strangely healing effect. The conflict between the conscious life which she is obliged to live in the world and the private life, with the desires and needs of the heart and of instinct, is quieted, and the split between inner and outer finds at least a temporary reconciliation. This is the value to be found by a voluntary return to the customs of the primitive woman. Naturally, here we are not suggesting a return to primitive customs as such; that would be merely a regression to superstition. What is meant is a conscious understanding of that which to the primitive was an unconscious working out of a projected psychological urge, and the following of a course of action suitable to the meaning and intent of this urge, clearly recognized, however, as psychological.

When a woman at the "dark of the moon" is disturbed by a sense of disharmony in herself, irritability, inertia, or restlessness, she may be able, by deliberately taking time to be alone, to gain a unity of psychological aim within herself, which the primitive woman found, perhaps, through submitting to the imposed taboo. A period of introversion and seclusion of this kind is often very valuable, but it must be a real introversion, a *turning within,* more actively undertaken than a mere submission to physical necessity.

In the practice of such voluntary self-seclusion many women find that the irritation or restlessness which have ordinarily disturbed them, disappear and that instead of being pulled down and depleted by the monthly period they have gained a contact with the deeper sources of their own feminine nature. Others, however, find that what lies below the surface is at variance with their conscious idea of themselves. The dark side of instinct may raise its head and confront them in the quiet of their time alone. Such an experience may be very disturbing, but to have the unknown adversary out in the open is far less disturbing than not to know what one fights. A woman who meets such things in the darkness of her own heart can, for the future, meet her conflict consciously instead of being the unconscious victim of unreconciled and opposing attitudes within herself. The outcome in either case is that the instinctual energy, formerly manifested only in disturbances of her conscious attitude, will become available for life. Sometimes this new energy flows naturally into her relationships, deepening them, and sometimes it finds an outlet in creative work, while at others it supplies the motive power which makes it possible to build a more complete personality founded on the dark as well as the light aspects of her psyche.

The second aspect of the old taboo customs, namely, the woman's segregation from the group, has also its psychological significance. Her segregation was an attempt to cope with the daemonic effect that her condition had upon men. It will be recalled that the old taboos stated that at her period the woman's presence would unman men, would destroy the virtue of the war-bundle and make arrows glance aside and render spears harmless against the enemy. Put into less concretized form this means that primitive man, under the temptation of aroused instinct, could not hold to his intention to hunt or fight. His resolution leaked away, for only a little of his energy was under the control of his will, much remained the slave of his instinct. This aspect of woman's rhythmic nature is masked today. Civilized man has far more conscious control of his own actions and his energy than his primitive forefathers. But the old problem still exists although it is no longer projected to the physical condition of the woman. It is now a psychological one. For still at times some women function as little more than feminine nature-beings, in whom instinct, sex, lives not mediated by human qualities: love, ruth, scruple. Such women are indeed ruthless, unscrupulous, not because they are vicious or degraded but because they have not attained as yet to human consciousness. The workings of this phase of feminine instinct will be taken up later. It is a phase which all women experience to greater or lesser extent in the cyclic rhythm of their instinctual lives.

For the conscious life of woman, with its daily routine and its more significant events, is lived, as it were, over an underlying pattern of rhythmic change determined by her moonlike quality; her reactions to the problems and happenings of life are dependent to an extent of which few women are aware on the phases of her inner instinctual rhythm. In Western countries, the modern woman, for the most part, pays no attention to the changing moods of her own nature and tries to live as though she were not profoundly affected by its stages. For she has it in her power either to disregard the underlying rhythm of her being or, if she is a more discerning person, she can seek consciously and deliberately to bring her life and activities into harmony with it. It is not merely a question of refraining from over-strenuous activity at her periods, nor is it only a matter of arranging her life so that she does not have difficult emotional problems to meet when she is physically and psychologically least able to handle them. There is a further problem involved which concerns the larger issues of fate and self-determination.

It is hardly necessary to point out that by moon-phase no reference is intended to the changes in the lunar planet, nor does it refer only to the physiological changes in the woman's sexual cycle, although this biological rhythm is in some strange way related to the psychological rhythm which is the real meaning of the moon cycle of woman. The interaction between the happenings in these two realms are so close, so intimate, that in the present state of our scientific knowledge it is almost impossible to say of many emotional experiences what part is biological and what psychological and, furthermore, which is cause and which effect. This being the case, we have to hold a tentative attitude about this problem and content ourselves with observing "things as they are," leaving their explanation to the future. So in the question of the moon-phase of woman certain rhythmical psychological conditions and happenings occur in her experience and also in her physical make-up. She is subject to a rhythmic law but we cannot say that these two things are necessarily correlated, evidence either for or against such a statement is lacking. The following illustrations are for this reason given rather tentatively.

In her emotional life it seems that a woman's ability to respond to the opportunities life brings her depends very largely on her moon-phase and this seems to be true in other realms as well. If the moment of the moon is favorable her love can well up and respond to the man who attracts her, but if it happens to be an unfavorable moment she remains cold and unresponsive, even though she may want to respond.

I remember hearing the story of an abortive love affair whose miscarriage seemed to be largely due to this uncontrollable factor. A man and woman met and were much attracted to each other. Circumstances threw them together for about a week on two occasions. Then they each returned to their homes in different towns, arranging, however, to meet again, for it so happened that his business took him to her town from time to time. From then on, however, fate was against them. For each time that he came she was in an off-phase and the incipient relationship gradually faded out. Such an outcome might just be called hard luck, or it could be taken more seriously. If her rhythmic changes were accepted by the woman as inherent in the nature of things she might say with the ancients that the goddess Ishtar, the moon, had gone to the land of No-Return, and so men and women could not love, they could only wait for her to come back.

This rhythmic coming and going of energy may work in the same way in other realms. For instance, life may at last present a woman with an opportunity for work or for a spiritual adventure for which she has long waited. If the moon is favorable she is able to take the step which will lead her out into a freer life of greater opportunity, but if the moon is not favorable she may see her longed-for chance slip by and be unable to do anything effective to seize it.

In such cases it seems as if her own nature were against her, frustrating her dearest hopes. Small wonder that the ancients spoke of the moon as being goddess of fate. The moon cycle does indeed appear to determine the fate of woman and, in a love affair, of man too. The realization of this aspect of her fate makes submission to the moon cycle more difficult. It requires an act of devotion deeper than at first seemed necessary, if a woman is to live her life in harmony with the rhythm of her own nature.

Yet when she recognizes that this all-powerful fate is *not* wielded by some outside power, by an inaccessible deity of the moon, but is instead the expression of the essential nature of her own being, she will feel very differently about it. For the rhythmic life within her is determinant of her own life, while her conscious wishes and impulses do not necessarily coincide with her deepest needs. No human being is wise enough to know from his past experience what course his life should take in the future. He is wiser than the average if he can look back

Fig. 18. The Phases of the Moon.

and estimate justly about the past. He is much wiser than the average if he can make a balanced judgment about the present, but how can he hope to include also the future? The part cannot comprehend the whole. Consciously he can only look forward in complete blindness to the future. But his future is surely determined by his own true nature. If he did but know that nature, he could trust himself confidently to it, leaving it to work itself out unerringly to its inevitable end. The only trouble is that we do not know, and we try to make up the deficiencies of our knowledge by our conscious aims and desires. But for woman, at all events, the "moon goddess," that is, the feminine principle within her, plays a hand and she usually holds the trump cards.

The dream of a modern woman may illustrate this point better than I can explain it. She dreamed that a drama was to be performed against a stage-set or background depicting "the Phases of the Moon," or "the Phases of the Goddess"; both terms were used in the dream. She drew the accompanying picture (figure 18) to show what she saw of the stage-set in her dream. The play she associated to the drama of life, representing the outer happenings, birth, marriage, death, work, and social relationships. All these events were to be played on the visible stage. Behind them, that is, on a deeper psychological level, the drama of the gods was to take place. This drama, since the dreamer was a woman, was represented by the phases of the moon. In the picture we see the goddesses, or rather the various phases of the one goddess, each in relation to one quarter of the moon. They all hold the crux ansata, symbol of eternal life.[6] Each figure has a fishskin garment, which is the garment of her instinct, making her a mermaid or fish, inhabitant of the sea, the unconscious. Fish were sacred to Atargatis, the moon goddess of Askalon, and both Atargatis and Derketo, a form of Ishtar, were sometimes represented with fishes' tails. Possibly this representation of the goddess signifies the extreme unconsciousness of much of feminine instinct. For the fish is cold-blooded, very far from human. It acts in accordance with the laws of its own nature entirely without scruple. The fulfilling of its instinct is all that counts, the effects even of its actions are not recognized as such. When, therefore, the goddess is worshipped as half-fish it must be this blind adherence to natural law that is venerated—not a law recognized intellectually and respected by a conscious act of the will, but the law which moves unseen in the watery depths of the unconscious, which can only be followed by a blind devotion. To us with our Western viewpoint such a following of unknown laws seems entirely unredeemed, quite unhallowed, but to the ancients a service of this character was highly meritorious. They did not, of course, take such an attitude of blind devotion as the guide to conduct in daily life, but only as a religious act of self-sacrifice to be performed perhaps once in a lifetime only, or in some cases as a ritual which recurred from time to time.

In this picture the fish-garment covers the woman's body, one-half or three-quarters, whatever the phase of the moon may be to which she is related. At full moon she steps completely out of her fishskin, she is the bright or "light" woman, completely revealed, entirely human. It might be supposed that during the period of the dark moon she would be completely fish, entirely under the dominion of instinct. In the picture the

6 Compare the picture of the "Emblem of Isis," figure 14.

dark moon, the dark woman, would stand behind the Sun Goddess, Sekhet, Goddess of Life. But this phase is not shown, for this phase of the woman is taboo; it is nonhuman, daemonic; it may not be spoken of, nor may it live in the light of day. It belongs to the sphere of the woman's mysteries. For a man to look upon a woman then is "sickness and death."

The daemonic, nonhuman aspect of woman can be translated into the terms of everyday experience somewhat as follows: If a woman acts, in any situation, as nothing but female, yin, refusing to give expression to the human considerations which would moderate her yin-like effect, she catches the man by *his* instinct. He is very apt then to get ensnared in a way which undermines him. Such a situation has often been described in novels and plays where a woman uses her power over a man to induce him by means of her sex appeal to stay with her when his duty or honor call him away. The typical story is that he must join his regiment. When he goes to say goodby to her she coaxes him to remain or is so alluring that he forgets his obligation, and the army entrains without him. All true women blame the woman who acts in this way, rather than the man. They know that such an action takes an unfair advantage of the man's vulnerability.

A woman who truly loves her man feels under an obligation not to tempt him by her feminine charm, but to safeguard his honor. She will in the circumstances described above, even hide her attractions, veil herself, so that by her self-discipline he may be released to follow the path of discipline too. Sometimes a woman is not conscious of the power of this feminine, this yin, quality in herself. Then a disastrous effect of this kind may come to pass while she remains unaware of the part she has herself played in her lover's undoing. Other women are quite aware of their power over men and use it unscrupulously for personal advantage. Such a woman seems to offer the man love and understanding while in reality she is only giving the rein to her own desire for power. If such a woman would stop to question her own motives she might readily see that her pleasure lies chiefly in the satisfaction of her vanity, fed by his flattery, and in the sense of importance she gains from his infatuation.

A more conscious, more developed woman knows of this

danger, and is scrupulously careful to guard against producing such a disastrous effect. For only through the discipline of desirousness can love and psychological relationship between man and woman be safeguarded. Such a woman does consciously and voluntarily what the primitives sought to accomplish through their menstrual taboos. For it might well be said that a woman who allows her yin-like nature to act in an unrestrained way is in a dangerous state and should be segregated. She is a public menace. The Hindus, whose allegorical sayings stand between the concretization of the primitive and our Western psychological abstractions, were aware of the danger of the dark aspect of woman's nature. In the *Satapatha Brahamana* it is said that when the moon is dark it comes to the earth and waits in the place of sacrifice. During that time men must fast. For to suffer from this coming of the moon power and yet not to give way to it requires self-discipline, sacrifice of the egotistic desires, sacrifice of autoerotism. On the man's part, of the autoerotic desire which demands physical satisfaction whenever sexuality is aroused, and on the woman's, sacrifice of the self-love which always seeks to possess the man and which can be so easily flattered by the ease of his conquest. The ego takes as its own that which happens of itself, by the power of the moon. This attraction between a man and a woman is, however, a nonhuman effect. If it is mistaken for human love it can only cause unhappiness and disaster. The ancients have left it on record that men must fast when the moon comes to the earth, that they must refrain from self-indulgence, and for women more elaborate rituals have been prescribed by means of which that which belongs to the gods can be given to them and thus be separated from that which belongs to human beings.

The woman who dreamed this dream did not know these things. The meaning of such a dream can only be sensed at the time, but bit by bit life reveals its significance. These significances are not visionary, unreal imaginings; they are intuitively perceived *realities* which condition this woman's unconscious functioning. But we can go a little further than that, for this picture takes on the form of an impersonal myth, it corresponds to the myths of the Moon Goddess, found alike in ancient times and among primitive peoples. It is, so to speak, a modern myth, an expression by a modern woman of psychological facts which function in the depths of all women, expressions of the feminine principle, the Eros. On this principle all womankind, and the individual woman also, is based, her experience of life itself is colored by her moonlike changes.

7

THE MAN IN THE MOON

The discussion of the monthly cycle of woman has taken us rather beyond the stage where the moon is considered to be a vague, ill-defined fertilizing influence, having a particular effect on women. We must now take up the more organized beliefs about the moon, where this power becomes personified to form a god or goddess.

The most primitive belief about the moon is that it is a *presence* or a fertilizing influence. As religious forms became more organized the moon became definitely a *person,* first a man, later a god, a fertilizing male deity or power.

The moon is so regarded in some of the most ancient cultures. In the Iranian, for instance, which preceded the Persian, and flourished on the borders of the Persian Gulf in the thousand years or so before 1600 B.C., the moon was held to be a Great Man and was venerated as such. This moonman was at first thought of as living in the moon a life exactly like our earthly life. Our Man in the Moon doubtless is his descendant. Sometimes this moonman was believed to be incarnated on earth when he appeared as a very powerful king. Later the kings of a certain line or dynasty were all considered to be incarnations of the moonman. Many ancient kings wore a horned headdress emblematic of the "hornéd moon." By a natural transition the king who was thus adorned became not only the moon but also the bull. For horned animals, especially the bull and the cow, are among the animals associated with the moon. Bull's horns were worn as a ceremonial headdress by Celtic, Egyptian, and Assyrian kings, as well as others, indicating that to these peoples their king was an incarnation of a horned deity.

In later times it was said that the king who was actually reigning was not himself the moon, but that he was a representative of the moon, was perhaps descended from the moon. For instance, Genghis Khan, the Mongolian Emperor of the thirteenth century A.D., is said to have traced his ancestry to an ancient king whose mother had been impregnated by a moon ray, although it was recognized that of course such things did not happen any more.

The Chief of Einu in the Polynesian Islands was called The Lord of the Moon and in Samoa when the Chief died they said "The Moon has fallen" while in other tribes watch is kept for the first rising of the crescent moon, and as soon as it is seen they cry to the king "Your life has been renewed!" It is as though they feared that if the moon did not come again the king could not continue to live.

Thus the myths embodying the story of the moon gradually became crystallized. The changes observed month by month in the actual moon were narrated as though the moon were a living being. They were garbed in human guise, for they were felt to be in some way typical of things that happen to men upon the earth. We now recognize that this sense of appropriateness refers to a psychological correspondence, not to some half-forgotten historical event of the heroic age. The myth which grows up about a natural phenomenon represents a perception of an inner subjective truth "projected" to or perceived in the outer world. But the primitives naturally did not know this. They merely reported in story form the truth whose origin they never suspected. So the waxing and waning of the moon is anthropomorphized, making a moonman who is represented as a sort of hero figure, living in the moon, while at the same time he is the moon itself.

The typical story is that the moonman begins his career when the waxing crescent first appears, by fighting the devil of darkness who has eaten up his father, the old moon. This devil of darkness is represented in the old pictures as a sort of dragon. The hero overcomes the devil and as the moon comes to fullness, he reigns triumphant on earth. He is a wise and great king. He creates order in the tribe and establishes agriculture, teaching his people when to sow and when to reap. He is also a maker of laws and the judge of men whose hidden motives he is able to bring into the light.

These qualities of the great heroic moon king fit in with the earlier unformed myths and superstitions which have already been outlined. There the beneficent power of the moon marks off time, so creating order, for the changes of the moon formed primitive man's first calendar; in particular the succession of moons regulated agricultural activities. In the later myth the moon hero is said to have taught men how to cultivate the fields. Before his coming, that is, before the organized cult of the moon, men must have lived only in nomadic tribes without agriculture.

This phase of the hero's life lasts during the bright period of the moon. He has no sooner reached the zenith of his power, however, than the old enemy who conquered his father begins to attack and pursue him. He is finally overcome, and the devil eats him up also. The moon wanes and the king is said to die, strangely enough, by fragmentation. We shall meet this theme again when we consider the story of Osiris whose body was cut into pieces and scattered. The piecemeal eating doubtless refers to the nightly "bite" which is taken out of the moon in its gradual waning.

After his death the moonman goes to the underworld, for he has been swallowed by the dragon, whose belly *is* the underworld. His sojourn there continues during the dark of the moon. While he resides in the underworld he is not dead nor just passive, but exercises his old function of judge. Now, however, he is judge of the souls of the dead who are the inhabitants of the underworld, for, as in all dragon myths, the dead are all swallowed up by the monster. At the end of this period the cycle repeats itself. His son fights the devil and overcomes him for a brief period, becoming in his turn king by the power of the moon.

This myth clearly represents the changes of the moon in its various phases, as they were observed by primitive man. But it is something more than a myth representing astronomical events, since the changes of the moon are related throughout to man himself. The facts are "contaminated" with psychological or subjective material. Man's own inner unseen life, not recognized as within himself, was projected outside his psyche, its activity being ascribed to the moon.

This moonman, who represents an unrecognized part of the human psyche, does for the primitive tribe what the tribesman of that age was unable to accomplish by his own intelligence. He establishes order, teaches the art of agriculture, is judge and giver of laws. These things are first products of thought, but thought not as a function of human consciousness, but culled out of the functions of the moon, whose influence on primitive life in unlighted villages is more profound and more impressive than we realize. Primitive man has no clocks, no calendar. He does not know how many days make up a year, or perhaps a very wise medicine man or chief may know. But the ordinary man does not know and could not keep count of the days even if he did know their number. For many primitive people even today cannot count more than the fingers of both hands, while others have words only for one, two, three, four, and many. The rhythmic changes of the moon, however, gave him a means of reckoning time which was invaluable to him and set him calculating. Thus the time for sowing and reaping was reckoned by moons, so that naturally it was felt that the moonman had taught the art of agriculture. The council of elders met by the light of the moon after the day's work was done. If any crime had been committed in the tribe the case would be investigated by moonlight, and in this way the moon was felt to be judge. On bright nights, too, the old men sat around the fire, undisturbed by the jungle fears which oppressed them when the nights were entirely dark, and originated those early ruminations and speculations out of which organized thought evolved. So that to this day, words which have to do with mental activity are in most languages cognate with the names for the moon.

In a somewhat later form the moon is represented as a god. This change in characterization marks a step forward in the development of man's consciousness. For the gods are not just the highest kinds of men, supermen, they clearly belong to the spirit world, or, as we should say, to the psychological realm. In their groping way those early people were trying to distinguish between what was objective and what subjective in their observations. When they relate a myth of the gods which is yet in some curious and inevitable way linked with natural phenomena, they are dimly recognizing that the story is a record of a spiritual drama, which we now know takes place in the unconscious, but which they only saw in its reflection in the outer world, in this case in the moon. The psychologist would say they only saw it projected into the object.

The moon gods are still of very early date so that we have

not any very consecutive record of them. Hur was the moon god of the Chaldeans, whose capital city was named after the god and was called Ur or Hur. This was the city, it will be remembered, from which Abraham was said to originate, about 1900 B.C. The various art objects which have recently been discovered at Ur have given us a glimpse of that very ancient civilization. In the Burbur dialect Khaldi is the exact equivalent of Hur. The Chaldeans were thus either moon worshippers or perhaps were inhabitants merely of a town dedicated to or called after the Moon God.

Sinn was the moon god of Babylonia. His worship flourished for many centuries. It probably began about the time when the Babylonians absorbed the culture of Ur and Eridhu, both centers of moon worship, which must have been about 1800 B.C. It continued into the thirteenth century B.C. when we have a record that King Kuri-Galzu restored the temple to the moon god, Sinn, at Ur. During all this long period the moon was the supreme deity in Babylon, although during its course Shamash, the sun god, arose, but he was never considered as powerful as the moon god. Another change was also initiated during this phase in the rise to power and favor of the moon goddess, Ishtar, who was said to be the daughter of Sinn. In the course of time her worship came to supersede that of the older moon god and the transition, of which we shall have occasion to speak later, was made and the moon lost its male sex and became feminine.

Sinn has much more character for us than Hur for his story is clearly told in many pictures of him which are preserved on coins and tablets, and it is also told in the cuneiform inscriptions which have been found and deciphered. Something of his power and his attributes are also known from inscriptions and prayers addressed to him. He is called Father of the gods, the Lord of heaven whose sickle shines among the gods. An ancient hymn addresses him thus "Sinn, thou alone givest light from above; thou art the light of the world." In the pictures we see him enthroned on the crescent, or on the holy tree, or embarking in his moon barge in which he sails the night sky, or fighting the devil who would devour him. (Figures 19, 20, 13, 44.)

Like the moonman he has two aspects or phases, one lived in the upper world and the other, during the dark of the moon,

Fig. 19

Fig. 20

Fig. 21

Fig. 22

The Babylonian Moon God Sinn

Fig. 19. Sinn enshrined on the crescent and surrounded by the circle of the full moon.

Fig. 20. Sinn enthroned on the crescent. Before him is the morning star, Ishtar, who in later centuries will replace him as chief deity of the moon. The crescent throne rests upon the Sacred Moon Tree.

Fig. 21. Sinn enthroned, holding the moon as his emblem. Two hounds, one coming and one going, represent the waxing and the waning moon.

Fig. 22. Sinn receiving a worshipper brought to him by Ishtar. The god is here represented as black, which probably indicates the dark or under-world phase.

(Figures 19, 20, and 21 are from *Sur le Culte de Mithra*, Felix Lajard, 1847; fig. 22 is from *Ancient Pagan and Modern Christian Symbolism*, Thomas Inman, 1876.)

in the underworld. But in the story of Sinn a further differentiation has taken place. The time of brightness is now divided into three periods, each of which is ruled over by a separate aspect of the god. Sinn thus becomes a triune god, composed of three persons (figure 21). It is expressly stated in the texts that Sinn

89

is each of these three persons who rule over the segments of the moon's bright period. This is probably the beginning of the division of the moon month into four-week periods, the fourth week being the period of darkness. These three persons or gods are Anu, Enlil or Bel, and Ea. An early text reads: "The moon is during the period of his visibility, in the first five days, the god Anu; from the sixth to the tenth day, the god Ea; from the eleventh to the fifteenth day, the god Enlil."[1]

The name of this moon god, Sinn, is familiar to us in Mount Sinai, which means Mountain of the Moon. This fact throws an interesting side light on Jewish history for it will be recalled that it was on Mount Sinai that Moses received the tablets of the law. Sinn, as moon god, was the ancient law giver long predating Moses. It was therefore in a very appropriate place that he sought and found the divinely given tablets.

Mēn or Mene was the Phrygian moon god. His name is of especial interest to us because of the curious coincidence that the Latin word *mens* means month. These two words, however, do not seem to have come from a common root. Osiris is the Egyptian moon god. The story of his life and death is known to us in much greater detail than is the case with any other of the moon gods. Its discussion will be reserved till the section on Isis and Osiris.

The story of the moon god's career follows a pattern similar to that of the moonman. There is, however, one important difference between them. The moonman lives through only one cycle of the moon's changes and then, eaten up by the devil of darkness, dies. He is replaced by his son, the young moon, who may also live but through the brief period of the moon's brightness. The moon god, in striking contrast, is immortal. He lives and suffers and dies but he comes again, reborn with the new moon. He is the pattern of the dying and resurrecting gods. His life occurs in a series of phases. When the moon is bright the god is in his upper-world phase. When the moon is dark, the god has gone to the underworld, but he will surely return. His relation to human beings changes with his changing phases. In his upper-world phase he is invariably beneficent, having the attributes of truth, justice, constructiveness and fertility. In his underworld phase, however,

1 H. C. Rawlinson, *The Cuneiform Inscriptions of Western Asia* (London, 1861), III, 55-3.

he is destructive to earth dwellers. He sends storm, flood, death, and disaster. Nevertheless, in his underworld phase he brings light to the underworld, he is judge of the dead and the mediator between man and the gods, and in his moon boat he carries the souls of those who should be redeemed, from the underworld up into the sun. He is thus the bringer of the hope of immortality.

The god who goes to the underworld and preaches to the souls in hell is a familiar figure to us from the Christian narrative. It is interesting to note that this function which is characteristic of all the dying and resurrecting gods probably dates back in its earliest form to the old moon gods.

Many pictures of the ancient moon gods have been preserved which show the various episodes in their histories. Sinn as we have seen is often represented like a "man in the moon," enthroned on the crescent. Sometimes the picture shows him being besieged by a dragonlike monster who is about to devour him. On certain coins this same dragon is seen devouring a crescent moon. In other pictures Sinn is wholly human in form, he is seen receiving worshippers or judging the dead in the underworld. In the latter capacity he is not infrequently represented as black, indicating that he is here in his underworld phase as the dark moon. (See figure 22.)

The moonman or moon god who was gradually evolved from the earlier ideas of the moon as fertilizing influence, retained the functions and powers which had formerly been ascribed to the moon. Indeed he came into being, as it were, by a concentration of the rather diffuse power which the moon had before dispensed. This moonman or moon god became the one giver of growth and fertility. For instance, the king, who was the earthly representative of the moon, was usually the rainmaker, and if the harvests failed he would bear the blame, perhaps even pay for his failure with his life. The moon god also inherited the moon's powers of fertility in regard to animals and human beings, so that he was approached by childless women with gifts and prayers that he would remove their curse of sterility.

It will be recalled that among the most primitive tribes it was felt that women and animals could only bear young by the power of the moon, a feeling which was crystallized among certain tribes into the belief that the moon was the real husband of all women, who conceived not by human seed but by the impregnation of a moon ray. It is not surprising therefore that in religions where the moon god is worshipped we should find that a marriage ceremonial is celebrated between the women worshippers and the god or his human representative. At first this custom was carried out in the case of every ordinary marriage as a purely secular measure, a necessary proceeding to ensure that the marriage should be fruitful. The king or headman, as the impersonation of the moon, slept with the bride on the first night of the marriage. This custom survived in France into the middle ages in the Seigneur's right. A similar marriage ceremonial came to form the central rite of the woman's mysteries in many ancient religions. This is a *hieros gamos,* a sacred marriage or holy matrimony which was thought to be absolutely necessary, not only for the fertility of the women who took part in it, but also for the crops and herds of the community.

In many religions these "mysteries" were performed annually and constituted one of the chief religious festivals. They are the basis for many of the fertility rites which have been so often described in connection with antique religions, and they have survived in the Spring carnival which still takes place preceding Lent, for Lent and Easter are festivals associated with the moon. These rites are connected with the dying and resur-recting gods, who are moon gods, or are sons of the Moon Mother.

During these festivals it is reported that the women dis-played an abandon and gross sensuality which did not represent their normal characters at all. The participators might be respectable members of the society in everyday life. But at the time of these rites it was their duty to indulge in the grossest sensuality in order to stimulate the fertilizing powers of the god. Obscene jests and actions were a part of this deliberate attempt to arouse the god, and the lasciviousness which was displayed was intended to excite the Heavenly Bridegroom to bestow his fertilizing powers abundantly on the tribe.

Briffault gives the reason for these customs in the following passage: "The explanation of the sensual and sexual character of [these] religious rites lies in the notion that every function of woman, whether as mother, as wife, as supplier of food, as cultivator of the soil, as sorceress, witch, prophetess, or priestess, postulates her union with the god who is the bestower of these powers. The indecency so conspicuous as a feature of all heathen religions has everywhere reference to that union, in some form or other, of women with divine beings. The union of men with goddesses plays virtually no part in those conceptions and practices. It is to women that the sacred marriage with the Divine Bridegroom is a functional necessity; men do not require to be united with a divine bride to fulfill their functions. But every religion, from the most primitive to the highest, is pervaded with the idea that union with a god, a *hieros gamos,* or "Holy Matrimony," is a necessity to every woman." [2]

As we saw above, the Maori believe that the moon, which among them is considered to be only a vague power or influence, is yet the only true husband of every woman. So in religions which are further advanced, having developed a deity from the earlier concept, this god is also considered to be the true husband of every woman and as we have just seen woman's mysteries were enacted every year during which each woman of the community in her own person, or in the person of a chosen surrogate, united or sought to be united with the god.

This moon god, however, is not only bestower of fertility upon woman but is also her guardian and protector. His monthly cycle of change corresponds to her cycle. His activities are hers. So that we find moon gods caring for agriculture, a specifically feminine task, spinning, weaving, making pots, carrying water and firewood, cooking, and even acting as midwife. Now all these things are women's occupations. It is almost as though the moon god, patron of women, must himself be a woman in disguise. Indeed the moon god is usually rather feminine in type. Some of the moon gods are actually androgynous, both male and female. Sinn, the moon god of Babylon, is addressed by his worshipper as: "Mother Womb, begetter of all things, O Merciful Father who hath taken into his care the whole world."

It is not surprising therefore to find a tendency in many places to consider the moon deity as a woman. She becomes a goddess but still retains something of her male characteristics. In Babylon, the moon god, Sinn, was gradually replaced by the goddess, Ishtar, who is described as Mother of the Moon and

[2] Robert Briffault, *The Mothers* (New York and London, 1927), III, 207–208.

also as Daughter of the Moon. She, like Sinn, her predecessor, is also androgynous, being invoked as "Oh my God and my Goddess." In Egypt one of the earliest forms of the moon goddess Isis was Isis-Net who was both male and female. The Greek moon goddess, Artemis, is also considered to be both male and female. Plutarch says: "They call the moon the Mother of the Cosmical Universe having both male and female nature."

The transition from moon god to moon goddess which took place in many of the ancient religions was probably related to the rise of sun worship. For the sun god took over some of the attributes of fertilizing deity from the earlier moon god. Certainly this was the case in Babylon where the worship of the sun god, Shamash, gradually increased in importance. Shamash, the Sun, was originally the son of the Moon, and his worship and honors were definitely inferior to those of the all-powerful Sinn, Lord of the Gods. But when the goddess Ishtar became par excellence the moon and the woman's deity, Shamash was relieved of a formidable rival, for Ishtar could be Mother of the Gods without infringing his dignity. A somewhat similar transition occurred in Egypt where the earlier and exclusive claim of Osiris to be supreme Lord of the Heavens was challenged by the latecoming sun god, Ra. The worship of Ra was fostered by the priestly cult of Heliopolis for reasons of political power and it came to have official recognition. But the spiritual religion of the country remained centered in the worship of Osiris and Isis, his wife and sister, who is Mother of all Nature and Goddess of the Moon.

Consequently in later religions we find the moon typically represented by a goddess and her son, who dies and is born again. This mother goddess is the heavenly representative of womanhood. She is The Mother, or The Woman. She is immortal. She does not die as her predecessor the Moon God did, but lives eternally, the prototype of woman, the eternal feminine. Associated with her is a young man, her son, who dies and resurrects just as the earlier moon god did. He is in fact the direct descendant of the moon god and carries the values which might otherwise have been lost in the change.

This goddess is Heavenly Mother, Mother of the Moon God, indeed she is Mother of God. She lives eternally and it is her unchanging, enduring character which is her most marked characteristic. She is the power behind God, or to quote Briffault's summing up "She is . . . the fatal goddess, the Goddess of Fate, and often therefore the inexorable one, the goddess of death whom even the efforts and entreaties of her son cannot mollify." [3]

This brings us to the last phase of moon worship, where the moon is Mother. As we have seen, this grew out of a more primitive concept of the moon as fertilizing male. It is a very natural transition. First there is the fertilizing influence of the moon which bestows the power to reproduce upon the female. Then this influence is concentrated into a personified being, a moon god, who directly impregnates his women worshippers, and then, by a sort of enlargement of the concept, the moon becomes the creator, the Great Mother of All. She is Mother of the Moon God, but he is also her spouse. His power is bestowed upon her as it was formerly bestowed upon the women worshippers of the moon god. She is herself fertilized by him. Thus is represented a concept of perpetual generation. The mother gives birth to the son and is in turn fertilized by him, or as it also has been expressed, the moon god or goddess is androgynous, both male and female, able to reproduce from himself alone.

This mother who is All-Giver, mother of gods and men and of the creatures of the field, occurs again and again in primitive mythologies. Sometimes she is the Moon Mother and again she appears as the creative Earth Mother or as Mother Nature. In many systems these two concepts are closely interwoven so that it is hard to say of some ancient mother goddesses whether they are primarily moon deities or earth deities. For they were each regarded as representing the same generative power. The Chaldeans, Greeks, Scandinavians, Hindus, and Chinese speak of their mother goddesses sometimes as lunar and sometimes as earth deities. This seems a little incongruous to us, today, but to more primitive people the rationale offered no difficulties, and indeed if it had, there was the myth of the origin of the moon to explain the identity of the earth and moon attributes. According to this myth, which occurs in both the old and the new worlds, the original source of both earth and moon was a World Egg, the moon, which split into two parts, one remaining in the sky as moon and the other becoming the earth. That

[3] *Ibid.*, III, 48.

first World Egg *was* the mother from whom all things came. Both parts of the Egg have been called the Woman, or the Mother. All earth mothers, Bachofen has pointed out in his *Das Mutterrecht,* lead a double life as Earth and as Moon. Nevertheless they all derive from the Great Mother, the Moon. The earth is but a part of the great cosmic World Egg. She is in fact the Moon's daughter. Plutarch in his *Isis and Osiris* tells us that: "The Egyptian priests style the Moon the Mother of the Universe," which includes the earth and in some places also the sun, for the son of the moon mother is sometimes a moon god but occasionally he is the sun god.

In all ages and in all places men have conceived of a Great Mother, a Great Woman, who watches over mankind from the sky or from the place of the gods. This concept is to be found in practically every religion and mythology whose contents have come to our knowledge. These Great Mothers whose worship has dominated the religious thoughts of peoples far removed from each other in time, space, and culture, have an essential similarity which cannot but amaze us. The Great Mother was worshipped in ancient Babylonia, in the Near East, in Egypt, in Rome, in medieval Europe (even to this day among the peasants of Europe), in the Celtic countries, in ancient Mexico, among the North and South American Indians, in Africa, in Australasia, in Polynesia, in India, and in Ancient China. In all these places, and no claim is made that this is a complete list, the Mother has certain clearly defined qualities. She is a goddess of the moon and partakes of the characteristics of the moon, and, in a peculiar sense, she is the woman's deity. It is indeed strange that legends which have taken their origin so far apart should yet be so similar. The only possible explanation is that the myths represent a psychological reality which has been perceived by these widely separated peoples, not in the form of abstract thought, but as an image rising from the unconscious and projected into the outer world as a divine being, in this case as a deity of the moon. For as Jung has clearly demonstrated [4] the gods are principles or forces which function apart from man's conscious volition and to whose fiat he must needs bow.

The myths of the Moon Goddess and the characteristics she

[4] Compare Jung, *Contributions to Analytical Psychology,* trans. by H. G. and Cary F. Baynes (New York and London, 1928), p. 161.

possesses shadow forth a truth which could not be perceived directly by human beings, namely: the inner subjective reality of feminine psychology. In the past the Moon represented, and in man's unconscious imagery still represents today, the picture or image of the feminine principle which functions in men as well as in women. But while in women's psychology it is the dominant principle, it is for men the ruler of the night only, the *principle* under whose aegis the *unconscious* functions.

8

THE MOON MOTHER

The moon goddesses are many; yet as soon as we begin to study their attributes and characteristics and the stories of their lives we cannot fail to recognize that they are really all one and the same. Throughout Western Asia and in Asia Minor the chief deity was for many centuries a Great Mother goddess. She was called Magna Mater, or Dea Syria. She was known under different names in different countries and in different ages, but her life story, her attributes and characteristics, did not vary very greatly even though the name of the religion changed from place to place. The worship of this Magna Mater is exceedingly old. The origins are lost in the remote past but as far back as history can be traced we find evidences of a Great Mother goddess reigning supreme with her son who is usually also her lover.

Ishtar of Babylon is one of the oldest. Before the aboriginal Sumerians migrated to Assyria, prior to the third millennium B.C., she and her son Tammuz were already worshipped there. Astarte or Ashtart was the form of the Mother Goddess worshipped by the Canaanites, the Hebrews, and the Phoenicians, but she and her son Baal predated these peoples. Her name which so closely resembles Ishtar's is first mentioned in 1478 B.C., but even then her cult was already old, stretching back into the primitive Semitic days. Isis of Egypt, with Osiris and Horus, sons and lovers, was worshipped from about 1700 B.C. She was called Mother of the Universe and was giver of all life on earth. Cybele, Goddess of Earth and Goddess of the Moon, was worshipped in Phrygia before 900 B.C. She was the mother of Attis, another typical dying and resurrecting god. Anahita and her son Mithra were worshipped in Persia from about 400 B.C. The Celtic mother goddess Anu or Annis was revered from prehistoric times in Western Europe, as far west as Ireland. She also is Goddess of Earth and Goddess of the Moon. These deities are all equivalent forms as are also Aphrodite with Adonis, her son and lover; Anatis of Egypt; and Nana of Babylon. Cybele, the ancient Phrygian goddess, has been further identified with the Greek goddesses Rhea, Ge, and Demeter, earth mothers and moon mothers, and with the Roman forms Tellus, Ceres, and Maia. In medieval Europe the Virgin Mary and her son carried the same significance, and in the many legends which have gathered around her name, does so even today. It is probably not without importance that the worship of the Virgin as Mother of God first came into prominence in the Church at about the time of the Crusades when the ecclesiastical thought of the day was profoundly influenced by Eastern Asia and Syria where the Mother and her Dying Son were still so deeply revered.

Fig. 23. Selene, the Moon Goddess of Greece. (From *A New System or Analysis of Ancient Mythology*, Jacob Bryant, 1774.)

We do not ordinarily think of the Virgin Mary as being related to the great mother goddess of Syria, who was Goddess of the Moon and Mother of God, but psychologically speaking she was perhaps her direct descendant. In medieval art the Virgin was frequently represented enthroned on the moon, as Selene, the Greek moon goddess, had been before her (figure 23), and in the writings of the Catholic Fathers, the association of the Virgin with the moon is clearly expressed. We might conclude that this was symbol or poetic metaphor, perhaps, but the customs of the peasants in certain parts of Europe show that to the uneducated, at all events, the connection is more than a mere figure of speech.

Briffault has collected much interesting material which bears on this relation of the Virgin Mary to the moon and to the ancient moon goddesses.[1] She is called by orthodox Catholic Fathers, The Moon of the Church, Our Moon, The Spiritual Moon, The Perfect and Eternal Moon. She is said to control the moon and through it all the stars and planets; and she is called Star of the Sea and Ruler of the Ocean. The great luminaries which God provided, the sun to rule the day and the

[1] Robert Briffault, *The Mothers* (New York and London, 1927), III, 184.

moon, the night, Hugo explains as follows: "The former is a figure of Jesus Christ, whose splendid rays illumine the just who live in the day of grace; the latter is typical of Mary, whose mild luster illumines sinners mid the dreary night of sin." [2] And Innocent III makes the identification still more complete: "Towards the Moon it is he should look, who is buried in the shadow of sin and iniquity. Having lost divine grace, the day disappears, there is no more sun for him; but the Moon is still in the horizon. Let him address himself to Mary; under her influence thousands every day find their way to God." Hence in Catholic countries we find peasants constantly making this identification. In France they call the moon Notre Dame; in Portugal, The Mother of God.

In Protestant countries these ideas have been forgotten and it is true that Mary is not deified in the New Testament. But, after all, Christianity did arise in Syria, and a close contact was again made with Eastern ideas through the Crusades, in the eleventh and twelfth centuries, when religious orders were established and maintained for many years in Palestine. It is, therefore, not very surprising to find that the figures of the younger religion carried, and, especially for simple folk, still do carry, the significance of the older. For these forms and symbols arise spontaneously from the unconscious and represent psychological realities which human beings throughout the world have dimly felt to be true. We learn, for instance, that when Jesuit missionaries first went to China and to Mexico they found in both these places moon goddesses whose hieratic form and story coincided so extraordinarily with those of the Virgin Mary that an identification of the two by the converts to Christianity was inevitable.

Father Clavigero, in his *Storia Del Messico,* tells of the women of ancient Mexico holding up their children to the Mother Moon, praying her to give them an ever-renewed, eternal life like her own, and relates how, as the people were converted to the true faith, there arose on the site of the temple to their great goddess, the Mother Moon (who was called Tetevinan, The Mother of God) another church dedicated to the Virgin Mary, also called Mother of God whom they irresistibly identified with the moon, and besought in the same terms. [3]

2 *Ibid.,* III, 184.
3 *Ibid.,* III, 62.

Sir John Barrow, in his *Travels in China,* says that the "most common of female deities [in China] is Shing-Moo, or Holy Mother or Perfect Intelligence." [4] He speaks of the amazement of the early Jesuits at discovering in her the most striking resemblance to the Virgin Mary. They found her usually shut up in a recess behind the altar, the position of the Christian Lady Chapel; she was veiled and carried a child, sometimes in her hands, sometimes on her knees and had a glory around her head. Her story as well as her appearance was like Mary's for she conceived and bore her son while yet a virgin.

The close resemblance of the Moon Mothers to each other is most striking. For instance the virgin birth seems to be quite characteristic of the Moon Goddess and is so universal and so strange to our modern ideas that we need to take it up rather more in detail. The Great Mother is always represented as *Virgin,* in spite of the fact that she has many lovers and is the mother of many sons, or of one son, who dies only to be born again and again, year after year. This term "virgin" needs some investigation, for obviously, with its modern connotation of chaste, innocent, it cannot be used of the Magna Mater, unless we assume that she remains miraculously virgin in spite of experiences which would seem to make the term inapplicable. Frazer, however, has an illuminating statement on this point. "The [Greek] word *parthenos,*" he says, "applied to Artemis, which we commonly translate Virgin, means no more than an unmarried woman, and in early days the two things were by no means the same . . . there was no public worship of Artemis the Chaste; so far as her sacred titles bear on the relation of the sexes, they show that, on the contrary, she was, like Diana in Italy, especially concerned with the loss of virginity and with child-bearing. . . Nothing, however, sets the true character of Artemis as a goddess of fecundity though not of wedlock in a clearer light than her constant identification with the unmarried, but not chaste, Asiatic goddesses of love and fertility, who were worshipped with rites of notorious profligacy at their popular sanctuaries." [5] In a footnote Frazer comments on the line in Isaiah, "and a virgin shall be with child," and says that the Hebrew word here rendered as "virgin" means no more than

[4] J. Barrow, *Travels in China* (London, 1806), p. 473.
[5] J. G. Frazer, "The Magic Art and the Evolution of Kings," *The Golden Bough,* Part I (New York, 1917) , I, 36, 37.

"young woman," and that "a correct translation would have ob-
viated the necessity for the miracle." This comment does not
quite cover the point of difficulty, however, for whatever the
Prophet Isaiah may have meant by his saying, there is no doubt
that the Virgin Mary was venerated by the medieval church
and is still venerated by Catholics today, as virgin in our modern sense of the word, even though it is recognized by tradition
that she bore carnal children to Joseph after the virgin birth
of her Eldest Son, and is also hailed in Latin hymns as spouse
as well as mother of her Son. These things would form a fla-
grant contradiction or require an impossible miracle, if they
were to be taken as true on the objective plane. If, however, we
recognize religious concepts as symbolic and interpret these
contradictions psychologically we realize that the term "virginity" must refer to a *quality*, to a subjective state, a psychological attitude, not to a physiological or external fact. When
used of either the Virgin Mary or of the virgin goddesses of
other religions, it cannot be used as denoting a factual situation,
for the quality of virginity persists in some unexplained fashion
in spite of sexual experience, childbearing, and increasing age.

Briffault gives a clue to this enigma. "The word virgin," he
says, "is, of course, used in those titles in its primitive sense as
denoting 'unwed,' and connoting the very reverse of what the
term has come to imply. The virgin Ishtar is also frequently
addressed as 'The Prostitute'; and she herself says, 'A prostitute
compassionate am I.' She wears the 'posin,' or veil, which, as
among the Jews, was the mark of both 'virgins' and prostitutes.
The hierodules, or sacred prostitutes of her temples, were also
called 'the holy virgins.' . . . Children born out of wedlock
were called 'parthenioi,' 'virgin-born.' The word 'virgin' itself
has not, strictly speaking, the meaning which we attach to it;
the correct Latin expression for the untouched virgin is not
'virgo,' but 'virgo intacta.' Aphrodite herself was a Virgin." [6]

The Eskimo mother goddess has the same characteristic of
virginity in the old sense of the term. The Eskimos call her,
"She who will not have a husband." Demeter also is said to have
"execrated marriage." She presided not over marriage but over
divorce. The Chinese holy virgin, Shing-Moo, the Great Mother, conceived and bore her son while yet a virgin. She is ven-

<hr />

[6] Briffault, *op. cit.*, III, 169–170.

erated as a pattern of purity; her conception of the Holy Child is deemed to have been immaculate, but her ancient character is revealed in the fact that she is the patroness of prostitutes.

The term virgin, then, when used of the ancient goddesses, clearly has a meaning not of today. It may be used of a woman who has had much sexual experience; it may be even applied to a prostitute. Its real significance is to be found in its use as contrasted with "married."

In primitive times a married woman was the property of her husband, often bought for a considerable price from her father. The basic idea which underlies this custom still holds sway to some extent among us. In the period of "arranged marriages" and of "marriage settlements" the assumption that the woman was a purchased possession might be glimpsed beneath the decorous negotiations, and the custom of "giving away" the bride recalls the same underlying psychological concept, namely, that a woman is not her own mistress but the property of her father who transfers her *as property* to her husband.

Under our Western patriarchal system the unmarried girl belongs to her father, but in earlier days, as still in some primitive communities, she was her own mistress until she married. The right to dispose of her own person until she marries is part of the primitive concept of liberty. There are many evidences of a general careful guardianship of the young girls in primitive societies, both within and without the tribe; they are guarded, for instance, against violence and especially from "incest" with their "clan brothers," but with men of a clan into which they may marry they can follow their own wishes. This liberty of action involves the right to refuse intimacies as well as to accept them. A girl belongs to *herself* while she is virgin—unwed—and may not be compelled either to maintain chastity or to yield to an unwanted embrace.

As virgin she belongs to herself alone, she is "one-in-herself." Gauguin remarks on this characteristic of the Tahiti women in his book *Noa Noa*. To him it seemed strange. He tells how any woman would readily give herself to a stranger if he attracted her, but that she gave herself not to the man with whom she had intercourse, but to her own instinct, so that even after the relation had been completed she remained one-in-herself. She was not dependent on the man, she did not cling to him or demand that the relationship should be permanent. She was still her own mistress, a virgin in the ancient, original meaning of the word.

It is in this sense that the moon goddesses can rightly be called virgin. The quality of virginity is, indeed, characteristic of them. Other goddesses of ancient and primitive religions do not partake of it; they are not one-in-themselves. They have apparently no separate existence of their own, but are conceived of only as the wives or counterparts of the gods from whom they derive both their power and their prestige. Thus the goddess has the same name as the god, the same attributes and powers, or perhaps she has the feminine version of his more masculine qualities. They form a pair, undifferentiated except in sex. The goddess is merely mate to the god as the woman was to the man. Her name even was a matter of no concern. She was designated merely by the feminine form of the male deity's name. For example the wife of Faunus was Fauna; Dios was the feminine of Zeus, and Agnazi of Agni; Nut corresponded to Nu, and Hehut to Hehu. Even the primitive earth and sky gods formed a pair united in marriage, Mr. Heaven and Mrs. Earth.

Goddesses existing in this way as the counterparts of the gods are of distinct type. They represent the ideal of the married woman and personify that aspect of feminine nature which is clinging and dependent. They deify the domestic virtues of the wife, who is concerned only with the interests of husband and children.

This is the ideal expressed in such terms as "the two shall become one flesh." It is also the archetype underlying the story of the creation of Eve from Adam's rib. In such a situation the "entity" or unit is the pair, the married couple, the family. The members who make up this unit do not have a separate or complete existence, nor do they have a separate or complete character or personality of their own. For in such a marriage the man represents the male part of the entity and the woman the female part. The psyche itself, however, is both male and female. Each human being contains within himself potentialities in both directions. If he does not take up both of these aspects and develop and discipline them within himself, he is only half a person, he cannot be a complete personality. When two people form a complementary marriage, where all the male is in the man and all the female is in the woman, it follows that each of them remains one-sided, for the unlived side of the psyche, being unconscious, is projected to the partner. This condition may work fairly well so long as both are living and remain on good terms. But when one partner dies the other will find himself seriously at a loss and, perhaps not until then, when it may be too late, is it borne in upon him how limited and one-sided his life has been.

In Western patriarchal society, during many centuries, man was concerned to be dominant and superior, while woman was relegated to a position of dependence and inferiority. Consequently the feminine principle has not been adequately recognized or valued in our culture. And even today, when the outer manifestations of this one-sidedness have undergone considerable change, the psychological effects persist and both men and women suffer from a maiming of the psyche, which should be whole. This condition is represented by the goddess who is counterpart of the male god and nothing else.

The relation of the Moon Mother to the god associated with her is entirely different. She is goddess of sexual love but not of marriage. There is no male god who as husband rules her conduct or determines her qualities. Instead she is the mother of a son, whom she controls. When he grows up he becomes her lover and then dies, only to be born again as son. The Moon Goddess belongs to a matriarchal, not to a patriarchal, system. She is not related to any god as wife or "counterpart." She is her own mistress, virgin, one-in-herself. The characteristics of these great and powerful goddesses do not mirror those of any of the male gods, nor do they represent the feminine counterpart of characteristics originally male. Their histories are independent and their functions, their insignia, and their rites belong to themselves alone, for they represent the essence of the feminine in its sharpest contrast to the essence of masculinity. In Chinese philosophy the feminine principle, Yin, stands in direct opposition to the masculine principle, Yang. Yang is the bright, hot, powerful, creative energy, while yin is the dark, moist, shadowy, and receptive power which is also creative because it brings to birth and manifestation the creative stirrings of the yang energy. The yin is said to be of equal power with the yang because it brings *all* his stirrings into manifestation. In the Hindu system Shakti, the feminine creative power, or goddess, stands over against Shiva, the creative spirit, in mas-

their counterparts, not equal and alike,
but equal opposite

characteristics of being one-in-themselves, virgin, and bearing a son by immaculate conception, are not the only points, however, on which the moon goddesses from Asia, Europe, and the New World resemble each other. The myths of their life histories tally in an extraordinary fashion; their sons die and rise again; they are the mothers of all life on earth; givers of fertility; and also, they are the destroyers of the world, especially by flood.

In the Chinese myth of the great flood, the Moon Goddess sent her representative to earth, after the waters had subsided, to repeople the world. In the Babylonian account, Ishtar, the Moon Goddess, is reported to have both caused the great flood and to have saved a remnant of her people. Here her dual character is clearly seen, for she herself sent the flood and then lamented over the havoc she had wrought. On the *Eleventh Tablet of Creation* is told the story of the flood. It is called "The Lamentation of Ishtar at the Great Deluge." According to this ancient record the goddess Ishtar prophesied evil which immediately came to pass. If a person endowed with magic power prophesies, according to the "magic" way of thinking, she evokes that which she has prophesied, whether it be good or evil. We are still swayed by this old attitude when we feel it to be unlucky to suggest that something may go wrong, or that there may be an accident, or other misfortune, and we can still "feel" a hint of the dread which was caused by a witch's curse. For the curse was by no means only a wish that evil might befall, it was believed actually to bring to pass the evil that had been "wished on" the cursed one. This colloquial expression gives the nearest modern equivalent to the old concept of a witch's prophecy or curse. So Ishtar, who was a noted prophetess, as were all the moon goddesses in whom the dark side of the moon was represented, prophesied evil, thus bringing the flood upon the earth. Then when mankind and all the animals were threatened by the rising waters, she pitied their plight and saved them.

Spake Ishtar like a child uttered the great goddess her speech,
"All to corruption are turned and then I in the presence of the
gods prophesied and

As I prophesied in the presence of the gods e . . . . were
  devoted all my people and I prop . . .
I the mother have begotten my people and lik . . .
  the fishes they fill the sea
The gods concerning the spirits were weeping with me
The gods in seats seated in lamentation covered with their lips
  for the coming evil
               Six days and nights passed
The wind, the deluge, storm overwhelmed.
On the seventh day in its course, was calmed the storm and all
  the deluge
Which had destroyed like an earth quake,
               Quieted."

As the poem proceeds, Ishtar is depicted in the boat which she
has made and from which, like Noah from the Ark:

> "On the seventh day in the course of it
> I sent forth a dove and it left"
>
>   * * *
>
> "I sent the animals forth to the four winds" [7]

There was probably an earlier version of this myth which
makes the Moon God the central figure. Noah, in the Old Testament story, is probably a form of Nuah, a Babylonian moon
goddess, and like Ishtar, he saved a remnant of the world from
destruction in an ark which he built. Then when the waters
subsided, Noah, taught by a dove, the bird which is invariably
associated with moon deities, came out onto the land. The de-
populated earth was repeopled from him and his family alone.
He was thus the father of all who were born subsequently. As
he had taken with him in the ark one pair of each animal species he was thus the generator or creator of all animal life on
the renewed or redeemed earth.

The word *ark* is cognate with the Hindu word *argha,* which
means crescent, and also with the *arc* of a circle. The ark in
which Father Noah carried the animals over the flood was thus
a moon boat. This story is put into the form of history, in the
Old Testament, as is so much of religious myth. Even today,
controversy still centers around the problem of the factual basis

[7] George Smith, "Eleventh Tablet of Izdubar Legend," *Records of the Past*
(London, 1873–81), VII, 159.

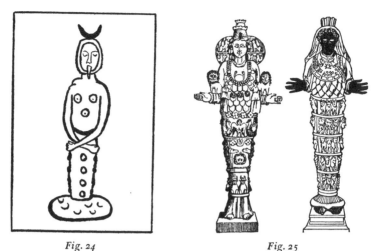

Fig. 24   Fig. 25

Fig. 24. An archaic statuette of Astarte, or Ishtar. (From *Religions de l'antiquité,* Georg Frederic Creuzer, 1825.)

Fig. 25. Diana, or Artemis, the "Many-Breasted", in her dual aspect, dark and light. (From *Ancient Pagan and Modern Christian Symbolism,* Thomas Inman, 1876.)

for the almost generally accepted legend of a great flood. Whatever may be the truth in regard to the deluge, it is clear that the story of the moon boat refers to psychological events. In the Chaldean story the whole happening is concretized. It is living men and animals who are transported over the floods to the "New World." In the Egyptian story Osiris, the Moon God, ferried the dead man who had been initiated into his rites, over the waters to the Isle of the Blest, and so gave him immortality. This also was a concretization. It was thought of as having an actual physical reality. But the Hindus, who were more psychologically minded than either the Chaldeans or the Egyptians, speak of the moon as carrying the souls of the dead over the waters to the sun where they live a redeemed life. This transition is represented in the Tantric diagrams of the Seven Stages of Consciousness. There the crescent moon is seen in the watery region, above which comes the fiery region of the sun. But already this is realized as symbol. The psychical is no longer projected into a concrete semihistorical happening, but the myth is recognized as representing stages of consciousness or of psychological development.

The moon boat of the Hindus carries the souls to the new world, the new incarnation, it is the boat of immortality. The Chinese moon goddess after the flood gives birth to all living things. It is a renewed world and a new creation. Men, women, and all animals arise from the different parts of her person. The moon goddess of Western Asia and of Europe similarly gave birth to all living creatures. The statues of Diana and those of the Asiatic moon goddesses in their hieratic form show animals and plants springing from heads, limbs, and breasts. For the Moon Goddess is the Many Breasted Mother of All, creator of all life on the earth. (Figures 24 and 25.)

The Moon Goddess is, in literal fact, the mother of all living things and yet, strange though it may seem, not only is she the life-giver but also the destroyer. She creates all life on the earth, and then comes the flood, which overwhelms it. And this flood is her doing, for she is cause of rain and storm and tide and also of the flood. But like Ishtar of Babylon, she laments at its consequences and does her best to save her children, who have all become "like the fishes of the sea." Similarly, though she stands passively by when her son is killed, the Moon Goddess mourns, as Aphrodite did, at the defeat and death of Adonis, an event that was commemorated annually, in the festival of the "weeping for Adonis."

In her role as giver of rain, too, the moon deity is quite unaccountable, for not only does she send rain in the spring, when it is needed for the young crops, but she also has a penchant for sending storms in August when they frequently destroy the very harvest which her bounty has provided. For this reason special rites were prescribed to induce the goddess to prevent the coming of these harvest storms. On the thirteenth of August there was a great festival of Hecate the moon goddess in Greece and of Diana her direct descendant in Rome, for the harvest ripens earlier in these southern countries than it does farther north. On this day the Goddess's aid was invoked to avert storms which might injure the coming harvest. This festival was continued by the Catholic Church. The date of August fifteenth was chosen for celebrating the feast of the Assumption of the Blessed Virgin. The connection between the pagan and the Christian ceremony is a very interesting one. The special feature of the Christian ritual centers round prayers addressed to the Virgin Mary, as they formerly were to the moon goddesses who preceded her, to turn aside storms until the fields are reaped of their fruits. There is a passage in the Syriac text of *The Departure of My Lady Mary from this World* which runs thus: "And the apostles also ordered that there should be a commemoration of the Blessed one on the thirteenth of Ab [that is August], on account of the vines bearing bunches of grapes and on account of the trees bearing fruit, that clouds of hail, bearing stones of wrath, might not come, and the trees be broken, and the fruits, and the vines with their clusters." [8]

Most primitive peoples consider the moon to be the great rain giver, a belief which seems to have some connection with actual observations of the weather. Farmers and seafaring people say that the weather changes at the new moon or when the moon passes the full. In primitive tribes rain making, a most important function, is usually in the hands of the women, who are believed to be in such a peculiar relation to the moon that they are likely to have a better chance of influencing the fickle deity in a favorable way. Even where a man, the medicine man or the king perhaps, as incarnation of the moon, exercises this function, he generally holds his office by virtue of and with the assistance of his wife or wives. Many interesting ceremonies connected with rain making have been gathered by Briffault and it is striking how general and conspicuous is the role that women play in them. [9]

The moistening power of the goddess depended not only on her control of the rainfall, for she was also believed to produce the dew. In Greece, the Moon Goddess was called the All-Dewy-One, and a dew service was held for her in Athens, when dew maidens danced about the statue of the goddess. [10] Dew is a symbol of fertility and a bath of dew was often prescribed, late into the middle ages, as a love charm. In short, as Plutarch says: "The moon, with her humid and generative light, is favorable to the propagation of animals and the growth of plants."

Ishtar, the Babylonian moon goddess, was connected with springs and dew, and bore the title All-Dewy-One. This epithet takes on a new significance for us when we recall how hot and dry Mesopotamia is. In the cold North a sun god is needed for

8 "The Departure of My Lady Mary from this World," *Journal of Sacred Literature and Biblical Record,* New Series, VII, 153.
9 Briffault, *op. cit.,* III, 9–21.
10 Jane Harrison, *Themis* (Cambridge University Press, 1912), p. 191.

fertility but in tropical countries the sun is an enemy of vegetation, while rain and dew cause the earth to bring forth the
green things. So the temples of the moon goddess were often
in natural grottos, where a spring represented the source of
life, and the perpetual greenness of the oasis in the desert wit-
nessed to the presence of the moon goddess, giver of vegetation.
Ishtar was also called Queen of the Dust and Mistress of the
Field, while she and her son Tammuz were both known by the
epithet Urikittu meaning The Green One. Plutarch, in his *Isis
and Osiris,* says: "The moon, having the light which makes
moist and pregnant, is promotive of the generating of living
beings and of the fructification of plants." And Macrobius, in
his *Saturnalia,* differentiates between the warmth of the two
great heavenly bodies with: "The heat of the sun dries; that of
the moon makes moist."

Like Ishtar, moon goddesses from whatever region were regarded as guardians of the waters, rivers, brooks, and springs
which, gushing forth out of the ground, were usually held sacred
to the goddess of fertility; probably because they so aptly symbolize that invisible hidden power of "bringing forth from
within" which is the peculiar characteristic of feminine creation.

The Moon Goddess was thus giver of life and of all that pro-
motes fertility, and at the same time she was the wielder of the
destructive powers of nature. To the ancients her contradictory
character was an essential factor, frankly recognized. But viewed
from our rational and causal standpoint a deity can be either
friendly or malicious, but cannot be both. From the Christian
point of view it is well-nigh impossible to conceive of a god
who is at once kind and cruel, who creates and destroys. For
God is conceived of as good: evil is always the work of the devil.
But to the worshippers of the Moon Goddess there was no contradiction. Their supreme deity was like the moon, not like
the sun. She was dual in her very nature. She lived her life in
phases, manifesting the qualities of each phase in turn. In the
upper-world phase, corresponding to the bright moon, she is
good, kind, and beneficent. In the other phase, corresponding
to the time when the moon is dark, she is cruel, destructive, and
evil. It is not that these goddesses are undifferentiated or unreliable. For as, from the first day when the slender crescent appears in the sky, it can be relied on to increase in size and

brightness, night by night, till the full moon, and thereafter to decrease, until the brightness of the moon "has been eaten up" by the dark moon, so the goddess turns first her beneficent face and then her angry aspect towards men.

In some cases this dual character of the Mother is represented in religious art by portraying her face as part dark and part fair. Father Clavigero describes the statue of the Mexican moon goddess in the ancient temple referred to above as similar to the black-and-white Greek Erinyes; the upper part of the face was pure white while the lower part, from the mouth down, was black. Among the Ainus of Japan the Moon is clothed in a black-and-white garment. The ancient Egyptians often represented their Isis as a black woman holding the infant Horus in her arms, on the other hand she was shown in her upper-world phase as fair. There are statues of Artemis, which are exact counterparts of each other except that one is fair and the other black (figure 25), while as we have already seen, Sinn, the moon god of Babylonia, was represented as black when in his underworld phase (figure 22).

There are in Europe to this day certain shrines of Mary, Mother of God, Moon of the Church, in which the image of Mary is black. These shrines of the Black Virgin are all wonder-working and are very highly esteemed, being visited by pilgrims from far and wide.

The Church of Notre Dame de la Recourance in Orléans has a statue of the Black Virgin, which is miracle-working and is considered particularly holy. In times of great danger or present calamity it is carried through the streets in procession. A statue of the Black Virgin in Notre Dame de Monserrat depicts both Virgin and Child as black. In the north rose window of the Cathedral of Notre Dame at Chartres, the Virgin is dark of complexion and her Child is fair, while in the crypt is the most ancient statue of the Black Virgin beside a deep and dark well.

Henry Adams remarks, in his *Mont Saint Michel and Chartres,* that in this particular church Mary the Virgin did not hesitate to admit Mary Magdalene and Mary the Gypsy to her society. Mary the Harlot was black in character; Mary the Gypsy, or the Egyptian, was black in face. In a Roman Catholic book of the Saints is recorded a legend of this Egyptian Mary to the effect that, wishing to go to the Holy Land on a pilgrimage, her only way of obtaining passage was to offer herself as a prostitute to the sailors on a vessel bound for that shore. Thus she earned her way to the Holy Land, where she lived for years as an anchorite in the desert.

There is another very ancient shrine of the Black Virgin at Einsiedeln in Switzerland, whose origin is lost in the mists of antiquity, although there is a local legend to the effect that the statue was blackened by fire. This Black Virgin has an Egyptian or Moorish appearance. She stands on the moon. She is wonder-working and is visited by cripples and invalids who make long pilgrimages to kneel before her and implore her aid. There is a large monastery nearby whose monks worship and tend the Black Virgin daily. She has her own little chapel at the west end of the church, where she stands on the moon, eternally. And out in the *place,* in full daylight, is a statue of the White Virgin, poised, precariously, on a dragon.

In the foregoing examples the moon is represented by *one* deity, who like the luminary she personifies, changes her appearance and is alternately dark and light. These two aspects of the moon are represented in other religions by two separate goddesses. The history of Greek religion gives an instance of the change from one form to the other. In the earliest days the moon was represented by Selene alone. She was a rather neutral, indeterminate figure and was later replaced by two distinct characters, Aphrodite, the Bright Moon, and Hecate, the Dark Moon. In still later times, however, the Moon Goddess was sometimes called Hecate-the-Three-Headed. (Figure 39, and frontispiece.) This is a combined form composed of Artemis, Selene and Hecate. It represents the moon in its three phases: Artemis is the crescent or waxing moon, Selene the full moon, and Hecate the waning and dark moon. To us it may seem strange that the moon in its totality should be represented by Hecate, the dark moon. We might expect the moon to be represented by Artemis or Selene. For in our modern view the positive or bright aspect of things is always considered to be the most powerful and dominant and to it we give the greatest emphasis and the most constant attention, disregarding the dark and shadowed side as far as possible. But to the Greeks the *power* of the moon was represented by Hecate, the Dark Moon.

113

The rites of this goddess were performed at night, and were especially concerned with placation in order to turn aside her wrath and the evil she so often wrought. She is Dea-Triformis of the Cross Ways who leads travellers astray, and, as Queen of the Ghosts, she sweeps through the night followed by her "dreadful train of questing spirits" and baying hounds (even as late as medieval times witches were "seen" flying through the air headed by Hecate herself). She is goddess of storms, of destructions, of the terrors of the night. "For," as Plutarch says, "the waxing moon is of good intent, but the waning moon brings sickness and death."

The Moon Goddess, however, is not only Goddess of Storms and of Fertility, that is of disturbances and creations in the outer world, she is also goddess of disturbances and of creative activity which take place in the inner world. She is responsible for lunacy and, on the positive side, is Giver of Vision. Cybele and Hecate were both called Antea, which means the Sender of Nocturnal Visions, while Museos, the Muse-man, was one name for the son of Hecate, or Son of the Moon. Magic, inspiration, and understanding are her gifts.

The ancients knew no inner or psychological realm, to them the inner world was conceived of as the underworld, the spirit realm, the place where all spirit things dwelt. We still, to a lesser extent it is true, but in some measure, think of inner creative activity as uncanny or mysterious, to us it smacks somewhat of the underworld. But to the ancients all subjective life was still in the unconscious, in the hidden, terrifying depths of the underworld darkness. Thus the Underworld Queen is mistress of all that lives in the hidden parts of the psyche, in the unconscious as we should say. She is the Goddess of Magic and of magicians. Contact with the dark side of the Moon Goddess was considered to be the sole reliable instrument for the working of magic. Pindar tells us, for instance, that Aphrodite, the Bright Moon, taught her son Jason, when he needed the help of magic powers, "how to draw down the dark moon," showing that although she herself did not have the power of black magic, she could yet invoke Hecate (the ancient idea of invoking someone included compelling their aid) whose magic had a universal application. Magic connected with love, metamorphosis, and *pharmaka*, medicine in the primitive sense of "magic," potent healing or destructive substances, were hers in a peculiar sense. It is interesting to note that the shrines of the Black Virgin in Europe today are reputed to have great wonder-working and healing powers (powers of *pharmaka*) often in excess of the power of the shrines of the Virgin in her White aspect. The powers connected with love and metamorphosis are of particular interest in this study as they recur again and again in the interpretation of modern moon symbolism.

In many primitive tribes the beneficent aspect of the moon is overlooked entirely and she is thought to be only evil in her effects. The evil aspect, however, usually applies chiefly or entirely to men. To women the moon is generally of "good intent." The moon is in fact the First Woman whose influence on men is invariably evil. It is not only in the Genesis story that man puts all the blame for his troubles onto the woman. When we consider "the woman," the moon, as representing the feminine principle and when we realize that for men this feminine principle which is so foreign to their own masculine nature, yet governs their unconscious, we understand why it is that all his mistakes can, justly enough, be blamed on "the Woman." Only, the blame should not fall on the actual flesh-and-blood woman who is his partner, but on the Old Woman in himself, the anima, who indeed causes most of the unexpected troubles which upset his calculations, while if she gains the upper hand in his psyche, he will "lose his manhood," as the primitives believed. He will then be dominated by his unconscious feminine soul, his anima, a condition which imparts to a man a sort of "womanish" character.

W. H. Keating in his *Expedition to Lake Winnipeck* states that among the Winnebagos, the sun is believed to be propitious to men; but the "Moon, on the contrary, they held to be inhabited by an adverse female deity, whose delight it is to cross man in all his pursuits. If during their sleep this deity should present herself to them in their dreams, the Indians consider it enjoined on them by duty to become *Cinaedi;* and they ever after assume the female garb." [11] The Cinaedi were homosexual men; they wore women's clothes, performed only women's tasks, and often, even, took husbands. As we shall see later this is not

11 W. H. Keating, *Narrative of an Expedition to the Source of St. Peters River, Lake Winnipeck,* 2 vols. (London, 1825). See E. Carpenter, *Intermediate Types Among Primitive Folk* (London, 1914), p. 44.

the only instance of men being compelled to sacrifice their manhood and their fertility when called to the service of the Moon Goddess.

But while to men the Moon is most harmful, is indeed the "dreadful Goddess," she is usually helpful to women, perhaps because they are of the same nature as herself. She demands from women not the sacrifice of their power to reproduce but instead she gives them the gift of fertility and is their chief refuge in the dangers and pangs of childbirth. The Moon Goddess is called upon by childless women, who want children and by pregnant women, who beseech her for an easy delivery, just as she was invoked for aid in making the fields fertile and the harvest plentiful.

Diana, for instance, was famed for blessing women with children. She presided over childbirth and was called Opener of the Womb. Euripides tells us that in her capacity of midwife, Artemis, the Greek prototype of Diana, would not even speak to childless women. Cumant reports of Anahita, the Mazdian moon goddess, that she "purifies the seed of males and the milk and womb of females," and that she was also invoked by marriageable girls and by women in childbirth. Aphrodite, too, was goddess of sexual love. A reminiscence of her reputed power yet lingers in the term Aphrodisiac. Artemis, Anaitis, Aphrodite, and Ishtar are all goddesses of sexual love, not of chastity, and of each it is said that they encourage women to be fruitful and multiply.

The contradictory character of the Moon Goddess is thus resolved. For her good and evil aspects are seen to be not absolute but relative. Her power works evil under certain circumstances but good under others. To men whose nature is in opposition to her cyclic character she is apt to be particularly dangerous. To women who have within them this same peculiar quality which the Moon Goddess epitomizes, the power she wields is far less likely to be destructive and indeed if the woman is in a right relation to this principle of her own nature, the goddess blesses her with fertility and with magic power.

Just how a woman in the twentieth century can bring herself into this right relation to the moon principle is a very difficult question. A closer inspection of the ancient rites of the moon goddesses may perhaps give a clue to the solution of the problem which is felt to be of vital importance in the present day.

9

THE VIRGIN GODDESS

During the long ages of human history woman has gradually evolved out of the purely instinctive stage which is still represented by the dark moon. The tendency to function indiscriminately from the animal-like level of her feminine nature has been checked by the conventional laws which gradually grew up and have been in force for so long, regulating especially the behavior of the sexes towards each other. For the daemonic, nonhuman manifestation of instinct is like a tide, which can easily swamp all human values. Conventional standards were established, indeed, to prevent such inundations. For when the tide of unconscious instinct rises it can sweep away all human safeguards and destroy all those values which have been laboriously built up throughout the ages of civilization.

Life within the limits of the conventional code has become so mechanical and sterile, however, that many people, today, are seeking again a direct contact with the sources of life which can grow out of a freer relation to instinct. Women in particular, have rebelled against the restrictions imposed upon them by the moral requirements of the Victorian age, which have indeed seemed to be especially unfair to them, owing to the different standards in vogue for men and women. But as soon as a woman releases herself from the purely conventional ways of thinking and acting this nonhuman aspect of instinct begins to well up within her. Perhaps for the first time in her life she finds herself attractive to men, able, without herself being involved, to attract them and hold their attention. By allowing herself to act according to instinct without conscious criticism of what she does and without paying attention to the implication of her words and deeds, she becomes the medium of the eternal feminine which is irresistible to a large proportion of

117

men. The uprush of feminine instinct in such a woman may be like a flooding from the unconscious which threatens to swamp all the specifically human values which she formerly seemed to possess when she controlled her life by conventional standards.

The rising of instinctive femininity which sweeps through a woman as part of the experience of her moonlike quality, if left to itself would reduce her from the human level to that of an instinctive animal. The myths of the moon and the picture described in Chapter 6 suggests that it would make her into a fish. She would be in fact, in her effects, much like a mermaid, or one of the Sirens who are proverbially the undoing of men. These mythological creatures, half-fish, half-woman, are represented always as concerned only with themselves, they were autoerotic. They conquer men not for love of the man, but for a craving to gain power over him. They cannot love, they can only desire. They are cold-blooded, without human feeling or compassion. Instinct in its daemonic form, entirely non-human, lives through them. This unmediated living of instinct has a strangely attractive effect on men, it catches their attention and infatuation. Such women steal the man's soul, but they do not themselves experience the passion, the desires, the griefs, of instinct. The lower part of the body is fish, not woman.

This aspect of feminine nature corresponds, perhaps, to the coldness of the moon. The sun shines by its own light, while the moon's light is only reflected. The sun is bright and hot in itself; the moon in itself is cold and dark. The sun has everywhere represented the masculine or yang power, the moon the feminine or yin. Yet we are not accustomed to think of a woman as being cold and a man hot. Men are generally considered to be relatively without feeling, that is cold; and women, who are actuated so largely by feeling, are considered warm or glowing. But while men can be cold and materialistic on the business side of life, it is well to remember that there is a type of woman who can be terribly cold on the feeling side. In his *Cakes and Ale*, Somerset Maugham coined a phrase which conveys the exact shade of meaning, "A woman with a heart of gold and an eye to the main chance."

These are the women who play the role of anima to men, as a game, a technique—deliberately repressing their own reactions so that they may the more surely get what they want. This subject has been discussed at length in the chapter "All Things to All Men" in *The Way of All Women.*[1]

It is relatively rare to find a man who is not touched to warmth in an erotic situation, but there are whole classes of women who, even while living erotically, are as cold as icebergs and as calculating as stockbrokers. The coldness of the moon and the heartlessness of the Moon Goddess symbolize this aspect of feminine nature. In spite of its lack of warmth and its callousness, partly perhaps because of its very indifference, this impersonal eroticism in a woman often appeals to a man; for her real indifference to him and his welfare may be hidden under an exceedingly personal manner and apparent concern. If the man is immature in his own emotional development his feelings remain sentimental, and he will be flattered by this apparent interest in his intimate and personal life. He will feel that this woman has a peculiar connection with him in things which are ordinarily secret, which only a mother knows or cares about. It gives him a curious feeling of warmth and closeness, almost a sense of body contact which is well-nigh irresistible. In this way the woman finds a chink in his personal dignity and reserve through which she can enter. She touches him where he is soft and yielding, where his defenses do not serve him any more. His conscious judgment of the situation and of her character is nullified, lulled to sleep by the narcotic of this animal-like instinctive contact. He is readily misled by the ease of this intimacy into the delusion that she has some, almost uncanny, knowledge of him, for she seems to know all about him without his having to tell her anything. This knowledge seems to constitute a deep bond between them and it is often taken as evidence that there is an inherent similarity in their natures. The man feels her to represent his other self, his inevitable mate. And it does not occur to him that he has been the victim of a trick. The personalness of his own feelings has betrayed him. He is vulnerable because of his own lack of development in relation to the nonpersonal Eros. Only by creating a relation to the feminine principle can he learn to distinguish between the false and the true in a woman's attitude to him.

Strangely enough, women can produce this almost magic

[1] M. E. Harding, *The Way of All Women* (New York, 1933).

effect on men most readily when they are themselves least involved, or are involved only on a power basis, seeking conquest, not love. When the woman herself is immune to love, and regards it only as a game, a technique, she plays the role of Siren to greatest advantage. The more impersonally skillful she is the more likely is it that the man will become hopelessly enmeshed.

For this reason the woman who finds her satisfaction through the attentions she can command, and the emoluments which come to her from the admirers she attracts, must not fall in love. Only so long as she herself is not emotionally involved can she control the situation. If she falls in love she becomes at once, through her own participation in the hopes and fears, the joys and griefs of her love, a part of the plastic material of life. She is no longer an impersonal actor in the human drama but is herself the one acted upon.

In the play *Maya* just this outcome is shown. The heroine is a prostitute, presented in her various relations to a whole series of men. She can play the role of mother, wife, sweetheart, meeting each man and comforting him according to his need. But when the man, who had loved her in her girlhood, comes and demands that she show herself as she really is, all her ability to carry the situation vanishes. She is overcome by hysterical emotion and frantically tells him to go. In face of his reality she can no longer play a role, converting herself into the particular woman-phase he desires, and she finds herself pitifully, tragically, incompetent to be a real person. For she has wasted herself in an empty game, and now there is no "herself" that she can be.

A woman of this kind is never profoundly or spontaneously aware of herself and her own instinct. Femininity shows itself in her only in the presence of men, either in response to the man's desire or, quite as often, as the expression of her own desire to conquer him. Her sexuality has been pressed into the service of her ego and functions as a part of her desire for power. Such a woman has no deep instinct or passion of her own. Her mood and her actions merely reflect the man's wishes. She has no individual contact with the Eros principle, and in the absence of his desire she can bring him nothing. She has a technique for catching his interest; her own involvement is not erotic but depends on the desire for ego- and power-satisfaction.

A woman of this kind may be aware to some extent of the nature of her own involvement or she may be most amazingly unaware. She may even be convinced that she falls in love with the various men whom she meets and subdues. But if the situation progresses to a point where something more is required of her than dalliance, the true character of her emotion is likely to be revealed. When put to the test of life, the real selfishness and coldness of her nature will certainly show themselves. If, for instance, she marries one of her "conquests," he will soon discover that her idea of love is that she should be waited on and pampered, while he is expected to offer unflagging devotion, which must not waver even when she pursues her "mission" of being kind to other men—that is, when she continues to subdue the hearts of all the men who cross her path. And indeed her cold-blooded exploitation of his love does not stop at this point, for when love-making should give place to the fulfillment of passion, she usually proves to be cold or even entirely frigid. A woman of this kind is in fact aptly symbolized by the mermaid whose cold and fishy tail is the dark and sinister reality underlying the charming naïvety represented by her perpetual preoccupation with comb and glass.

This aspect of feminine nature is represented by the dark moon, or the very early phase of the new moon. When a woman lives in this phase of her nature only, she is not individual, not human. She is, instead, the personification of a nature force, or rather, perhaps one should say that her effect on men is *as though* she were a force of nature.

When the moon is seen as crescent, the rest of the moon's disc is dark and is for that reason not visible. It is not that a black body is to be seen in the sky. We know that the moon still exists but we cannot see it. At the most the whole circle may be outlined, perhaps, by a faint luminous line, but the dark side of the moon, by far the larger part, is not clearly visible. This might be interpreted, perhaps, by saying that the dark side of the woman's moonlike nature should remain obscured. It is not only dark in its nature but should also be hidden. It is a thing *in* the night, and should not be dragged out into the light. In the picture of the Phases of the Moon reproduced in figure 18, the woman representing the dark moon is hidden from view. It seems as if this modern woman's intuition taught her that the dark aspect of the woman's cycle should remain a mystery. In fact, if an attempt is made to bring these obscure movements of the feminine spirit too clearly into the light of consciousness, they either disappear from view or they become hostile and take on an evil aspect.

The dark moon was, as we have seen, considered to be negative, even hostile to man. For instance, in the service called Hecate's Supper, food was taken for the dread goddess, at dead of night, to the crossroads and left on the ground. The worshipper then withdrew from the place without looking back, for he must not see her in her dark phase. Similarly the moon aspect of woman must not be looked at.

With modern Western peoples there is no longer a question of the need to segregate women at the menstrual period for fear of physical contamination, nor is there any question of secluding women at all times, as the Mohammedans have done, but a problem in regard to the daemonic attraction of women, who are in the psychological condition which we have been considering, still remains unsolved. In the past this situation was taken care of by providing all young and attractive women with chaperones and duennas who sought to safeguard their charges, by careful surveillance, from the more serious indiscretions into which their own undisciplined feminine instinct might be expected to lead them. Today, chaperones are out of date and young people are given complete freedom to experiment with life as their impulses dictate, a freedom which is also not infrequently taken by their elders, who might be expected to have a deeper understanding of life. Understanding of life, however, is only gained through a knowledge of oneself and one's own motives, and, where a woman's development is still so immature that she is compelled by impulses arising from the unconscious to attract and dominate men through the power of her feminine instinctiveness, she has no consideration to give to more human values, but acts in a purely egotistic and destructive way.

Feminine instinctiveness is not necessarily destructive, however. If it is made to serve the ends of human love and cultural development, it is a force of great value. It is not evil in itself; but neither is it good in itself. It is energy, which can be used for either good or evil. Energy, if left to itself, however, produces only nonhuman effects. It always runs downhill, it never builds up. Human intervention is needed to convert energy into work through which something of value can be achieved. So that when a woman gives herself over to the flow of this instinctive energy, neither love nor psychological relationship will be the outcome. When related in this primitive way to instinct she is a social danger. But we have no system for protecting men from her baneful influences, and she is as a rule the last person to recognize the evil effects which follow in her train, consequently she is not likely to undertake to abide by "taboo" regulations of her own free will. Furthermore men, as a rule, do not recognize the danger either, so that they do not want her segregated, at all events, until after they have been so severely burned that they become embittered against the whole sex. But women usually are not slow to recognize when one of their number is in this stage of development and they do attempt in a rather unconscious way to build a psychological wall about her. The older and more experienced women say that she will probably get over it, while the younger ones, who are most likely to suffer on account of the vulnerability of their men, are usually hostile to her.

Sometimes the woman herself may come to realize what is happening, either because of the barrier which grows up between herself and other women, or, more often, because of the repeated disasters which follow her infatuations. In this way she may become disgusted with herself and long to change. H. G. Wells once wrote a story about a mermaid, who fell in love with a human who came to bathe near the rocks where she was wont to sit combing her hair. For the first time in her life she really fell in love. But she was a mermaid, she could not love as a human woman would. For all her longing she could never become a "real-maid." All she could do was to lure her lover to a watery grave.

The "mermaid" phase of the modern woman may denote a complete lack of psychological development, the woman having remained in an animal-like at-one-ness with nature, which has never been broken by any human awareness, or, perhaps more often, the woman of today comes into this state because she has found the conventional ways of behaving entirely sterile, dry, infertile, like the Wastelands of the Grail legend. The coming of the flood of instinct resembles the deluge through which Ishtar brought moisture to the desert land. But in the myth her children all became like the fishes of the sea, truly a cause for lamentation. No woman, however, who has experienced this fructification, would wish to go back to a conventional attitude as a means of controlling the dark feminine force which acts through her. She knows from her experience of the power of the goddess that the conventional woman is no true woman, is, indeed, little more than an automaton. But no sooner is a modern woman released from the yea and nay of Mrs. Grundy, than she finds herself immersed in instinctive desires and ways of acting which threaten to drown all that is human in her. She cannot go back but must ask herself whether there is any way forward. Can she be saved from drowning in the flood, and yet not lose the values of the life-giving moisture? In the moon myths this question is answered. It is repeatedly recorded that when the moon sent the deluge upon the earth she also provided a means of salvation, a boat which carried the chosen ones of her children to a new world where they could live redeemed lives. The boat that she provided was an ark, a crescent moon boat, and in this her people were carried to the sun, the place of warmth and light.

We have to ask what is the psychological meaning of this ark, this crescent boat. Surely it means that redemption from the cold-blooded attitude of the unconscious waters of instinct, representing the dark of the moon, is to be found by gaining a different relation to the moon goddess. Instead of being engulfed by the waters of the moon, the initiate can embark in her boat and so become one of her company. It is a religious symbol with which we are very familiar. The salvation is to be found by taking a new attitude towards the power of instinct, involving the recognition that it is, in itself, not human, but belongs to the nonhuman or divine realm. To enter the boat of the goddess implies accepting the uprush of instinct in a religious spirit as a manifestation of the creative life force, itself. When such an attitude is attained, instinct can no longer be regarded as an asset to be exploited for the advantage of the personal life; instead it must be recognized that the personal I, the ego, must submit itself to the demands of the life force as to a divine being.

The chief characteristic of the goddess in her crescent phase is that she is virgin. Her instinct is not used to capture or possess the man whom she attracts. She does not reserve herself for the chosen man who must repay her by his devotion, nor is her instinct used to gain for herself the security of husband, home and family. She remains virgin, even while being goddess of love. She is essentially one-in-herself. She is not merely the feminine counterpart of a male god with similar characteristics and functions, modified to suit her feminine form. On the contrary she has a role to play that is her own, her characteristics do not duplicate those of any of the gods, she is the Ancient and Eternal, the Mother of God. The god with whom she is associated is her son and him she necessarily precedes. Her divine power does not depend on her relation to a husband-god, and thus her actions are not dependent on the need to conciliate such a one or to accord with his qualities and attitudes. For she bears her divinity in her own right.

In the same way the woman who is virgin, one-in-herself, does what she does—not because of any desire to please, not to be liked, or to be approved, even by herself; not because of any desire to gain power over another, to catch his interest or love, but because what she does is true. Her actions may, indeed, be unconventional. She may have to say no, when it would be easier, as well as more adapted, conventionally speaking, to say yes. But as virgin she is not influenced by the considerations that make the nonvirgin woman, whether married or not, trim her sails and adapt herself to expediency. I say whether married or not, for in using this term *virgin* in its psychological connotation, it refers not to external circumstances but to an inner attitude. A woman who has a psychological attitude to life which makes her dependent on what other people think, which makes her do and say things she really does not approve, is no virgin in this meaning of the term. She is not one-in-herself but acts always as female counterpart or syzygy to some male. This "male" may be an actual man, her father, or husband, or some man whose opinion she esteems very highly, or it may be some quite abstract *idea* of what people think, or an even more remote opinion, formulating itself as "one must do this to be liked," or "a girl should act thus and so if she wants to get married." These ideas and opinions are manifestations of the male within her, her own animus, and she is related to this psychological male in much the same way as many married women are related to their husbands.[2] A woman with such an

2 Harding, *op. cit.*, "The Ghostly Lover".

attitude is not one-in-herself, she is dependent upon someone or something outside her own psyche. Her qualities and characteristics are determined by that other, just as the characteristics of the Egyptian goddess Nut were dependent on those of her syzygy Nu, or the Latin Fauna on Faunus. The woman who is psychologically virgin is not dependent in this way. She is what she is because that is what she is.

This sounds, perhaps, unattractive. And if the motive that displaces the law of convention is merely egocentricity the cure would indeed be worse than the disease. The step, intended to release from the bondage of society, would prove to be regressive, leading away from a disciplined and civilized state into barbarism. But when the motive is not a personal one but is concerned with a nonpersonal goal, namely with gaining a right relation to the "goddess," to the principle of Eros, the result is freed from egotism and selfishness. The truth in the woman's action then has the tang and headiness of an intoxicating drink, while she herself is seen to be not an egotist but a personality of more profound significance.

How then can an ordinary woman release herself from her ego orientation? It is so natural to be on the lookout for the main chance, to want to make the best of life for oneself. This is a difficult problem but perhaps the ancient teachings about the moon may give us some light on it. For the primitive conception of the moon, as both giver of fertility and destroyer of life, was gradually replaced by a more developed ritual and myth regarding the feminine principle as embodied in the Moon Goddesses, who were virgin, one-in-themselves.

10

PRIESTS AND PRIESTESSES OF
THE MOON

The religious practices observed in the service of the moon deity range all the way from magical customs of primitive and savage people to elaborate rituals, carried out with all the dignity and solemnity that antique civilizations could muster. Obviously these religious practices cannot all be dealt with here. We must content ourselves with considering a few of the outstanding rites which seem to have particular significance for the present investigation.

We have already spoken of the rituals which are observed in certain tribes at the first appearance of the new moon, where all the people or in some cases selected individuals, cry to the king, moonman on earth, "Your life has been renewed." Others, as the Hottentots do, go out at the new moon and at the full moon and throw clay balls into the air as rain charms.

The persons who are entrusted with these services can hardly be called priests or priestesses but in other tribes, rather more advanced, certain women are definitely set apart as priestesses of the moon. It is a significant fact that everywhere the moon is served by women, although as we shall see later, men also played a part in her service but in a very different capacity. These women have charge of the magical practices intended to foster the fertilizing power of the moon. The most important of these functions are the care of the water supply and the tending of a sacred flame, or sacred fire representing the light of the moon, which must not be allowed to die. In addition, in many places these priestesses receive the fertilizing energy of the deity in their own persons, as women, a function which is performed for the benefit of the whole tribe.

The making of rain and the magical control of the weather

are perhaps the most important functions of the magician of primitive tribes. This function is closely related to the moon and is almost invariably in the hands of women. Even where a man, the chief, or the man magician, is officially the rain maker, further inquiry usually reveals the fact that he holds his office by virtue of his relation or marriage to a woman who is the real medium of the magic power. For instance, in Africa rain making is generally the function of a sacred king, a moonman, but his powers are usually dependent on the help of certain women, who gather the necessary herbs or pour the water used as a charm, or clean out the springs or water holes as part of the ritual. In many tribes, however, rain making is carried out entirely by the women and these ceremonies must not even be seen by a male. The women taking part in the rites are usually naked. They visit the water springs and clean them out, then draw fresh water and throw it over themselves. Sometimes this ceremonial is performed by one woman or girl alone, who is for the time being considered priestess of the moon deity.

Where the sacred fire of the moon is tended by Vestal priestesses, they are usually responsible also for the rain rituals. This was the case in Peru, where the priestesses of Mama-Quilla were vestals and also rain makers, just as in ancient Rome, the Vestal Virgins, guardians of the sacred fire of Vesta, performed a ceremony at the Ides of May, the time of the full moon, to regulate the water supply. This included throwing twenty-four manikins into the Tiber, a substitute for the human sacrifice, which had formerly been made to the river.

The shrines of the Moon Mother were usually in groves, where there was a spring, often in a grotto where the water trickled directly out of the rock, while ceremonies of water drawing and pouring were a constant feature of her service. In Egypt a vase of water was carried in the annual procession of the Phallephoria, in front of the image of the phallus which represented Osiris, and, similarly, water jars and water pourings played a large part in the service of other moon deities, givers of rain and dew whose gift of moisture was thus at once extolled and besought.

In these ways the Goddess was venerated as giver of dew and rain, and at the same time the ceremony was intended to foster her moisture-giving proclivities. Ancient and primitive religious rites have usually this double intention. Water is poured out to induce the goddess to send rain; it is a sort of reminder, a powerful suggestion, having its origin in mimetic magic. And also her powers are felt to be increased by the service given, by the water poured out. The rite is thought to be especially efficacious when water is scarce and it is thus a costly sacrifice. Sometimes, indeed, in severe drought a more costly fluid still is dedicated to the goddess. A cow is led out to the fields and there milked, the milk being poured out on the parched ground. This sacrifice is felt to be particularly pleasing to the Moon Goddess, who is also the Heavenly Cow.

These customs, silly and superstitious as they must seem to us when viewed as a means of affecting the weather, may have a significance that is to be taken entirely seriously when looked at as having to do with the projected parts of the human psyche. The religion of primitives and the ancients had to do not only with objective phenomena, but also with their own unconscious psychological contents, which were projected to the object. Practices, which cannot change the weather or cause a Goddess of the Moon to alter her mind, may yet be efficacious in charming the unconscious of the believer. Could these magical practices give us a hint, perhaps, as to how our own psychological weather, our moods, may be altered?

The fertilizing power of the moon was symbolized by its light. But this "symbolizing" was no abstract intellectualized concept. To antique man, as to the primitives, the light of the moon *was* its fertilizing power. Moonlight falling on a woman as she slept might in very fact generate new life in her, an actual flesh-and-blood child. And so we find that the light of the moon is, as it were, tended or encouraged by lights on earth. Torches, candles, and fires are burned in honor of the moon and are used as fertilizing magic, being carried, for example, round the newly seeded fields to aid the germination of the grain, just as Hecate's torches were carried around the freshly sown fields, long ago in Greece, to promote their fertility.

This idea of the fertilizing power of the moon being actually fire is a very common one. It is thought that this power can be hidden in wood or tree where it lies sleeping in latent form, and can be drawn out again by rubbing, the primitive way of producing fire. The Huitoto, for instance, say that fire was first obtained from the moon by a woman. And there is another primitive myth, which states that an old woman, probably the moon herself, who is so often called the Old Woman, made the first fire by rubbing her genitals, while in the Vedic hymns of a far higher culture, Agni, the fire spirit, is also regarded as being hidden in the sacred wood, from which he is born again through rubbing the fire stick.

The Moon Goddess was, indeed, thought of as being actually the fire or the light of the moon, which could lie latent in wood. This is attested by the legend that Orestes brought the worship of the great goddess to Italy, after slaying King Thoas, by concealing her image in a bundle of faggots, which he took with him. Thus the goddess was, as it were, the flame latent in the bundle, waiting to be brought to life again by certain rituals. In Italy they named her Diviana, which means *The Goddess*, a name that is more familiar to us in its shortened form of Diana. For Diana, the Huntress, was none other than the Moon Goddess, Mother of all animals. She is shown in her statues crowned with the crescent and carrying a raised torch. The Latin word for torch or candle is *vesta*, and Diana was also known as Vesta. So that the bundle of faggots, in which she came from Greece, was really an unlighted torch. In her temple a perpetual fire was kept burning and her chief festival was called the Festival of Candles or of Torches. It was celebrated on August the fifteenth when her groves shone with a multitude of torches. This day is still celebrated as a Festival of Candles, but the torches are no longer lighted in Rome for Diana, but for the Virgin Mary. It is the day of her Assumption. On this day of Diana's old festival it is Mary who is carried to the heavens above, to reign there as Queen of Heaven.

Another ancient festival of candles celebrated long ago for a moon goddess is now repeated on the same date, February the second, for the Virgin Mary, Moon of our Church, as the Fathers call her. This is the Festival of Candlemas. It corresponds in date and customs to the Celtic Holy Day of St. Bride or St. Brigit. St. Brigit is the Christianized form of the ancient Celtic goddess Bridgit or Brigentis, a triune moon goddess whose worship was at one time very widespread. On February the first, as today in the Catholic Church at the Festival of Candlemas, the new fire was kindled and blessed.

A feast of lamps was also celebrated at Sais in Egypt in honor of Isis-Net. The ceremony took place in an under-chapel beneath the temple. Lamps were carried in procession around the coffin of Osiris, for it was by the power of light, symbolizing the life-giving power of the moon, that Isis could rekindle life in the dead Osiris.

Another custom in regard to the tendance of fire is of interest here. A perpetual fire was kept burning at Tara, the seat of the ancient Irish kings. On Midsummer Eve the fire was extinguished and was rekindled the following day, on the Feast of Beltane, which was originally a moon, not a sun, festival. On taboo days sacred fires are usually extinguished, signifying that then the deity has gone to the underworld. In the Catholic Church, for instance, the light which burns before the altar is quenched on Good Friday, when Christ has left the earth and descended into Hades, and is relighted on Easter Saturday. In the Eastern or Greek church the coming of the new light is one of the most important ceremonials of the year. Pilgrims congregate in Jerusalem in order to be present at the kindling of the new fire and to take home a taper lighted from the sacred flame. At the special morning service the archimandrite goes apart and remains in communion with God until the new fire is miraculously kindled. It is a rebirth of the light, symbolizing the return of Christ from the underworld, where in striking resemblance to the moon deities of an earlier time, he remained after his death, preaching to the souls in Hades.

In Babylon and in the Jewish law it was prescribed that there should be no fires kindled on the Sabbath, the Nefast, or taboo day. This ordinance, as we have seen, was connected with the belief that the Moon Goddess was under a menstrual taboo at that time. Similarly the tribes of the Orinoco also put out their fires during an eclipse of the moon, which is to them an inauspicious day.

The sacred fire was conceived of quite definitely as the spark or power of fertility. In the north of England, for instance, Candlemas used to be called The Wives Feast Day because it was regarded as a fertility festival. An interesting custom which survived in Scotland till as late as the end of the seventeenth century, bears witness to this fact. On Candlemas Eve a sheaf of oats was dressed in women's clothing. This "woman" was laid in what was called "Brigid's bed," and a wooden club was placed beside her. The women of the village sat up and kept a torch burning in the room all night long.[1] This drama was clearly a fertility rite. For "Brigid" refers to the Celtic goddesses who were known as the Three Brigids representing the three phases of the moon. So on the festival night the moon's fertilizing power, its light, was symbolized and invoked by the torch that was kept burning beside the corn woman in her union with the wooden pole, symbol of the phallus. The custom seems to say that the corn woman could not give rise to a new harvest unless she were energized by a sacred marriage blessed by the fertilizing power of the moon.

In many places a perpetual sacred fire was kept burning in the temple of the moon goddess, guarded and tended by a group of priestesses dedicated to its service. They were usually called Vestal Priestesses after the Vestal Virgins who tended the perpetual fire in the temple of the goddess Vesta in Rome. They did not marry, except under certain ritual conditions, but in some cases, they were considered to be "wives" of the king, although they were still called virgin, and not infrequently the king owed his pre-eminence to the fact that he was so "married" to a Vestal Priestess. This was the case in Rome, and indeed, many of the early kings were sons of Vestal Virgins. Frazer notes that at her consecration each girl received the name of Amata, or beloved, which was the title of the wife of the legendary King Latinus.[2] In many places these priestesses were sacred harlots, who gave themselves to strangers and to the male worshippers of the Goddess. The term virgin was thus clearly used in its original sense of unmarried. For these women were pledged to the service of the Goddess, their sex, their attraction, their love, were not to be used for their own satisfaction or for the ordinary purposes of human life. They could not unite themselves to a husband, for their woman's nature was dedicated to a higher purpose, that of bringing the fertilizing power of the Goddess into effective contact with the lives of human beings.

Closely associated with the symbol of the fire, maintained in the temples of the Moon Goddess, to embody or represent her power of perpetual fertility, are to be found certain ex-

[1] T. Banes, "Candlemas," *Hastings Encyclopaedia of Religion and Ethics* (New York and Edinburgh, 1909), III, 192.

[2] J. G. Frazer, "The Magic Art and the Evolution of Kings," *The Golden Bough*, Part I (New York, 1917), II, 197.

plicitly phallic objects which were venerated side by side with the Goddess herself. In Rome, for instance, in the temple of the goddess Vesta, a god, Pales, or Pallas, was also worshipped. He seems to have been identical with Priapus, and was represented by a phallic image. These two together formed the deity Pabulum which is Food.[3] The union of the moon goddess and the phallic image recalls the Scottish Candlemas custom of Brigid's Bed mentioned above, which was intended to secure a good supply of food.

The phallic god, Pallas, was not considered to be a rival deity but rather the associate of the Goddess. Each carried the symbol of fertility, but only when they were united in their functions was the "mystery" fulfilled. A similar connection existed in the case of other moon goddesses. For instance, the lover of Selene was Pan, and there has recently been discovered at the Acropolis, a tunnel leading from the temple of Aphrodite down to the temple of Eros which is below it. It is believed that at night a maiden descended by this tunnel carrying sacred objects. The visit doubtless represented a sacred union or marriage between Eros and Aphrodite.

Now these three gods, Priapus, Pan, and Eros, are all phallic or erotic gods. They do not carry the same significance as Tammuz, Adonis, and Attis, who are vegetation gods. Hence, when they are worshipped in company with the moon goddesses, their rites do not signify the fertilizing power of the moon married to the fruitfulness of earth, but rather the union of the masculine essence or principle with the feminine power.

This same idea that the divine power is manifested through the union of male and female is expressed in a symbol which is sometimes found representing the goddess Cybele, who was one form of the Magna Dea. She is represented as a lunar crescent in perpetual union with the sun. A similar symbol is found in Celebes in modern times. There an ithyphallic[4] god is worshipped as the supreme deity. He, like Pallas in the temple of Vesta, is served by priestesses. His supreme revelation is in the form of a symbol of the lingam and yoni (male and female genitalia) in contact. His chief festival is held at the first full moon after Ramadan. His connection with moon worship is established by this date, for Ramadan is the fast of

3 Briffault, *The Mothers* (New York, 1927), III, 18.
4 Ithyphallic is a Greek word meaning "with erect penis."

lamentation for Tammuz, son of Ishtar, who died and went to the underworld. The festival of the phallic god of Celebes proclaims that God is manifested anew at the first full moon, in the *union* of the male and female power. God is not here represented as existing either in the erect phallus, or in the all-embracing woman, but he shines out, comes into manifest being, in the *moment* of union, in the act through which tension is released and energy put forth.

To symbolize this truth of God as manifest, potent, in the union of male and female, the union, that is, of masculine and feminine principles, women, at their initiation into the mysteries of the Great Goddess, sacrificed their virginity in the temple, by entering into a *hieros gamos,* or sacred marriage, which was consummated sometimes with the priest, as representative of the phallic power of the god, sometimes with the phallic image itself, and sometimes with any stranger who might be spending the night in the temple precincts.

In this transition of the partner to the *hieros gamos* we see clearly the attempt to make of the act an impersonal ritual. At first it was the priest, who was not considered to be a man like other men, but was believed to be an incarnation of the god; he was recognized as functioning only in his office. In other cases the image of the phallus of the god was used. This rite was entirely without personal connotation. When the "stranger" enacted the part of the priest or the god, too, the impersonality of the situation was evident. The rite was performed by two people who had never seen each other before and would in all probability never see each other again. Indeed the regulations prescribed that the stranger should depart before daylight. In this way the nonpersonal, or divine aspect of the rite was impressed upon the participants.

It seems to have been a quite general custom for the moon goddess to be served by virgin priestesses, who were hierodules, or sacred prostitutes. In the temples of Ishtar, they were called Joy-maidens, and the term Ishtaritu, used to describe them, is the equivalent of the Greek hierodule meaning sacred prostitute. In some places these priestesses had sexual congress only with the man who impersonated the moon god, like the Vestal Virgins who were considered to be wives of the kings. But more often the sacred marriage could take place with any male worshipper or initiate who sought for union with the goddess. A sacred marriage of this kind probably formed part of the initiation of men to the mysteries of the goddess.

The priestesses were usually dedicated to the service of the Goddess for life. They remained in the sanctuary and performed the sexual rites, as they were prescribed, in addition to their other functions of tending the sacred flame and performing the water rites. They did not enter into secular marriages. They were virgins. But in addition to these sacred harlots, other women who were not pledged to a religious life were required to prostitute themselves once in their lifetime in the temple.

In his *History* Herodotus writes: "The worst Babylonian custom is that which compels every woman of the land once in her life to sit in the temple of love and have intercourse with some stranger . . . the men pass and make their choice. It matters not what be the sum of money; the woman will never refuse, for that were a sin, the money being by this act made sacred. After their intercourse she has made herself holy in the sight of the goddess and goes away to her home; and thereafter there is no bribe however great that will get her. So then the women that are tall and fair are soon free to depart, but the uncomely have long to wait because they cannot fulfill the law; for some of them remain for three years or four. There is a custom like to this in some parts of Cyprus."

The custom of religious prostitution was practiced particularly by the royal women of Greece and Asia Minor. The king was then regarded as an incarnation of the god, and his sisters and daughters, by becoming priestesses and mating with him, relived with him the myth of the union of Aphrodite and Adonis. For the mating of the god and goddess was "deemed essential to the propagation of animals and plants, each in their several kind; and further, the fabulous union of the divine pair was simulated and as it were, multiplied on earth by the real though temporary, union of the human sexes at the sanctuary of the goddess for the sake of thereby ensuring the fruitfulness of the ground and the increase of man and beast." [5] In Babylon also the daughters of noble families prostituted themselves in the temple of Anahita, the Mazdian moon goddess, dedicating, as it were, the first fruits of their womanhood to her.

In later times in Greece, when the social feeling against

5 Frazer, *op. cit.*, Part IV, I, 39.

promiscuous sexual relations, at least for women, was more developed, women who went to the temple of the goddess to perform the ancient ceremony, were allowed to sacrifice their hair instead of their virginity as a sort of symbolic surrender of their womanhood to her. But on the occasion of the ceremonial they still spent the night in the temple, a vivid reminder of the origin of the ritual.

In the worship of Cybele, whose symbol of the crescent moon was often shown in perpetual union with the sun, the initiate recited the following confession which is recorded by Clement of Alexandria.

> I have eaten from the timbrel,
> I have drunk from the cymbal,
> I have borne the sacred vessel,
> I have entered into the bridal chamber.

The first two lines obviously refer to a communion meal. That which was eaten was in all probability a cake of barley meal or of some other grain. This symbolized the body of the god, son of the mother; the drink was probably either of wine or of blood, or of wine as the symbol of blood. The Moon God was believed to have taught the knowledge of the vine as well as how to grow grain. He *was* the fruit of the corn and in some cases was also considered to be himself the fruit of the vine, his blood being the wine. Or perhaps the drink may be considered to be the Soma drink, wine of the gods, which was brewed from the moon tree and whose earthly counterpart was an intoxicating drink variously called "soma," "hoama," or "moly." The third line "I have borne the sacred vessel" refers to the carrying of the *kernos* which was a vase or bowl divided into many separate compartments, intended to contain different fruits and grains. In the center was a candle or torch representing the light of fertility whose power caused the fruits of the earth to grow. The initiant carried the sacred vessel, thus enacting the part of priest or priestess. The vase or vessel represented the womb of the Great Mother, giver of all life and increase, and was frequently used as a symbol or emblem of the goddess herself. The Virgin Mary for instance is called the Holy Vase, recipient of the fertilizing power of the Holy Spirit, from which Christ was born. Isis was symbolized by

136

the vase of water, where the water was the fertilizing power of Osiris caught and contained in the Vase of Isis, by which it was brought into manifestation in material form, namely the whole of nature.

In this confession the initiant declares: "I have borne the sacred vessel, I have become the recipient of the creative power of god." And the confession ends with the statement: "I have entered into the bridal chamber."

This was evidently a deeply significant experience. The concreteness with which it was enacted may repel us with our conscious morality and our rationalistic attitude but we cannot fail to appreciate the sincerity of those who took part in the ceremonial. To them it was in very truth a *hieros gamos,* a sacred marriage. In it they dedicated their most precious function, namely their reproductive power, to the goddess and avowed that for them spiritual fulfillment, attained through union with the godhead, was more important than biological satisfaction or ordinary human love.

It may seem strange at first sight that women should be required to sacrifice or give up their virginity to the goddess of love. It might be expected that she would bestow upon her worshippers gifts enhancing their attraction for men instead of demanding the sacrifice of their feminine function in her service. Frazer raises this problem and in answer to it he says: "The gods stood as much in need of their worshippers as the worshippers in need of them." [6] The goddess, the all-powerful deity of fertility, represents the creative power which resides in all female things and this power is renewed by the service rendered her in the *hieros gamos,* for as women sacrifice or give up the personal use and control of their feminine power to her, her divine power is enhanced, it shines forth anew. These things are not easy to express in words, they are more feelings than concepts, nor can they be grasped rationally, but we can perhaps intuitively sense something of this kind as being the essence or significance of the experience which lay behind the confession: "I have borne the sacred vessel. I have entered into the bridal chamber." Nevertheless the *relation* which the ancients sought to establish between men and the gods they themselves called The Mysteries. The experience *is* a mystery which can be un-

[6] *Ibid.,* Part I, I, 31.

derstood only when it is recognized that the "gods" are not beings external to man but are rather psychological forces or principles which have been projected and personified in "the gods." They overshadow man, but their roots are buried in the hidden depths of the human psyche.

In the mysteries, the chief priestess who impersonated the Moon Goddess, herself, was "married," once a year, to a man impersonating the male principle, the Priapic God. While the mystery was enacted in the holy place, the worshippers kept vigil in the temple. At the consummation of the rite attendant priestesses came forth from the sacred shrine bearing the new Sacred Fire which had just been born through the renewal of the power of the goddess, and from the new fire the household fires of all the worshippers were relighted. This rite recalls the similar ceremony performed to this day on Easter Saturday in Jerusalem.

The priestesses of the Moon Goddess in addition to performing those offices which represented the goddess in her fertilizing and life giving activities, had also to impersonate her in her dark and destructive aspect. The Vestal Virgins, it will be recalled, threw twenty-four manikins into the Tiber each year, and infant sacrifices were regularly performed in honor of, certainly, some forms of the goddess. It is recorded, for instance, that around the sacred stone which represented the goddess Astarte, hundreds of skeletons of human infants have been found. She was the goddess of untrammelled sexual love and first-born children and animals were sacrificed to her.

The chief priestess of the Celtic moon goddess was required to act as executioner whenever a human sacrifice was made. She had to kill the victim with her own hands. After a battle, for instance, the prisoners were so sacrificed, their heads being cut off, while they were held over a silver cauldron in which the blood was caught. One of these cauldrons was discovered in Jutland and is now in the Museum at Copenhagen. It is embossed with figures which not only show scenes of battle but also depict the Moon Goddess and the sacrificial ceremonial.

The silver vessel was called the Cauldron of Regeneration. It is the cauldron of the Moon Goddess who was the giver of fertility and of love. The blood poured into it must have formed a regenerating drink, or possibly bath. It is also recorded that the cauldron must be boiled until it yielded "three drops of the grace of inspiration," so that it is also the cauldron of inspiration, giving a drink like the soma mentioned earlier. MacCulloch informs us that this Celtic cauldron is probably the forerunner of the Holy Grail of the Arthurian Legends. He says: "Thus in the Grail there was a fusion of the magic cauldron of Celtic paganism and the sacred chalice of Christianity, with the products made mystic and glorious in the most wonderful manner." [7]

The Grail is a mysterious symbol. It is sometimes spoken of as a Chalice in which a spear, perpetually dripping blood, is thrust; and sometimes as a stone: or again as a food-bearing dish. It is always associated with a king who is either dead or mortally ill. This king is called the Fisher. His country, like himself, is sick, dried up, barren. It is called the Wastelands. In this old Celtic legend we have elements that correspond to important details in the myths of other moon deities.[8] The lands are waste because the Moon God has gone to the underworld and the moisture that he alone can bring is withdrawn. The chalice containing blood is the sacrificial cauldron of the Celtic moon goddess. To drink from that vessel bestows regeneration, renewal, perhaps immortality. As stone, the Grail is obviously a symbol for the Moon Mother herself, who, in many ancient religions, as we saw above, was worshipped under the form of a stone or cone. As food-bearing dish, the Grail is the symbol of the Goddess of Agriculture and of Plenty. In the Celtic version, the Fisher King, guardian of the Grail, suffers perpetual sickness, being neither dead nor alive, but suspended in a half-state between life and death, until the mystery of the Grail should be revealed to a mortal man, who has achieved that illumination through his courage and endurance. Then the Fisher King will be restored to life and the Wastelands will become fertile once more.

Such is the legend of the Grail and, as Jessie Weston points

---

[7] J. A. MacCulloch, *The Religion of the Ancient Celts* (Edinburgh, 1911), p. 383. *See also* J. A. MacCulloch, "The Abode of the Blest," Hastings' *Encyclopaedia of Religion and Ethics* (New York and Edinburgh, 1909), II, 694.

[8] In the Arthurian cycle, recorded by Chrétien de Troyes and in *The Mabinogion*, the old Celtic legend has been "Christianized." Thus the grail represents the chalice used at the Last Supper, and the spear dripping blood is the one used by Longinus to pierce the side of Christ. These sacred objects were believed to have been carried to Britain by Joseph of Arimathea and housed at Glastonbury.

out, it is clearly the story of an initiation.[9] The ordeal always requires that the hero shall ask a certain question: namely "What do these things mean and whom do they serve?" Failure to do so means that the mysteries continue in their eternal round, but no one is served thereby, and the lands remain waste. But if the question *is* asked and the meaning is made conscious, then the spell is broken, the king is healed and peace and plenty are restored to the lands.

There is a very interesting variant of these archetypal happenings recorded in the story of Isis, where Maneros, the Fisher, falls into the sea and is drowned.[10] In this legend the reason why the Fisher is dead, or mortally sick, is recounted. In the Grail legends this point is never made very clear, though in Wagner's *Parsifal*, his condition is ascribed to his failure to keep his vow of chastity. Maneros fell overboard because of his inability to endure the sight of Isis' grief over the dead Osiris; he could not stand the "awe of the Goddess."

Other examples of a Cauldron of Regeneration are to be found in the cauldron of the Alchemists and the cauldron of the Chinese and Hindu philosophies. In all these instances the cauldron is believed to have power to change the base material into the spiritual, the mortal into the immortal. It brewed the drink of immortality and of spiritual regeneration, and also the drink of inspiration. However, it could be used to brew "medicine," magic, powerful stuff, which was not beneficial but harmful. Just as the witches of the Middle Ages and of folklore were said to brew love potions, or fertility medicine for the fields or for barren women; or might instead produce baleful effects such as storms, illness, and fits, or even death. One reason for the extraordinary persistence of the witch cults in the Middle Ages, a persistence which survived wholesale massacre, burnings, and torturings, was doubtless that the women who took part in them really believed that the fertility of the countryside depended on their activities. Their religion had an extraordinary hold upon them. Its symbols must have sprung from a very deep level of the unconscious, for, as the records of the witch trials bear witness, they inspired hundreds of simple countrywomen to face a horrible death without flinching.[11]

9 Jessie L. Weston, *The Quest of the Holy Grail* (London, 1913).
10 See Chapter 13, p. 174.
11 See M. A. Murray, *Witchcraft in Western Europe* (Oxford, 1921).

The sexual rites of the witches carried the significance of a union with the divine power as well as being a magic rite to secure fertility. But as the religion had already been superseded by Christianity its symbols had dropped into the unconscious and appeared from there in negative form. The phallic god in the witch cults was no Bright Son of the Moon Mother, but was the Son of Darkness, the Devil. His rites, however, were still carried out at the new and full moon. The witch rites also included a *hieros gamos,* a sexual union either with a man who impersonated the devil, or more often with the image of a phallus. These rites correspond to those practiced in the ancient mysteries of the Moon Goddess.

The Moon Goddess was attended primarily by priestesses; but she also had priests attached to her temple. Like the priestesses they also took upon themselves vows which were not required of the ordinary man, nor even of the initiate who was not a priest. The ordinary man resorted to the temple of the goddess to take part in the *hieros gamos,* perhaps once in his life, at his initiation. It was a sacrament of union with the divine feminine nature and was also a ritual for the renewal of his powers of fertility. But the priests who were vowed to the service of the goddess for life, had a characteristic which seems very strange in the devotees of a goddess of fertility and in a temple where the phallic emblem is so directly venerated. These priests were eunuchs, or they were treated in some way as women, for instance they had long hair and women's clothes.

In certain tribes the priests of the moon wore feminine garb habitually, in others they wore masculine clothes when serving the male powers of nature, but feminine ones when serving the female powers; as Adolph Bastian reports, they learned "the idea of sex change from the Moon." [12]

The outstanding example of the ancient moon goddesses being served by eunuch priests is to be found in the worship of Phrygian Cybele. The emasculated men who were dedicated to her worship were considered to be incarnations of her son Attis, who was himself a moon god, wearing the crescent as a crown and in typical fashion, both son and lover of his mother, the Moon Goddess, Cybele.

The myth of Attis relates that he was about to wed the king's

[12] Adolph Bastian, *Der Mensch in der Geschichte* (Berlin, 1912).

daughter when his mother, or his grandmother, who was in love with him, struck him mad. Attis, in madness, or ecstasy, castrated himself before the Great Goddess. Annually in a worship dating from 900 B.C., on March the twenty-fourth, Cybele's grief for her son is celebrated. The lamentation for Attis recalls the grief of Ishtar for Tammuz and of Aphrodite for Adonis.

But in the worship of Cybele a special element was given great prominence. The third day of the festival was called the *Dies Sanguinis*. In it the emotional expression of grief for Attis reached its height. Singing and wailing intermingled and the emotional abandon rose to orgiastic heights. Then in a religious frenzy young men began to wound themselves with knives; some even performed the final sacrifice, castrating themselves before the image of the goddess and throwing the bloody parts upon her statue. Others ran bleeding through the streets and flung the severed organs into some house which they passed. This household was then obliged to supply the young man, now become a eunuch priest, with women's clothes. These emasculated priests were called *Galloi*. After their castration they wore long hair and dressed in female clothing.

A similar ceremony of castration took place in honor of Syrian Astarte of Hierapolis, of Ephesian Artemis, of Atargatis, of Ashtoreth or Ishtar, of Hecate at Laguire, and also of Diana whose statue was often represented with a necklace of testicles; sometimes the bloody organs of emasculated priests were hung about her neck. These goddesses were all served by eunuch or emasculated priests.

Other rites which were performed by men in service of the Moon Goddess included circumcision, a symbolic castration, and flagellation. This last rite was apparently never practiced by women but in certain communities many boys submitted voluntarily to whipping in honor of the Goddess. The castigation was often so severe as to endanger the lives of the devotees. However, in the frescoes of the Villa des Mystères, at Pompeii, where the initiation of a young woman to the Great Mother is represented, the neophyte is shown crouching at the knees of an older seated woman while undergoing flagellation.

Circumcision and flagellation are symbolic of a kind of mitigated castration. They are perhaps equivalent to the mitigated sacrifice of the women, the loss of whose hair was permitted at the time of the dedication in the temple, instead of the sacrifice of their virginity.

These are the sacrifices which the Moon Goddess demands, not, it is true, from every man, but from a few selected or representative men. To them she appears in her dark and terrible form, demanding mutilation or even death, for human sacrifice as we have already seen was included in her worship.

In these bloody rites the dark or underside of the great Goddess is clearly seen. She is in very truth the Destroyer. But strangely enough her destructive powers seem to be directed less against women than against men. The chosen man must sacrifice his virility completely and once for all, in a mad ecstasy where pain and emotion were inextricably mingled. The woman, on the other hand, must present the first fruits of her womanhood. It was a sacrifice of a very different nature. For as the primitives say, "The Moon is destructive to men but she is of one nature with women and is their patron and protector."

11

THE SACRED MARRIAGE

The ritual of the virgin goddesses demanded a *hieros gamos,* a sacred marriage in which the woman's sexual and love life was dedicated to the goddess herself through an act of prostitution performed in the temple. In the days when the worship of the Moon Goddess flourished there were not only *secular* harlots who practiced "the oldest profession in the world" for their own economic advantage and in response to a social demand, but in addition, as we have seen, there were *sacred* harlots, whose earnings were not their own property but belonged to the goddess whom they served. The occupation of these women carried no social reproach, on the contrary they were held in honor, and indeed every woman, high or low, was obliged, in certain countries, to prostitute herself in the temple once in her lifetime.

These practices seem to us, with our Puritan background, merely licentious. Yet we cannot overlook the fact that they were developed as part of a religion, a means of adaptation to the inner, or spiritual realm. Religious practices are based on a psychological need. The inner or spiritual necessity was here projected to the world of concrete fact and met through a symbolic act. If the rituals of sacred prostitution are examined in this light it becomes evident that the ancients felt it to be essential that every woman should once in her life give herself, not to one particular man, for love of him, that is for personal reasons, but to the goddess, to her own instinct, to the Eros principle within herself. In that *hieros gamos,* that holy matrimony, it did not matter who the man might be, provided only that he was *not* the chosen man. He must be a stranger. It did not matter even what kind of experience the woman had. The man was not chosen for his virility, as a fit impersonator of

Priapus. The temple of Ishtar, or of Aphrodite, would have been frequented, indeed, by men in need of strengthening; the old and others, whose virility was failing, would naturally seek a renewal of their waning powers in the precincts of the Goddess who gave "fertility to man and beast." For the woman the significance of the experience must have lain in her submis- sion to instinct, no matter in what form the experience came to her.

In the myths of the Moon Goddess these psychological real- ities are expressed in concrete form, and ancient man lived them in actual fact. He projected his psychological content and was compelled to live his symbolic drama *as though* Ishtar and Aphrodite were actual anthropomorphic goddesses; *as though* the demands of the feminine principle were to be met through external action. He was incapable of recognizing in them, as we are increasingly doing today, psychological principles which make demands upon us for changes in our psychological atti- tudes. A modern woman in seeking to establish a relation to the "Moon Goddess" or feminine principle within herself may have to submit to her own instinct, recognizing it not just as an in- tellectual concept but in fact, as a determining influence in her whole life; or she may need to accept the Eros order of *related- ness* and submit herself and her own wishes to that order.

In the ancient world only a few women lived their whole lives as prostitutes in the temple of the Moon Goddess; while the average woman played this role only once in her life. This act involved taking the responsibility of her own instinctual life upon herself. She performed her part because *she* needed to. Her act concerned her relation to the goddess of love and did not concern her relation to a husband, possible or actual. It had nothing to do with her economic security, as marriage had, but only with her relation to her own instinct. It is the hardest thing in the world for anyone, for a woman especially, to acknowledge and accept her love for another human being if it is not reciprocated. It is far easier to reject the love, to say, "I don't care for him either," or "he is not worth breaking one's heart over," or even to repress the love altogether and keep one- self entirely unaware that anything more than the surface has been ruffled. But the woman who is virgin, and who has per- formed the sacred marriage in the temple of the goddess, will not act so. She, realizing that the love aroused in her is a manifestation of the goddess of love, will recognize it and the suffering that it brings as part of her experience of the feminine principle. Indeed it may be that the recognition of her own love, unreturned on the human plane, may itself be of the nature of the *hieros gamos,* the marriage with the god which makes women virgin. Philo of Alexandria wrote many years ago: "For the congress of men for the procreation of children makes virgins women. But when God begins to associate with the soul, he brings to pass that she who was formerly woman becomes virgin again." The same idea is expressed in a sonnet by John Donne (1573 to 1631). It is as follows:

> Yet dearely I love you, and would be lovéd faine,
> But am betroth'd unto your enemie:
> Divorce mee, untie, or breake that knot againe,
> Take mee to you, imprison mee, for I
> Except you enthrall mee, never shall be free,
> Nor ever chast, except you ravish mee.[1]

These things seem to say that psychological virginity can only be attained through the ravishment of a god, through a *hieros gamos,* or holy matrimony. The accompanying pictures were drawn by modern women who had experienced something of the kind. These women were not artists as is clear from the crudeness of the drawing. The first picture (figure 26) was drawn by a woman who had not at that time had any psychological analysis. She drew the picture in an attempt to understand the meaning of a crisis through which she was passing. Her emotion expressed itself in the words of Donne's poem with which she was familiar. The second picture (figure 27) was also drawn by a woman, who, however, had already had considerable experience of the unconscious through

Fig. 26. Drawing entitled "Nor Ever Chaste Unless Thou Ravish Me".

1 John Donne, "Sonnet," *Oxford Book of Mystical Verse,* ed. by D. H. S. Nicholson and A. H. E. Lee (Oxford, 1917).

146

Fig. 27. An "unconscious" painting by a modern woman.

analysis. She too painted her picture in an attempt to clarify what was the nature of the emotion that she was experiencing.

Pictures drawn in this way to express an emotion whose nature and cause are unknown, are not produced as works of art, but solely as a means of clarifying and making conscious the unknown factor in the depths of the psyche whose presence is only felt through the emotional disturbance it produces. They are technically called "unconscious drawings" although naturally they are not produced in a state of unconsciousness. The term merely means that they are drawings of something which is relatively unknown and whose significance is usually entirely obscure. They portray, in fact, images which arise from the unconscious much as the images of dreams do. To occupy oneself with these images through the actual work involved in painting the picture has a curious effect. In the first place the image itself becomes clearer and more definite, it frequently seems to come to life and may begin to move and change its character during the actual process of painting, so that it may be necessary to paint a second picture or even a series, showing how it evolves. At the same time the mood or emotional conflict becomes clarified. It also changes and develops with the change in the unconscious image. Consequently when a woman in an emotional crisis or conflict has painted a picture such as the above, she usually finds herself greatly released, even if she does not understand what it is she has drawn. If she can come to understand the significance of her drawing she will naturally be still further relieved, for the painting is like an oracle, which has come from the depths of her own being, and contains a wisdom which is beyond her present conscious attainment.

In both the above cases the picture represents the woman's present suffering in the guise of a ritual, having a religious, that is a spiritual or psychological significance. These women were each suffering a sense of being in some way "ravished" by life or by the circumstances in which they were placed; that is to say their love, their interest, their emotional investment in life, was bringing them no return in the values that this world holds dear: human love and understanding, or other recognition. The picture of this suffering showed in each case that the human frustration was like a ravishment, which was being committed, not by some hostile or destructive force but by a bird, the Great Heavenly Bird, messenger of the moon, the Dove of Aphrodite.

In Christian symbolism a similar idea is familiar to us in the Spirit of God who is the Holy Dove. In certain medieval paintings the Conception of the Virgin Mary is pictured, much as in these modern drawings, as a ravishment by the Holy Dove. This image seems to express a universal fact of the human psyche, found alike in the religions of the ancient moon goddesses, in medieval Christianity, in the mystical writings of ancient philosophers, and of Elizabethan poets, and, today, in the unconscious drawings of modern women. These things seem to say that woman can only become one-in-herself when she is fully awakened to the possibilities slumbering in her own nature, has experienced what it is to be set afire with passion, carnal and spiritual, and has devoted her powers to the service of the god of instinct. Then when the nonpersonal, the divine energy has been aroused in her she attains chastity of soul, singleness or wholeness of her being, by dedicating her deepest emotion to the gods of instinct, by whatever name she may call them.

In this way she releases herself from her ego-desirousness, from her identification with her own instinct and its needs. This is the meaning of the Union with God, the sacred marriage in the temple of the goddess of the moon, who is always also deemed goddess of sexual love; she is source of the power to love as well as of the power of fertility. Those who were initiated to her mysteries attained a share of her power within themselves, they partook of her nature through a mystical union with her. We are familiar in our Christian teachings with the idea of union with God to be attained through specially ordained sacraments. Baptism, immersion in the waters; Communion, the sharing of consecrated food, eating of the body of the God, are dramatic representations of stages of initiation, which are lived in an actual ritual of the outer life and have as goal, union with God. In the Roman and Greek Catholic Churches marriage, also, is considered to be a sacrament, the actual sexual union of the man and woman is taken as a symbolic union of the soul with God. The idea of union with God, of a sacred marriage, a *hieros gamos,* is carried a step further in symbolic evolution when a woman becomes a nun. A symbolic marriage is then performed, and she becomes the Bride of Christ.

To the Christian mystics the sacraments were lived not only in the rituals of the Church but also in the inner and secret experiences of their private meditation. The theme of the divine union and of Christ as the Heavenly Lover, Bridegroom of the Soul, pervades much of the writings of the saints. The terms in which these mystical experiences are couched can leave little doubt that the spiritual experience was closely connected with an actual erotic involvement although not with a human partner.

In the religious practices of the Magna Dea a similar erotic experience, a marriage in the temple, formed part of the initiation, and certainly in the later days of the initiation to Isis, as described by Apuleius, the revelation of love as distinct from desire formed the central teaching of her mysteries. Then again the Moon God of Babylon was known to his ordinary worshippers as Sinn, but he had also a secret or cult name which was only revealed to initiates. This name was Wadd, which means friendship or love. In the ancient religions the symbolic

149

drama of the gods, that is of the spiritual or psychological life, was completely projected, so that the rituals were lived in concrete form. Little by little through the ages, as man's psychic life has come to be recognized more clearly as within, these rituals have become more and more separated from concrete reality, have become more and more symbolic. This is naturally a great step in advance, but it carries also a danger, for if the ritual loses entirely its connection with the instinctual sources from which it arose, it loses its power to renew or redeem, for it has become merely an abstraction and has lost its connection with the primal sources of life. In these days, when we have grown so far away from our humble beginnings, we need to contact again these life-giving symbols.

The crescent, emblem of the almost nonhuman desirousness of instinct, hardly emerged as yet from the flood waters of the unconscious, represents the level of development of the ordinary man and woman, but the Sufis, the mystics of Islam, have progressed much farther in their psychological development and understand more clearly the inner meaning of their own religious teachings. They speak much of the love of God, which they differentiate into three stages: *Rida,* satisfaction; *Shavg,* longing; and *Uns,* fellowship or intimacy. These they take as a drama, outwardly lived, which represents the progressive stages of union with God. Rabi'a, a woman mystic who lived about the eighth century A.D., wrote the following poem about the third stage of love, *Uns* or intimacy:

I have made Thee (God) the Companion of my heart,
But my body is available for those who desire its company,
And my body is friendly towards its guests,
But the Beloved of my heart is the Guest of my soul.[2]

In this poem is expressed the attempt to achieve a transformation from the concrete, the material, into the unseen, the spiritual. For the spirituality of the woman must be distilled from the concrete experience; it cannot be obtained directly. This distillation process is discussed in the *I Ching,* the sacred book of the Chinese, in the homily on the *Cauldron.* To the Chinese the cauldron has the same significance as to the al-

[2] M. Smith, *Rabi'a, the Mystic* (Cambridge University Press, 1928), p. 98.

chemists, it, like the Grail, is the vessel of transformation, or as the alchemists would say, of transmutation. It reads:

"All that is visible must grow beyond itself, and extend into the realm of the invisible. Thereby it receives its true consecration and clarity and takes firm root in the Cosmic order." [3] In the case of the experience of love of which Rabi'a speaks, the attempt to obtain transformation is by the downward-going road. For the Moon, goddess of women, is Queen of the Night, and the dark moon leads even to the underworld. Mystics in all ages have recognized that transformation may take place through the downward-going road, although we, with our Western philosophy of progress, advance, and the increased control of life through rational science, have lost sight of this fact. The Gnostics said for instance: "To go up or to go down, it is all the same," and William Blake wrote that it matters little whether a man take the right road or the wrong one, provided he follow it sincerely and devotedly to the end, for either road may lead him to his goal. So here, too, we must recognize that, although the road of the crescent leads downward, yet it also may lead to transformation of the personality, to a real rebirth of the individual.

The moon stands, indeed, for the great principle of transformation through the things which are lowest. That which is dark and cold and moist, which hides from the light of day and from man's enlightened thinking, holds also the secret of life. For life renews itself again and again, and when at last, through his repeated experiences, man understands, he will grasp the inner meaning which until that moment lies concealed within the very texture of the concrete happening. For the ritual of the *hieros gamos* is religious. Through the acceptance of the power of instinct within her, while at the same time renouncing all claim to possessiveness in regard to it, a woman gains a new relation to herself. The power of instinct within her is recognized as belonging not to herself but to the nonhuman realm, to the goddess, whom she must serve, for whom her body must be a worthy vessel. Through such an attitude she is transformed. The conventional control of her egotistic desirousness is no longer needed because it has been in actual fact transformed. What was formerly "I want, I must have" has been

[3] Richard Wilhelm and C. F. Baynes, trans., *The I Ching* (Bollingen Series XIX, New York, 1950), Hexagram 50.

replaced by the capacity to love. And the woman, instead of being merely a manifestation of nature, a mermaid, is reborn a human being with a human spirit.

The meaning of this sacrifice in the temple, of this *hieros gamos,* thus begins to emerge. Through it the woman who has been initiated is released from the domination of her own unconscious instinct with its desirousness and craving for power. Through submitting to her instinct instead of demanding that the man submit to it, she becomes virgin. In this ritual the woman recognizes and asserts, in the most emphatic and incontrovertible manner possible, that her sexuality and the emoluments it can bring are not her own, her possession, but represent the demands of life itself, which flows in her, and whose servant she is; her body, her psyche, is but the vehicle for life's manifestations. This is her submission to instinct. Until she has submitted in this way she is no virgin in the religious meaning of that term and cannot be united to the Eros, the feminine principle, the Magna Dea, which should rule her from within. For, as certain Gnostic writings state, only as a pure virgin can the spirit of man achieve union with God.

The need for the dedication of the woman's sexuality in the temple was explained by Frazer, it will be recalled, in terms of the ancient conception of a god who always had need of sacrifice from his worshippers, for his power depended on the service given to him by human beings. This old concept finds a new and more spiritual expression in the writings of later religious mystics. Meister Eckhart repeatedly asserts that God needs the worship of men and is born ever anew within the soul of the devout worshipper. Angelus Silesius and other religious mystics of many religions proclaim the same truth. So long as God is conceived of as a celestial Being entirely outside of man, absolute, not relative to man, the doctrine of his dependence on the service of his worshippers is the blackest heresy. But when God is conceived of as a personification of a psychological principle it is obvious that the power of God is enhanced by sacrifices such as we have been considering. In each woman who sacrifices her personal and egotistic grasp on the emoluments which the life-principle can bring her and submits herself to the movement of life within, the power and significance of the Eros principle itself, or as one might say, the power of the Moon

Goddess, shines forth more clearly. When she renounces her personal claims, the energy or libido formerly bound up with the determination to get her own way, flows into the feminine truth for which she made her sacrifice. Thus, as Meister Eckhart put it, God is "born anew within the soul," the Eros is raised in this particular woman's heart to a place above her personal desires.

From this experience is born the power to love another. Before she has undergone such an initiation, her love is no more than desire. She cannot even see the difference between "I love you" and "I want you to love me"; cannot differentiate between "I love you" and "I want the satisfaction you can bring me." But when she has passed through an inner experience analogous to the ancient prostitution in the temple, the elements of desirousness and possessiveness have been given up, transmuted through the appreciation that her sexuality, her instinct, are expressions of a divine life force whose experience is of inestimable value, quite apart from their fulfillment on the human plane.

It is impossible to explain the transformation that takes place when instinctive love is accepted in this way and assimilated, for it is one of those mysterious and inexplicable changes which belong to the realm of the psychological, the realm where physical and spiritual meet. The transformation from physical to spiritual is indeed a never-ending mystery which is beyond our human understanding. It is, however, a matter of actual observation that through an experience of this kind love emerges, a love which sees the situation of the other person and can unselfishly sympathize and appreciate. The Moon Goddess in her role of prostitute is constantly stated to have this kind of love. Ishtar announces herself, "A Prostitute compassionate am I." Compassion is also one of the chief characteristics of the Virgin Mary who, while never spoken of as a sacred prostitute or hierodule, had certainly experienced a corresponding submission through which she gained her title of Virgin.

The love which is born from the initiation in the temple is maternal in character. The legends and myths are unanimous in stating that the goddess as virgin conceives by an immaculate conception. The outcome of the *hieros gamos* is that the virgin is with child. Her child is the hero, the savior, the redeemer. He is the man-god, partaking of the nature of both man and god. Psychologically, this child represents the birth of the new individuality, which replaces the woman's ego, sacrificed through the temple ritual. He is called the Holy Embryo, the Jewel in the Lotus,[4] he is the new personality born of her sacrifice. He is the young Moon who fights and overcomes the same devil who conquered his father. He is thus the "one who goes beyond," and represents the rebirth of hope and the possibility of transcending the past. Through the power of the *hieros gamos,* the complete sacrifice of egotism and of the possessive attitude towards oneself and one's own emotions and instincts which that ritual involves, is born this Hero-child, the ability to start again, even after disaster and failure and to start on a different level with new values and a new understanding of life.

[4] Richard Wilhelm and C. G. Jung, *The Secret of the Golden Flower,* trans. by C. F. Baynes (New York and London, 1931).

12

ISHTAR

To recapture in any adequate way the significance which a god or a religious symbol has held for a people of a bygone time is always exceedingly difficult. For a symbol is the concretization of an actual living spirit or feeling which is yet not completely known or realized. So long as the spirit is living everyone senses its meaning and its power, although none of them could define it exactly. We do not need to explain today, for instance, what the flag means to us, indeed we cannot *explain*. In the same way the gods of old were "taken for granted" in their own times. No one wrote a reasoned contemporary account of their significance or of the spirit or feeling they carried for their own people. Only when the cult of the god was already declining did certain writers feel it to be necessary to preserve in "texts" a value which was in danger of being entirely lost.

Consequently our knowledge of the worship of the Great Mother is somewhat scanty. The rituals of her temple were either so well-known in her own day that they needed no written exposition or they were mysteries revealed only to the initiates— known to the general public, if at all, in symbols which are not particularly enlightening when uninterpreted. As far as written information is concerned, there are occasional references and allusions in the literature of the periods in which the Moon Mother flourished. Certain passages also occur in the writings of a later period which give a philosophical or metaphysical explanation of the older religion. These occur particularly in Greek writings of the Gnostic period. In addition there have come down to us a few ritual hymns and prayers addressed to the Mother, especially to Ishtar and to Isis, and a multitude of sacred objects and pictures whose meaning looked at with the eyes of the rational intellect can only be dimly discerned. If, however, we regard them as symbols, referring to psychological, instead of historic, facts, their inner meaning often flashes out in unmistakable clarity.

The Moon Goddess whose worship spread perhaps farthest during the days of antiquity was Ishtar of Babylonia. She was worshipped under many different names in the different countries where she was venerated. She was Ashtarte in Canaan; Attar in Mesopotamia; Ashtar in Moab; Athtar in Southern Arabia; Astar in Abyssinia; Atargatis in Syria; Astarte in Greece; while Artemis seems to be the general term used for any of the many manifestations of this great and all-powerful goddess—the Magna Dea of the East (figure 28).

Fig. 28. Ishtar as Goddess of Fertility. Sumero-Acadian, ca. 2000 B.C. (From *Encyclopédie de l'Art*, "L'Art de Mésopotamie Ancienne au Musée du Louvre," vol.i, p.263, fig.B, Editions TEL, Paris.)

Her counterpart in Egypt was Isis, whose worship spread to Greece and Rome and continued to flourish well into the early centuries of the Christian epoch. The story of Isis and the materials about her worship are so important that they will be considered in a separate chapter.

Ishtar is a personification of that force of nature which shows itself in the giving and the taking of life. She is the Mother of All, the Many-breasted Artemis (figure 25). She bears the titles Silver-Shining, Seed Producing, and Pregnant. She is the goddess of fertility, giving the power of reproduction and increase in the fields and to all animals including man. By a natural transition she becomes goddess of sexual love and the patroness of prostitutes. She is the Opener of the Womb, the one refuge of mothers in the pangs of childbirth. Thus all life emanates from her; plants, animals, human beings are her children.

But like the moon gods, Ishtar has a twofold character. Not only is she the giver of life but she is also the destroyer. For she is the moon itself, in whose waxing all things grow and in whose waning all things "are minished and brought low." But this is not the end, the crescent comes again. Light succeeds darkness even as darkness overcomes the light. The Moon Goddess appears once more in her creative and beneficent phase.

Ishtar thus ruled, successively, over all the moon cycles or months of the year; and the fertility of the year, all that was born during the twelve months, was considered to be her offspring. This idea was beautifully expressed in the belief that her son, Tammuz, was, actually, in his own person, the vegetation of the whole earth. He is called Urikittu, the Green One. In the myth, with the attainment of manhood, he becomes her lover. Year by year, however, she condemns him to death and at the turning of the year, about the time of the summer solstice, he perishes and goes to the underworld. In Mesopotamia, the green of spring is very short-lived. It is burnt up by the summer sun, and so the death of Tammuz does not come in the autumn but early in summer. At his death, the goddess and all women with her mourn for him, in the month called by his name, Tammuz, or Du'uzu. Very ancient hymns of lamentation for Tammuz have been preserved to this day. One Babylonian text dating from about 2300 B.C. runs as follows:

> Arise then, go, hero, the road of "No-return."
> Alas, hero! warrior, Un-azu;
> Alas, hero! hero, my god Damu;
> Alas, hero! son—my faithful lord;
> Alas, hero! Gu-silim [1] the bright-eyed;
>
>   *   *   *
>
> Alas, hero! thou who (art) my heavenly light;
>
>   *   *   *
>
> Alas, hero! brother, mother, heavenly vine.
> He goeth, he goeth, to the bosom of the earth—
> He will cause abundance for the land of the dead.
> For his lamentation, for the day of his fall,
> In an unpropitious month of his year.
> To the road of last man's end,
> At the call of the lord,
> (Go), hero to the distant land which is not seen. [2]

[1] Silim is the moon.
[2] T. G. Pinches, "Tammuz," Hastings' *Encyclopaedia of Religion and Ethics* (New York and Edinburgh, 1909), XII, 189.

The ritual mourning for Tammuz recalls the annual fast of lamentation for the death of Adonis. In the Greek myth, Adonis was killed by a bear, one of the animals sacred to Aphrodite, his mother. The bear is frequently associated with the Moon Goddess, indeed, the Celtic goddess was almost a bear, herself. So that in the myth Adonis is really killed by one aspect of his own mother. In another version of the story, it was Ares, a former lover of Aphrodite, who assumed the form of a wild boar, in order to kill Adonis. Frazer describes an ancient monument in the Grove of Lebanon, at Aphace, which depicts the story. The beautiful youth is represented with spear in rest, awaiting the attack of a boar. Aphrodite herself is seated in the background in an attitude of mourning. She is, Frazer suggests, the "Mourning Aphrodite of Lebanon" described by Macrobius.[3] This mourning of Aphrodite for Adonis or of Ishtar for Tammuz is the myth-origin of the fast of lamentation which formed a prominent ritual in the religion of the Great Goddess. In the Old Testament this fast is repeatedly referred to and its observance condemned by the Prophets. The cults of the Mother and Son, however, recrudesced again and again as rival to the religion of Jahweh. And, as we saw above, Ramadan, one of the most important religious observances of the Mohammedans, corresponds to the mourning for Tammuz.

Thus year by year, Tammuz perished and went to the underworld. Ishtar and all women mourned for him, and finally she undertook the dangerous journey to the land of No-Return, in order to rescue him. There her bright jewels were stripped from her as she passed each of the six doors which guard the place. And finally, when already deprived of her strength by the loss of her jewels, she had to fight her sister Allatu for the possession of Tammuz. In this form of the myth Allatu is Queen of the Underworld. More usually Ishtar is considered to be Queen both of the Underworld and of Heaven and Earth as well for as Moon she passes between the Upper and the Under Worlds. The loss of her jewels in six stages is the equivalent to the fragmentation of the Moon God, and represents the six nightly bites which are taken out of the moon in the six nights of the last quarter.

When the Lady Ishtar was away in the underworld, a time of

[3] J. G. Frazer, "Adonis, Attis and Osiris," *The Golden Bough*, Part IV (New York, 1917–19), I, 29.

terrible depression and despair fell upon the earth. For during her absence nothing could be conceived. Neither man nor beast nor plants nor trees could propagate, and worse than ever they could not even *want* to propagate. The whole world is described as being sunk in a kind of hopeless inactivity, mourning for her return.

In "The Descent of Ishtar to Hades" recorded on a cuneiform tablet we read as follows:

Since the Lady Ishtar descended to the land of No-Return
The bull does not spring upon the cow, the ass does not
bow over the jenny
The man no more bows over the woman in the street,
The man sleeps in his chamber
The woman sleeps alone. [4]

It was only after her return to earth that the power of fertility, and indeed of sexual desire as well, could operate once more. This is a very strange idea to us. Natural science presupposes that the instincts are *in* the living structure; that pollen and ovum meet through the operation of natural forces—chemiotaxis, wind currents, and the like—and that amongst animals, including man, the male seeks the female on account of his own instincts which are thought of as inherent in his natural make-up. But to the ancients the power of fertility and the attraction between male and female were gifts of the goddess, or perhaps were thought of almost as emanations from her. When she was absent in the land of No-Return, fertility and natural desire disappeared from the earth. When she returned the living spirit of fertility manifested itself once more among animals and plants alike. In a hymn she says: "I turn the male to the female; I am she who adorneth the male for the female, I am she who adorneth the female for the male." She was the awakener of the sexual impulse in animals and in men.

This concept is almost anathema to Western thought and yet perhaps, in a certain realm, it may be a more helpful way of looking at facts than the usual scientific or materialistic one. If we remember that the gods are projections of the unrealized forces of the unconscious, we can say it is *as if* the power of

4 Robert W. Rogers, *Cuneiform Parallels to the Old Testament* (New York, 1926, Abingdon Press), p. 126.

attraction between man and woman were a gift of the goddess, which is operative when she is present on earth, but which is utterly unattainable when she is absent. For certainly everyone will agree that more enters into the relation between a man and a woman than can be explained on purely materialistic grounds. Else why should their rapport, their physical rapport even, vary so much from one occasion to another. Some essential factor comes and goes without the conscious volition of those most concerned. It does indeed seem as if the goddess of fertility had withdrawn herself.

Of course such a statement is nonsense if we look at it with the cold eye of objectivity. The moon as a heavenly body or as a mythological goddess is far removed from the daily problems of modern men and women. But if we remember that the ancients, under the guise of the goddess and her adventures, were depicting the movements of a psychological force operating in man's unconscious, we shall not need to be so sceptical of their observations. The ancients knew much of the working of these unconscious forces for they recorded them in an entirely unbiased fashion. We, however, are biased, we disregard everything which does not fit in with our preconceived theory of scientific, that is materially observable, data. But the workings of psychological factors, especially those in the unconscious, are not susceptible to direct observation and experiment. These things we exclude as irrelevant, but the ancients noted them and incorporated them into their religions. It is worth-while, therefore, to ask further about Ishtar and how she functioned.

When she was absent, man and beast lost their power of fertility and their desire. When she returned, because she was the Goddess of Fertility and of Sexual Love, love sprang up again throughout the whole world. The powers of love and of fertility were the effects of a living spirit which she carried with her and which affected everyone like an infection or contagion. She herself was imbued with this same spirit and gave herself freely to her love whenever it was aroused. Tammuz, the vegetation of the earth, was reborn year by year as her son, and year by year reunited to her as her spouse. But the seductive goddess had many other lovers. She was revered as the all-accepting one. Little shrines containing her image were set up in the houses in ancient Babylon, where she was represented nude and seated in

Fig. 30

Fig. 29. Ishtar Kilili, "She Who Peers Out." Ivory panel from the palace of Assurnasipal, ninth century, at Calah. (From *Mythology of All Races,* vol.v, Stephen Herbert Langdon, 1911.)

Fig. 29

Fig. 30. Derketo and Ouanes, God of the Primal Waters (From *Sur le Culte de Vénus,* Felix Lajard, 1837.)

a window frame. In this aspect she was called Kilili Mushritu, that is "Kilili who leans out," the typical pose of the prostitute (figure 29). In the Gilgamesh epic it is told how she finally tried to seduce Gilgamesh, but he was the hero, whose task it is to overcome the goddess.

This theme of Gilgamesh, the hero, is a late one. It is most important, however, for our discussion as it represents a time when mankind was beginning to sense that the gods might perhaps be overcome by human beings and their powers incorporated into man himself. This was an almost superhuman task and was naturally not to be attempted by everyone. Only the hero could undertake it; he alone could fight against the gods and usually he paid dearly for his impious audacity. But the hero myths are a pattern for us, today, for only by a similar adventure can we hope to overcome the "gods," those projected forces of the unconscious, and annex their powers as parts of human psychology. Gilgamesh reproached the goddess bitterly for her fickleness and was scornful because she was so universally accepting. Yet because she was a goddess she must act according to her nature; and her nature is such that where she loves there must she give herself. For like the moon she can never be possessed. She is ever virgin.

This conception of the nature of the goddess is in marked contrast to the ideal of marriage as exemplified by such deities as Hera. There fidelity to the given word is the principle which is worshipped. In the case of Ishtar it is loyalty, not to a contract, but to the *actual feeling*, the reality as it lives in the moment. This is the principle which was worshipped as the woman par excellence—the Magna Dea.

From the inscriptions and invocations which have been preserved on monuments, coins, and the like, we can gather something of the ancients' conception of her qualities and power. She is represented as All-Goddess, Queen of Heaven, The Honored One, The Heavenly Cow. She was born from the sea foam. In one form she was even represented as half fish, a sort of mermaid or leviathan, inhabitant of the primal waters. In this form she was called Derketo, an epithet which is also applied to Atargatis, the Phrygian moon goddess. Lucian in *De Dea Syria* says: "The image of Derketo in Phoenicia was a strange representation; half was a woman, and from the thighs to the extremities of the feet, it appeared as the tail of a fish." (Figure 30.)

Like her son, Tammuz, Ishtar is called Urikittu or The Green One, the producer of all vegetation. Her symbol was a conventionalized tree called Ashera, which was treated as if it were the goddess herself. She is also called Earth Goddess, Lady of Mountains, The Queen of the Earth and Mistress of the Field. Like Sinn, the moon god who preceded her, she is triune, for she is the moon in its three aspects. In her own person she is Goddess of Heaven, Goddess of Earth and Goddess of the Underworld.

In her bright or upper-world phase, Ishtar was worshipped as the Great Mother who brought fruitfulness to earth and cared for her children. She promoted the fertility of man as well as of the fields and of the beasts of the field. She was the goddess of maternity. As Queen of Heaven she was conceived of as leading the stars. She herself had once been a star, the morning and the evening star, who accompanied Sinn, the earlier moon god, as his wife. But later she replaced him and reigned in her own right. Then she became Queen of all the Stars and Queen of Heaven. She rode nightly across the sky in a chariot drawn by lions or goats. The zodiacal constellations were known to the ancient Arabs as the Houses of the Moon, while the whole zodiacal belt was called the "girdle of Ishtar," a term which refers to the moon calendar of the ancients, for whom the months were the twelve moons of the solar year. Thus Ishtar was the Goddess of Time, whose movements directed the sowing and reaping and controlled the annual round of agricultural activities. She was known as the moral governor of man. An interesting sidelight is thrown on the concept of the Moon as the governor of men, when we remember that the last Hebrew migration was from Sinim (that is, from the Land of the Moon) and that Sinai, the mount on which Moses received the Tablets of the Law, is the Mountain of the Moon.

As Queen of the Underworld, however, she became inimical to man and destroyed all that she had created in her upper-world activity. In this phase she was entitled the Destroyer of Life. She was Goddess of the Terrors of the Night, she was the Terrible Mother, goddess of storms and of war. She was also the giver of dreams and omens, of revelation and understanding of the things that are hidden. In a hymn recorded on one of the cuneiform tablets she chants:

Ishtar speaks "To give omens do I arise, do I arise in perfectness.
For my father Sinn,[5] to give omens do I arise, do I arise in perfectness." [6]

It was through her magic that men could obtain power and knowledge, often illicit knowledge, of hidden and secret things whose understanding brings power of itself.

The underworld of the ancients represents, as we saw above, the hidden and unknown depths of what we call the unconscious. But while we recognize, to some extent, that the unconscious is within us, the hidden part of our own psyches, they projected this unknown region outside themselves and thought of it as an actual geographical place, to which one might take a journey in a boat or chariot.

The statement that the Goddess of the Underworld had magic power is equivalent to saying that the unconscious works in a secret, unknown, that is, in a magic way. And indeed it is true that the unconscious has such a magic effect, as will be readily

5 Sinn—God of the Moon.
6 Rogers, op. cit., p. 162.

conceded by anyone who has even a slight acquaintance with it. We often suffer from its powerful and unaccountable workings and would gladly find some way, if we only could, of getting into a better relation to it. To the ancients the moon goddess was queen of this realm also. She had power there as well as in the upper world. A safe and helpful relation to the powers of the underworld was to be gained through a right approach to her.

Ishtar had taken the dread journey to the underworld and although she was sore beset, she eventually conquered the darkness and rose again as the new moon, small at first but with power to recreate herself. Jerimias notes that "The moon is, according to the Babylonian teaching, the star of the upper world. . . . She dies and rises again from the dead (. . . 'fruit which produces itself out of itself'); she symbolizes the power of life from the dead." [7] Thus, like Sinn, who preceded her, and like Osiris of the Egyptians, she becomes Goddess of Immortality, the hope of life after death.

In her ever-changing forms she plays all possible feminine roles. She is called daughter as well as sister of the moon god who is at the same time her own son. She is Woman, the impersonation, as the Chinese would say, of yin, the feminine principle, the Eros. To women she is the very principle of their being, to men the mediator between themselves and the secret spring of life hidden in the depths of the unconscious.

Perhaps the power and significance of this great moon goddess, Queen of Heaven, who fell into the waters of the Euphrates and was brought ashore by a troop of attendant fishes or water gods cannot be better indicated than by quoting a hymn which was sung in her honor. The hymn is found on one of the "Seven Tablets of Creation" which date from the seventh century B.C., though the hymn itself is probably much older. It has been many times translated. I give an abridged version taken from King's translation:

I pray unto thee, Lady of Ladies, Goddess of Goddesses!
O Ishtar, Queen of all peoples, directress of mankind!
O Irnini, thou art raised on high, mistress of the spirits of
    heaven;

[7] A. Jerimias, "Ages of the World," Hastings' *Encyclopaedia of Religion and Ethics*, I, 185.

Thou art mighty, thou hast sovereign power, exalted is thy name!

Thou art the light of heaven and earth, O valiant daughter of the Moon-god.

    Ruler of weapons, arbitress of the battle!

    Framer of all decrees, wearer of the crown of dominion!

O Lady, majestic is thy rank, over all the gods it is exalted!

Thou art the cause of lamentation, thou sowest hostility among brethren who are at peace;

Thou art the bestower of strength! (friendship)

Thou art strong, O Lady of Victory, thou canst violently attain my desire!

O Gutira who are girt with battle, who art clothed with terror,

Thou wieldest the sceptre and the decision, the control of earth and heaven!

Holy chambers, shrines, divine dwellings and temples worship thee!

Where is thy name not (heard)? Where is thy decree not (obeyed)?

*   *   *

At the thought of thy name the heaven and earth quake.

The gods tremble, and the spirits of the earth falter.

Mankind payeth homage to thy mighty name,

For thou art great, thou art exalted.

All mankind, the whole human race, boweth down before thy power.

Thou judgest the cause of men with justice and righteousness;

Thou lookest with mercy on the violent man, and thou settest right the unruly every morning.

How long wilt thou tarry, O Lady of Heaven and earth, Shepherdess of those that dwell in human habitations?

How long wilt thou tarry, O Lady, whose feet are unwearied, whose knees have not lost their vigour?

How long wilt thou tarry, O Lady of all fights and of all battles?

O thou glorious one, that ragest among the spirits of heaven, that subduest angry gods,

Thou hast power over all princes, that controllest the sceptre of kings,

That openest the bonds of all handmaids,

That art raised on high, that art firmly established, O valiant
    Ishtar, great is thy might
Bright torch of heaven and earth, light of all dwellings.

*   *   *

O goddess of men, O goddess of women, thou whose counsel
    none may learn,
Where thou lookest in pity, the dead man lives again, the sick
    is healed,
The afflicted is saved from his affliction, when he beholdest thy
    face!
I, thy servant, sorrowful, sighing, and in distress cry unto thee.
Look upon me, O my Lady, and accept my supplication,
    Truly pity me and hearken unto my prayer!
Cry unto me "It is enough!" and let thy spirit be appeased!
How long shall my body lament, which is full of restlessness and
    confusion?
How long shall my heart be afflicted, which is full of sorrow and
    sighing?

*   *   *

Unto thee therefore do I pray, dissolve my ban!
    Dissolve my sin, my iniquity, my transgression and my
    offence!
Forgive my transgression, accept my supplication!
    Secure my deliverance, and let me be loved and carefully
    tended!
Guide my footsteps in the light, that among men I may glori-
    ously seek my way!
Say the word, that at thy command my angry god may have
    mercy
And that my goddess who is wroth may turn again.
    Thou art the ruler, let then my torch flame forth!
    May my scattered strength be collected.

*   *   *

Let my prayer and my supplication come unto thee,
And let thy great mercy be upon me,

That those who behold me in the street may magnify thy name,
And that I may glorify thy godhead and thy might before mankind!

Ishtar is exalted! Ishtar is Queen!

My Lady is exalted! My Lady is Queen!

Irnini, the valiant daughter of the Moon-god hath not a rival.

*   *   *

O exalted Ishtar, that givest light unto the (four) quarters of
the world! [8]

Ishtar is "Diva Astarte, Hominum deorumque via, vita, salus:
rusus eadam quae est pernicies, mors, interitus"—Divine Astarte, the power, the life, the health of men and gods, and the
opposite of this which is evil, death and destruction.

[8] L. W. King, *Seven Tablets of Creation* (London, 1902), I, 223.

13

ISIS AND OSIRIS

In Egypt, as in Babylon, the worship of the moon preceded that of the sun. Osiris, god of the moon, and Isis, moon goddess, sister and spouse of Osiris, and mother of the young moon, Horus, appear in the religious writings prior to the Fifth Dynasty (*circa* 3000 B.C.) while the worship of Ra, the sun god, was not established until late in the Twelfth Dynasty, probably around 1800 B.C. Even then the worship of Ra did not supersede the worship of the moon. Instead, bit by bit, Osiris came to be assimilated to the sun god, so that in the later writings while many of the epithets appropriate to a sun god are applied to him, he yet retains the qualities and characteristics of a moon deity. He is the Moon but, when after his resurrection he attains immortality, he is hailed as Sun.

These changes took place gradually over a period of not less than 2500 years and even then the religion of Isis and Osiris was not dead, for it had a later revival in the Hellenistic period as one of the mystery cults which came out of the East and influenced most profoundly, first Greece and then Rome, during the centuries immediately preceding and following the beginning of our era.

It is difficult to give a concise account of the meaning and worship of Isis and Osiris because during the many centuries in which this religion flourished, changes took place in men's understanding of them. In the earliest records that we have Osiris seems to be a nature spirit, variously conceived of as the Nile or the Moon, which was thought to control the river's periodic floodings. He was a god of moisture, of fertility, and of agriculture. During the period of the moon's waning, Set, his brother and enemy, a tawny red, burning devil, ate him up. Set was said to have engaged a black Ethiopian queen to help him in his revolt against Osiris, probably referring to the drought and heat, which periodically came up from the Sudan and destroyed the crops of the Nile district. Set was Lord of the Underworld, in the sense of Tartarus, not of Hades, to use the Greek terms. Hades was the place where the shades of the dead awaited their resurrection, corresponding, perhaps, to the Catholic idea of purgatory. Osiris was Lord of the Underworld in this sense. Tartarus is the hell of the damned, and it was of this world that Set was the Lord.

In the earliest form of the myth, Osiris was the moon and Isis was nature, Urikittu, the Green One, of the Chaldean story. But later, she became the moon—sister, mother, and spouse of the moon god. It is this cycle which chiefly concerns us here. For bit by bit this primitive nature myth began to take on a deeper religious significance. Men began to see in the story of Osiris, who died and went to the underworld and was then restored to life by the power of Isis, a parable of the inner life of man, which they dimly felt should transcend the life of the body on earth. The Egyptians were a very concrete-minded people, however, and so they conceived of the immortality which was to be gained through the power of Osiris, in a completely materialistic way. It was for this reason that they preserved the bodies of those who had been "made into Osiris," by initiation, as recounted in *The Book of the Dead;* for they believed that so long as the physical body persisted, the soul, or Ka, also had a body in which it could live in the Land of the Blest, with Osiris, who, in a Pyramid text of the Fifth Dynasty, is called "Chief of those who are in the West," that is, the other world.

The ancient Egyptian texts and inscriptions are not the only source of information in regard to the religion of Isis and Osiris, however. For in the second century A.D. Plutarch, himself an initiate, wrote to Klea, who was also an initiate, a treatise on the meaning of the mysteries. Although the secrets of the mystery religion and the details of the initiations were held sacred by Plutarch, he was addressing one who already knew of what he was writing, so that by applying the knowledge of universal symbols which analytical psychology gives, it is possible for us, also, to read between the lines and glean a deeper understanding than would otherwise be the case.

A study of the religion which centered around Isis and Osiris is thus particularly valuable for our purpose in this book, because we have records, not only of the myths of the ancient gods, referring to the natural phenomena with which they are associated, but we have in addition, in the *Book of the Dead*, the mystery instruction for those initiated to the religion of Osiris in the early dynastic period, and also a philosophical treatise of the second century A.D., which gives us a glimpse into the hidden spiritual meaning of the mysteries as they survived into the early part of the Christian epoch.

This long series of texts gives a picture of the transition from primitive nature worship, through a period when some recognition was arising of the inner significance of the myths, up to the highest form of spiritual religion of the early Christian centuries. It forms a most interesting and suggestive bridge from the ancient concrete projection of all inner reality, to the psychological understanding of symbols which is possible for us in the present day.

The symbols of the ancient religions must, however, be accepted as representing the drama of the inner life of man. If they are not treated with a certain sympathy and respect they will not yield up their secret. To take them and explain them reductively is exactly equivalent to taking the spiritual achievement of Plutarch and reducing it to the primitive worship of the Moon or the Nile. It is true that the Great God, Osiris, was both Moon and Nile, and Isis was the land made fertile by Nile's risings and fallings, as well as being herself Goddess of the Moon. But these are also analogies, happenings in the external world which mirror and reflect the movements of the spirit, the Logos, which Osiris symbolizes, and the ever-renewing, all-accepting Mother Nature, whose ways are shadowed forth in the story of Mother Isis. As Plutarch says:

LXVI. Still there is nothing to complain of it [only], in the first place, they cherish the Gods in common with ourselves, and do not make them peculiar to Egyptians, either by characterising Nile and only the land that Nile waters by these names, or, by saying that marshes and lotuses and god-making [are their monopoly], deprive the rest of mankind who have no Nile or Buto or Memphis, of [the] Great Gods.

Indeed all [men] have Isis and know her and the Gods of her company; for though they learned not long ago to call some of them by names known among the Egyptians, still they knew and honoured the power of each [of them] from the beginning.

In the second place, and what is more important—they should take very good heed and be apprehensive lest unwittingly they write-off the sacred mysteries and dissolve them into winds and streams, and sowing and ploughings, and passions of earth and changes of seasons.

As those who [say] that Dionysus is wine and Hephæstus flame, and Persephone, as Cleanthes says somewhere, the wind that drives through the crops and is killed; and [as] some poet says of the reapers:

Then when they, lusty, cut Demeter's limbs.

For these in nothing differ from those who regard a pilot as sails and ropes and anchor, and a weaver as yarns and threads, and a physician as potions and honey-brew and barley-water; nay, they put into men's minds dangerous and atheistic notions, by transferring names of Gods to natures and to things that have no sense or soul, and which are necessarily destroyed by men according to their need and use. For it is not possible to consider such things in themselves as Gods.

For a God is not a thing without a mind or soul, or one made subject to the hand of man; but it is from these things that we deduce that those who bestow them on us for our use and offer them [to us] in perpetual abundance, are Gods.

Not different [Gods] for different peoples, not non-Greek and Greek, not southern and northern [Gods]; but just as sun and moon and earth and sea [are] common to all [men], though they are called by different names by different peoples, so of the Reason (Logos) that orders all things, and of one Providence, that also directs powers ordained to serve under her for all [purposes], have different honours and titles been made according to their laws by different [nations].

And there are consecrated symbols, some obscure ones and others more plain, guiding the intelligence towards the mysteries of the Gods, [though] not without risk.

For some going entirely astray have stepped into superstitions, while others, shunning superstition as a quagmire, have unwittingly fallen into atheism as down a precipice. [1]

The original story as told by Plutarch is that Nut (the Greek

1 G. R. S. Mead, *Thrice-Greatest Hermes* (London, 1906), I, 346–48.

equivalent is Rhea), the Mother of the Gods, who is the eternal flux, the chaos, united secretly with Seb (Greek Kronos), time, and conceived by him. When Ra, (Greek Helios), the sun, her rightful spouse, came to know of it, he cursed her, saying that she should not bring forth in year or month. This meant that she could only bring forth in a day that was not in the solar calendar. The goddess, in her predicament, went to Thoth (Greek Hermes), who is the Orderer, he who holds the scales of justice, the Measurer.[2] Thoth also was in love with her, so he agreed to help her. He went to Selene, the moon, and played a game of draughts with her for stakes. He won and took from her one-seventieth part of each of the lights, that is the days. He put these together and made in all five days. At that time the Egyptian year consisted of only three hundred and sixty days. So Thoth added these five days which were called the induced or intercalated days, making a solar year of three hundred and sixty-five days. They were added in July, the time when the Dog Star, Sothis, or Sirius, is in the ascendant. The Dog Star was considered to be the attendant of Isis, and her guardian. Nut brought forth her five children on these five days in July which were named the Birthdays of the Gods, and were observed as religious festivals by the Egyptians.

On the first day, Osiris was born and a voice came forth from the womb with him, proclaiming, "The Lord of all forth comes to light." He was the moon. On the second day, the Elder Horus was born, and on the third, Set, or Typhon, who "breaking forth with a blow, leapt forth from her side." He is the unruly, unmanageable, untamable one, who is forever enemy of Osiris. On the fourth day, Isis was born and on the fifth, her sister, Nephthys, whose name means End and Victory. She was thought of as the extreme edge of fertility where the Nile's waters only reached for a little while. So that Nephthys had only clandestine meetings with Osiris, but was married to Set, the ruler of the hot desert land. In another version it is said that Nut brought forth Isis as a dark-skinned child and called her the Lady of Love. We have already met the dark or black aspect of the goddess who is Lady of Love. Of the five days, the first, the third and the fifth were considered inauspicious. But the fourth, the birthday of Isis, was lucky.

[2] Thoth is a precursor of Osiris who later took over some of his attributes and became the Measurer, the Reason, the Logos.

In the myth it is related that Osiris and Isis had intercourse while in the mother's womb and that from that union the Elder Horus was born. Osiris was the Moonman, husband of Isis. He was killed by Set and avenged by his son Horus who reigned in his stead. The story is that when Osiris became king he set the Egyptians free from an animal-like existence, teaching them agriculture, and how to make wine, and laying down laws and teaching them to honor the gods. He then set out on a journey over the whole country educating the people and charming them with persuasion and reason, with song and "every art the muses give." For as we shall see later he was the divine Reason, the Logos, and Museos, and he also possessed the power of music and art. For the "Muse Man," the incarnate spirit of that art which affects man through his feelings, is a son of the Moon Mother. One of these moon sons is actually called Museos, which means Muse Man, and Isis herself is sometimes called First of the Muses.

While he was away, Isis his wife ruled and all went well, but as soon as he returned, Set, who symbolized the heat of the desert and unbridled lust, laid a plot to catch Osiris and make away with him. He made a casket exactly the size to fit Osiris. He then invited all the gods to a feast, having hidden his seventy-two followers close by. During the feast he displayed the casket which all admired very much. He promised to give it to him whom it should fit. So they all lay down in it in turn and it fitted none of them, until Osiris lay down. Then the ambushed men rushed out and fastened down the lid. They took the coffin and threw it into the Nile. It floated away and went out into the sea by "the opening that is known by the abominable name."

These things happened on the seventeenth day of Athur, or Hathor,[3] that is November, in the twenty-eighth year of Osiris' reign, or perhaps when he was twenty-eight years old. He lived or reigned through a cycle of twenty-eight periods or days, because he was the moon whose cycle is completed in twenty-eight days.

When Isis heard what had happened, she cut off one of her curls and put on mourning dress and wandered everywhere weeping and searching for the casket. The first news of it that

[3] Hathor was the Cow-Goddess, the Hornéd One, a very ancient mother goddess, with whom Isis is identified.

she got was from the babbling of children who had seen it float by, then her dog Anubis, who was the child of Nephthys and Osiris, led her to the place where the coffin had floated ashore in the Byblus country. It had come to rest by a heather bush whose growth had been so stimulated by its presence that it had grown all round the coffin and had completely enclosed it in the trunk of the tree. The king of that country had found the tree and taken it to make a rooftree for his palace. He had lopped off the branches and used the trunk, quite unaware that it contained the coffin.

When Isis reached the place where the tree had grown a daemon voice told her what had happened. So she sat down to wait and presently the maidens of the queen came to bathe. Then Isis made friends with them, curling their hair and scenting them with the perfume of her own body. When they went home to the queen she asked about the perfume and engaged Isis to be nurse to her child. Isis reared this little one by giving it her finger instead of the breast to suck and at night she "burnt round the mortal elements of its body" to give it immortality, while she herself, as a swallow, flew round the tree trunk in which was the coffin of Osiris. But the queen came in while this was happening and thought the child would be burnt to death. She took it from the fire and so robbed it of its immortality. Isis then declared who she was and begged for the tree trunk which contained the body of Osiris.

The names of this king and queen are instructive. Plutarch gives them as Malek and Astarte, or Ishtar, as though Isis perhaps has to recover the body of Osiris from her predecessor of Arabia.

Isis cut the casket out of the tree trunk and took it with her in her barge and sailed away. She took also the younger child of the king with her. As soon as she had got away she opened the coffin and threw herself upon the body of the dead Osiris in a paroxysm of love. The child saw her ecstasy of love and swooned away because "of the awe of her," and died, but some say that he fell overboard into the river. His name was variously called Maneros, which Plutarch tells us means Understanding of Love, or Diktys, The Fisher, a term we have already met in another connection. Isis then hid the chest while she went to find Horus, her son, whom she hoped would be able to help her to bring Osiris back to life. While she was gone Set went out hunting with his dogs towards the moon and found the chest. (Naturally the moon and the chest were together, for Osiris himself was moon.) He opened it and tore the body of Osiris into fourteen pieces and scattered them abroad. Here again we have the fragmentation, the fourteen pieces obviously referring to the fourteen days of the waning moon.

Isis heard what had been done and went in search of the parts of the body. She travelled far in her little boat and wherever she found one of the parts she made a shrine at that place. She managed to collect thirteen of the pieces which she welded together by magic. But the phallus was missing. So she made an image of this part and "consecrated the phallus; in honor of which the Egyptians keep festival even to this day," as Plutarch relates. This festival was called Pamylia, or Phallephoria which means Phallus-bearing. Isis conceived by means of this image and bore a child, Horus the Younger, who was lame.

Osiris then came from the underworld and appeared to the Elder Horus. He worked through him and trained him to take revenge on Set. The fight was long and hard but finally Horus brought Set to Isis his mother, bound. Isis, however, being Mother Nature who bears with all, would not consent to his being killed but released him. At this Horus was angry and laid violent hands on his mother, tearing off her crown, or possibly beheading her. When Thoth heard of this he made her a crown of cow horns, or gave her a cow's head in place of her own. Thus Isis also, as moon, was killed, or maimed by losing her crown of light, and was restored to life as the Hornéd Crescent, Hathor.

Such is the main outline of the myth. The religious ceremonials of Egypt were concerned with these happenings. The death of Osiris was enacted each year, and the wanderings of Mother Isis and her lamentations played a conspicuous role exactly as the mourning of Ishtar for Tammuz and of Aphrodite for Adonis, did in Arabia and the Grecian Isles. The final mystery of his resurrection and the public display in procession of the emblem of his power, the image of the Phallus, completed the ritual. It was a religion in which emotional participation in the grief and joy of Isis played a prominent part. In later days it became indeed one of the religions in which redemption was achieved through the emotional ecstasy by which the worshipper felt himself to become one with God.

In addition to the seasonal festivals, Osiris was venerated twice a month, at new moon and at full moon, that is on the first and the fifteenth of the month. These moon celebrations are the early precursors of our own weekly holyday. At first they were bimonthly but later they came to be celebrated at each of the four quarters of the moon.

Another most important element which entered into the religion of Osiris was unique in Egypt. The reigning king was thought of as an incarnation of Osiris, the Moonman, and this ritual of the Passion of Osiris was enacted by him in person. It came to be believed that he thus gained a personal immortality, for was not he Osiris, Lord of the Underworld? After a while, certain other privileged persons were permitted also to partake in this dramatic identification with Osiris and so the mystery initiation came into being. Apparently it was always held as for the few, not for the many. But certainly in later times a large number of people sought initiation and became Osiris too.

The coming to life again of Osiris himself, often called his rebirth, was enacted daily in the temple service, by passing the image of the god through the skin of a sacrificed animal. It is probable that the postulant for initiation was likewise hidden under an animal's skin and then at the moment of rebirth was drawn out from beneath it, just as the casket containing the body of Osiris went out of the mouth of the Nile into the sea by "the opening which is known by the abominable name." Thus he was reborn, the spiritual or immortal man being born out of his own animal nature, symbolized by the sacrificed animal.

The initiation also contained a dramatic representation of the whole story of Osiris and his passion, and the grief and joy of Isis. "I performed the Great Going Forth" as Igernefert relates of his own initiation, on a stele of the Twelfth Dynasty, dated about 1875 B.C. "I followed the god in his footsteps. I avenged Osiris on the day of the Great Battle, I overthrew his enemies." This was followed by the return of the Lord of Abydos (Osiris) to his palace and the proclamation that he who had been initiated was now reborn as Osiris.

Not only did the initiation bestow the gift of immortality, it also acted as a guide to the traveller in the Other World. *The Book of the Dead* gives directions to those who have been initiated, telling them how they are to act when they come to the land of the dead. It also gives very specific information about the burial rites which were necessary in order to secure life everlasting for the dead. These rites were apparently based on the acts of Isis in her dealings with the body of Osiris by which she brought him back to life.

It is said, for instance, that the goddesses Isis and Nephthys come to Osiris and say words of power and give him his limbs, heart and so forth, and say "She gathereth together thy flesh, she bringeth to thee thy heart in thy body," and so on, enumerating all the parts. Then these parts were reunited by Horus and his four sons. "Horus loveth thee. He hath filled thee with his eye, he hath joined his Eye to thee. Horus hath opened thine eye that thou mayest see therewith." [4] Isis, meanwhile, drove away the enemies of Osiris by magic.

The process of resurrection of the deceased is described at length in the *Book of the Dead*. In the Text of Teta, describing his initiation, it is said to him "Hail, hail, rise up, thou Teta! Thou hast received thy head, thou hast embraced thy bones, thou hast gathered together thy flesh. . . ." After this ceremony of collecting the parts, came the ceremony of Opening the Mouth, which was done by the Iron Forearm of Set. Then followed the ceremony of Supplying the Table (or Altar) with food, or conquering hunger by the Eye of Horus. "They who have eaten the Eye of Horus give him wheat, barley, and bees." The deceased then unites with the Goddess Nut, who is the Mother Goddess. "He smelleth the air of Isis," henceforth he is able to enjoy union with a celestial counterpart. The deceased obtained his soul and vital power by entering into the breast of Horus and through him he became one with Osiris, who was the first risen man. The deceased became so greatly identified with the Great God of Heaven that he also spat upon the face of Horus and made his eye whole, and upon the genitals of Set, which had been injured in the fight with Horus, that he healed them also. The text says: "Thou givest birth to Horus, thou conceivest Set. Thou givest birth to Horus in his name of He ruleth the earth and terrifieth heaven. Thou givest birth to Horus for Osiris, thou givest him life, thou givest him strength. . . ."

The blessed then rises like a bird-soul. "He rises like a lily,

[4] This and the following excerpts are quoted from E. A. Wallis Budge, *Osiris and the Egyptian Resurrection* (New York, 1911), I, 69–127.

in the hand and under the nose of Ra," and goes to the island of Sasa, the Island of Fire. That is to say, through the power of Osiris the moon, he has come over the waters of Death to the Sun, which is the place of fire. For in later Egyptian thought Osiris, who in his passion on earth was the Moonman, became after his resurrection one with the Sun. And so also the human being who was Osirified through initiation became Son of the Sun. This sequence of ideas corresponds in an extraordinary way with the Hindu teaching that the souls of the dead are carried by the moon over the waters to the sun.

When the deceased reaches the Island of Fire he "setteth right in the place of wrong." It will be recalled that the moon god whom he now impersonates, is god of right, law, and justice. He becomes "chief of knowledge great," "the wise one." Next he is met by the gods, who prove to be hostile to him. They do not want any invasion of their territory. But being equipped with strength and a knife he subdues the "dwellers in the darkness" and there is none that can resist his power in the horizon. The gods are then called upon to look at him and note: "Look ye at him as he taketh the form of a great god. He trembleth not, he is equipped. Observe all of you. He speaketh words to men. . . ." With words of power he cries out "I am pure, I am pure in Sekhet-Aar [5] (with) the purity of Ra in Sekhet-Aar." . . . "Behold he cometh forth this day in the real form of a living Spirit." He demands that the boatman, who sees always behind him, shall ferry him across. The deceased succeeds in making his way into heaven and the gods are terrified when they see him arriving. They discover that he is mightier than they. He hunts them through the fields of heaven, lassoes them, kills "and eats them, and thus absorbs into himself all their strength and vital power."

It is said of the deceased "He is a risen soul," he lives "on his fathers and feeds upon his mothers. He is the Lord of 'sagacity, his mother knows not his name.'" This refers of course to his mystery name, his name of power. The text continues "His doubles are behind him. . . . His serpent-guide is in his breast, a soul that sees, an uraeus of fire." His doubles are his Ka, his souls, and the uraeus was the sacred snake which was the emblem of the gods.

[5] Sekhet-Aar was one of the shrines of Osiris, in which he was known particularly as God of the Moon. In the Other World it became his throne.

In another text it is said: "He (the dead king) eats them [the god's] words of power, he swallows their spirits. The great ones of them are for his food in the morning, their middle [sized] ones are for his food in the evening, and the small ones are for his food in the night. The old ones, male and female, are for his caldrons." . . . "He eats the wisdom of every god, his period of life is eternity, his limit is everlastingness in this form of him. What he will he does, what he hates he does not." Among the powers he gains are listed: "He eats with his mouth . . . he unites with women. He is the sower of seed who carries off wives from their husbands to the place which pleases him, according to the inclination of his heart."

In the ancient Egyptian rituals, performed to procure resurrection, the eye of Horus played a very important part, as is seen from the passages quoted above. It was used to bring life to the body of the deceased whose members had been collected together. The eye represented the light of the moon which was felt to be the life-giving power of the god. Set was said to have swallowed the other eye when Horus fought with him to revenge the death of his father Osiris. Budge remarks "The Eye contained the life of Horus, and while it was missing he was a Dead God. Horus was a god and could bring himself back to life. But Osiris was a man and needed the help of Horus." This explanation gives us another form of the transition from moon-man to moon god, the father being man and the son, god.

These texts give a picture of the magical rites which were performed with the intention of gaining immortal life for the deceased in the time of the Sixth Dynasty. Later on it became customary to perform some such religious ritual during the life of the worshipper with the intention of making him immortal while in this life, that he might become a twice-born, a living spirit. It is an almost universal religious idea that the physical birth produces only a physical man and that the living spirit has to be brought into being by a second birth. We are all familiar with this teaching from the Christian rite of baptism, itself a rebirth ritual intended to bestow a living spirit upon the one baptized. Primitive initiations serve the same purpose. This rite to procure rebirth came to be the central purpose of the mysteries which developed out of the ritual which is outlined above. We have some record of these mysteries of Isis both in the *Isis and Osiris* of Plutarch, of which mention has already been made, and a further rather veiled account of such an initiation in *The Golden Ass* of Apuleius.

It is interesting to note that in the Hellenistic period the initiation was called the Mysteries of Isis. The moon goddess has by this time entirely replaced the moon god as giver of immortality. For although the object of the rite was that the initiant might *become* Osiris, he was raised from the dead by the magic power of the goddess and the rites were called by her name and were performed in the Isium, which was her shrine. Osiris was at this time worshipped only in his spirit form which was represented by the Bull Apis, but he was served by an Isiac Brotherhood.

As far as we can make out, after a period of preparation, which included fasting and continence and solitary meditation, the candidate for initiation was baptized on the first day of the ceremonies. Ten days later, he himself took part in the mystery drama. He first impersonated Set, or Typhon, to use his more familiar Greek name. He was made into a red ass, the animal form of Typhon, and as such was maltreated and abused, and underwent a ritual or simulated death. As Apuleius says, "I approached the bounds of death." Plutarch tells us that "every now and then at certain festivals they humiliate it (the shattered power of Typhon) and treat it most despitefully, even to rolling red-skinned men in the mud, and driving an ass over a precipice." [6] Typhon was the god of lust and desirousness, so that in this ordeal the initiant, while fasting and maintaining strict chastity, was tempted in every possible way. He had to experience his own instincts fully before he could be redeemed by the power of Isis. In reading Apuleius' account we cannot but feel the deep religious intensity and desire with which he seeks to be released from this form of the brute beast, through eating of the Roses of Isis. Then in the secret of the sanctuary the initiant became one with the dead Osiris. Lucius Apuleius writes about his own initiation: "Listen therefore, and believe it true. Thou shalt understand that I approached near unto hell, even to the gates of Proserpine [the underworld, or world of death], and after that I was ravished through all the elements, I returned to my proper place; about midnight I saw the sun shine brightly; I saw likewise the gods celestial and

---

[6] Mead, *op. cit.*, I, 305.

the gods infernal, before whom I presented myself and worshipped them." [7] He suffered a ritual death and was raised to life again through the power of Isis. The following morning the initiant, now made one with Osiris, was publicly proclaimed as one Osirified. He was led into the temple. There he stood on a pedestal facing the statue of the Goddess Isis herself. He was arrayed in the robe of Osiris, he carried a lighted torch and wore a garland of flowers on his head "with white palm leaves sprouting out on every side like rays." He says: "Thus was I adorned like unto the sun, and made in fashion of an image, when the curtains were drawn aside and all the people compassed about to behold me." In this way he stood on the pedestal and was hailed as a god.

The robe of Osiris which he wore is described as "lightlike" or "raylike," it was worn only once, at the initiation. The robe of Isis, on the other hand, which was also obtained through initiation, was many-colored and was worn at many religious ceremonials. Plutarch says of this: "Wherefore when they have once and once only received this (robe of Osiris) they treasure it away and keep it from all eyes and hands; whereas they use those of Isis on many occasions." [8]

The many-colored veil of Isis is the same as the many-colored Veil of Maya with which we are familiar in Hindu thought. It represents the many forms of nature in which the spirit is clothed. The idea is that the Creative Spirit clothed itself in material forms of great diversity and that the whole universe we know was made in that way, that it is the manifestation in material form of the Spirit of the Creator. Plutarch expresses this idea when he says: "For Isis is the feminine [principle] of nature and that which is capable of receiving the whole of genesis; in virtue of which she has been called 'Nurse' and 'All-Receiving' by Plato and, by the multitude, 'She of the ten-thousand Names,' through her being transformed by Reason (Logos) and receiving all forms and ideas [or shapes]." [9]

Thus the robe or veil of Isis is the ever-changing form of nature, whose beauty and tragedy veil the spirit from our eyes. This perpetual interplay in the manifest world, which includes

[7] Apuleius, *The Golden Ass,* trans. by W. Adlington, 1566 (New York: The Modern Library, No. 88), p. 294.
[8] Mead, *op. cit.,* I, 361.
[9] *Ibid.,* I, 333.

external objects, trees and hills and the sea, as well as other human beings, and also ourselves, our own bodies, our own emotional reactions even, the whole drama of the world, seems to have such an absolute reality that we do not question it. Yet in moments of insight, induced, perhaps, by pain and suffering or great joy, we may suddenly realize that *this* which makes up the obvious form of the world, is not the true, the real. The real, the eternal is a different kind of reality, which is, however, "bodied forth," to use a Gnostic term, in the interplay of this world's forces. Plutarch tells us that "the seat of Athena (that is Isis, as they think) at Sais used to have the following inscription on it:

> 'I am all that has been and is and shall be,
> and no mortal has ever revealed my robe.' " [10]

Mead interprets this saying as meaning "no one within duality has expressed or shown that in which this aspect of feminine life veils itself." This term "duality" refers to the conditions of life here on earth. For human beings, because they are both animal and spiritual in their nature, belong not to one but to two worlds.

A hymn addressed to Isis-Net expresses this same idea of the Veil of Nature which hides the mystery truth from human eyes. Net was a form of Isis, and was regarded as the Mother of All, being of both male and female nature. The text in which this hymn is recorded dates from about 550 B.C. but it is probably far older.

Hail, mother great, not hath been uncovered thy birth!
Hail, goddess great, within the underworld which is doubly
  hidden thou unknown one!
Hail thou divine one great, not hath been unloosed!
O unloose thy garment.
Hail, Hapt (Hidden One), not is given by way of entrance to
  her,
Come receive thou the soul of Osiris, protect it within thy two
  hands.[11]

The veil of Isis has other derivative meanings. It is said that the living being is caught in the net or veil of Isis, which

[10] *Ibid.,* I, 273.
[11] E. A. Wallis Budge, *The Gods of the Egyptians* (London, 1904), I, 459.

means that at birth the spirit, the divine spark, which is in everyone, was caught or embodied in the flesh. And it also refers to the fact that we all get entangled or caught in the net of nature. This net of nature is the same as the web of fate or circumstance. It is inevitable that we should get caught in our own fate, but we often regard our entanglement as a misfortune. For we long to be free to follow our own devices. If we accept this saying that the living being is caught in the net of Isis, however, we shall have to regard our own entanglement in life differently. For it is by such a process alone that the divine spirit can be caught. If it were not captured in this way it would wander free and would never have an opportunity to transform. The spirit of man must necessarily be caught in the net of Isis or it cannot be carried in her boat to the next phase of experience.

Isis, the moon, is also Mother Nature, who is both good and bad. She tolerates all things, just as in the myth she could not allow Horus to destroy Typhon utterly, for nature consists necessarily in growth *and* decay. That which is created must be destroyed if this world is to continue. Plutarch commenting on the fact that after the fight Isis let Typhon go says: "For the Mistress and Goddess of the Earth did not allow the nature which is the opposite of moisture [moisture being Osiris and its opposite Typhon] to be destroyed entirely, but she slackened and weakened it, wishing that the blend should continue, for it was not possible the cosmos should be perfect, had the fiery (principle) ceased and disappeared." [12] The weakening and slackening refers to the fact that Horus was said to injure the genitals of Typhon. Isis is shown as decreeing that there should not be perpetual harmony, with the good always in the ascendant. On the contrary she desires that there should always be a conflict between the powers of growth and those of destruction. The process of life consists not in unchecked progress but in the conflict between growth and decay. For this that we call the "process of life" is not identical with the well-being of the form in which life is temporarily manifested. This "process of life" belongs, not to a material world, but to that spiritual realm which underlies the material manifestation. In these ancient religious myths we thus find the problem of the

[12] Mead, *op. cit.*, I, 317.

persistent existence of evil already grappled with and, in their own projected terms, solved. Isis *would* not that Typhon should be utterly destroyed.

First Isis, like Ishtar, the Green One, of Chaldea, is Mother Nature, while Osiris is Moon. Gradually, however, Osiris became assimilated to the sun and Isis became moon in her own right. She was the Crescent, crowned with the headdress of cow horns, the Hornéd Goddess, the Cow, and as such was identified with Hathor the Cow-Goddess who preceded her. Osiris, too, was a hornéd deity, known as the bull god, Apis. For Apis was the spirit of Osiris, who was said to be "conceived whenever the generative light from the moon fastens on a cow in heat." This was, perhaps, the most sacred symbol of the Egyptians. A real bull, called the Apis, was reared at Memphis as the image of the soul of Osiris. Its food and care were under special ritual regulations. This bull form of the dying and resurrecting god is not exclusive to Osiris, however. Dionysus, also, was known in a bull form, called Zagreus, and this bull was torn to pieces by the Titans, just as the body of Osiris was torn to pieces by Typhon. Plutarch, indeed, states quite definitely that Dionysus and Osiris are the same.

Isis, both in the form of Nature and in the form of Moon, had, as we have seen, two aspects. She was the creator, mother, nurse of all, and she was also the Destroyer. Her name Isis means ancient, and she was also called Maat, which means Knowledge or Wisdom. Isis is Maat, the *ancient wisdom.* This means the wisdom of things as they are and as they always have been, the innate, inherent capacity to follow the nature of things both in their present form and in their inevitable development in relation to each other. It is the wisdom of instinct. To the philosophers of Hellenistic times she was The Wisdom, The Sophia. Osiris also represented knowledge, but his knowledge was the Reason, the Logos, which is that organizing, comprehending capacity which can map out, and foresee. He is the Logos, the Moon who meted out the heavens, portioning them into areas by his movements through the zodiacal constellations, and by his cyclic changes dividing the eternal flow of time into seasons and months, so teaching men law and order and justice.

The symbol of Isis is shown in figure 4. Sir Wallis Budge writes me that this was probably a womb with its dependent ovaries, meaning that the very nature of Isis is expressed in her generative power and also in the attraction woman has for man, from *ancient* days. It was said in the myth that Isis by her love drew forth again the potency of the dead Osiris. "Isis the magician avenged her brother. . . . She made to rise up the helpless members of him whose heart was at rest. She drew from him his essence and she made therefrom an heir. She suckled the child in solitariness and none knew where his place was." [13] Her love gave him back his potency, which Typhon, the Lustful, had destroyed.

In the mystery initiation of later centuries, as we have seen, the initiant had to impersonate Typhon, the Ass, and thus experience all his own lustfulness until he realized its utter inability to satisfy his human need. The truly human part of him, the spirit, was, as it were, killed by the domination of the Typhonic spirit, just as Osiris had been killed by Set or Typhon. Then, and not till then, could the love of Isis and his longing for her regenerate him. By her power and grace, he was restored to life, not any longer as brute beast, but as man, redeemed from his own animal passions, a living spirit like unto the gods, assimilated to Osiris, governed no longer by lust, but by the Reason, or Logos, which Osiris symbolized. This rebirth, however, could only be achieved by lifting the veil of Isis. By recognizing, that is, that this worldly show is only the garment of the true, the real, which lives on a different plane.

It is by the power of Isis, through her love, that the man, sunk in lust and passion, is raised to a spiritual life. But as we saw above, Isis is destroyer as well as life-giver. Her statues frequently represent her as black. The typical form is that of a Virgin and Child. Often she is seen suckling the infant Horus, for she is Nurse as well as Mother of all, she nurtures and fosters that to which she has given birth. Ancient statues of Isis with the Child have, in not a few instances, been taken over by Catholic communities who mistook them for representations of the Virgin Mary and the Infant Jesus. It is even possible that some of the shrines of the Black Virgin in Europe have really grown up around such statues of the Black Isis.

This mistake is not as incongruous as it might seem, for Isis,

[13] E. A. Wallis Budge, *Osiris and the Egyptian Resurrection* (New York and London, 1911), I, 94.

also, was believed to be Mother of God and was worshipped as virgin, just as were all the other moon goddesses whom we have considered, even though she was, at the same time, said to be the wife of the moon god. This aspect of her relation to the god is more emphasized in Egypt than in other countries. Pos-

Fig. 31. Isis. The Birth of Horus in the Papyrus Swamp. (From *Osiris and the Egyptian Resurrection,* Wallis Budge, vol.i, p.301. London, Philip Lee Warner; New York, G. P. Putnam Sons, 1911.)

sibly the greater emphasis on the wifehood of Isis is related to the persistence of Osiris as moon god. Usually the moon god comes to take a subsidiary place, giving way to the worship of a goddess, fairly early in the religious evolution, as it did, for example, in Babylon, where Sinn was replaced by Ishtar and her son, Tammuz. But in Egypt, Osiris, who is thought of primarily as Moonman, having been raised from the dead by the power of Isis, becomes immortal. He remains the moon, husband of Isis even though he is eventually made one with

Ra, the sun, while his son, Horus, who is a god from the beginning, able to raise himself from the dead by his own power, is the young moon more nearly equivalent to Tammuz.

The attainment of immortality by the moonman, Osiris, became a central teaching of the Egyptian religion, while in Babylon this was always a subsidiary belief. In Egypt we find both Osiris and Horus as moon deities, with Isis standing between them. In the mystery teaching of later centuries it is specifically stated that Isis was mother as well as spouse of the moon, referring in each case to Osiris. But the contradiction was never entirely resolved.

Isis as virgin, and unborn, conceived the Elder Horus and brought him forth (figure 31). It was said that Isis "brought forth of herself" her first-born, although the myth also relates that she united with Osiris in the womb of their mother Nut. She also conceived again after the death of Osiris, by means of the image of his phallus which she had made, and in this regard she is spoken of as "that Blessed and Incorruptible Nature according to which the Divine conceives itself . . ." [14]

Here again, then, we have the problem of virginity in a goddess who is both wife and mother. Philo of Alexandria, who lived 30 B.C. to 45 A.D., has a teaching on this subject which is very illuminating. He says: "For it is fitting God should converse with an undefiled, an untouched and pure nature, with her who in very truth is *the* Virgin, in fashion very different from ours. For the congress of men for the procreation of children makes virgins women. But when God begins to associate with the soul, He brings it to pass that she who was formerly woman becomes virgin again." [15] According to this concept the *hieros gamos,* the marriage with the god, creates the quality of virginity, it makes the woman one-in-herself. Through such an experience the woman comes into possession of her own masculine soul, which is then no longer projected entirely outside herself into a man who has for her the value of a god, with godlike authority. Thus she becomes complete, whole.

Isis, then, was virgin, and in the period of her mourning, she was black-robed, or was herself black. Like the Black Virgin of European shrines, who is so closely related to her, she

14 Mead, *op. cit.,* I, 291.
15 *Ibid.,* I, 218.

was a goddess of healing. Budge records that "Isis interests herself in healing men's bodies and to all who need her help she appears in dreams and gives relief." [16] She also brewed a medicine which would raise the dead. It will be remembered that of Ishtar it was said "Where thou lookest in pity, the dead man lives again, the sick is healed." Isis gave her medicine to Horus who not only came to life but became immortal. This medicine was called "moly" and is thought to be the same as soma or hoama, the drink brewed from the moon tree, which occurs in Persian and Hindu literature, and which, also, is said to bestow immortality.

The black statues of Isis had a further meaning. Plutarch relates that "the hornéd ones of her statues are representations of her crescent, while by the black-robed ones are signified the occultations and overshadowings in which she follows the Sun [Osiris] longing after him. Accordingly they invoke the Moon for affairs of love and Eudoxus says that Isis decides love affairs." [17]

At the Winter Solstice, the goddess in the form of a golden cow, covered by a black robe, was carried around the shrine of the dead Osiris seven times, representing the wanderings of Isis who journeyed over the world mourning for his death and searching for the scattered parts of his body. Her dirge has been preserved to us. It was called Maneros, which it will be recalled was the name of the child, son of Queen Astarte, who fell out of the boat overcome by awe, when he saw Isis, in her passion of love and grief, embracing the dead Osiris. His name, Maneros, means "Understanding of Love" (or perhaps Love of Understanding). The lament is as follows:

Return, oh, return!
God Panu, return!
Those that were enemies are no more here.
Oh lovely helper, return,
That thou mayest see me, thy sister,
Who loves thee.
And comest thou not near me?
O beautiful youth, return, oh, return!

[16] E. A. Wallis Budge, *Osiris and the Egyptian Resurrection* (New York, 1911), I, 13.
[17] Mead, *op. cit.,* I, 332.

When I see thee not
My heart sorrows for thee,
My eyes ever seek thee,
I roam about for thee, to see thee in the form of the Nai,
To see thee, to see thee, thou beautiful lov'd one.
Let me, the Radiant, see thee
God Panu, All-Glory, see thee again!
To thy beloved come, blessed Onnofris,
Come to thy sister, come to thy wife,
God Urtuhet, oh come!
Come to thy consort! [18]

One part of the ritual enacted to procure the resurrection of Osiris consisted in a dramatic driving away of Typhon the enemy who had killed him. This was doubtless at first a magic proceeding intended to prevent the drought from encroaching any further on the fertile regions which bordered the Nile, for the resurrection of Osiris was at that time a symbol for the annual flooding of the Nile on which the fertility of the land depended. Later the driving off of Typhon was incorporated into the initiation ceremonies recorded in the *Book of the Dead*. We do not know whether it played any part in the mystery initiations of Hellenistic times, but Plutarch mentions that in the driving off of Typhon use was made of the sistrum of Isis. The sistrum was a musical instrument made rather like a rattle. There was a hollow ball which contained four "things," which rattled when it was shaken. These "things" are said to be the four elements, earth, air, fire, and water, of which the universe is composed. Plutarch writes: "The sistrum also shows that existent things must be shaken up and never have cessation from impulse, but as it were be wakened up and agitated when they fall asleep and die away. For they say they turn aside and beat off Typhon with sistra—signifying that when corruption binds nature fast and brings her to a stand [then] generation frees her and raises her from death by means of motion." [19]

This seems to be exactly right from the psychological point of view. For Typhon is that desirousness which can only say "I want." Whenever anyone gets under this aspect of his own

[18] Emil Naumann, *History of Music*, trans. by F. Praeger (London, 1882), p. 40.
[19] Mead, *op. cit.*, I, 344.

nature the flow of life is dammed up and he finds only frustration. Everything seems to become heavy or sultry. Really he is himself in a heavy, sullen mood which will not allow of any compromise. It is not by getting what one wants, however, that one can be released from such a mood, but only by seeking for the actual truth of the situation. Relatedness, the law of Eros, demands that one's own desires shall not be taken as absolute but shall be adapted to the needs and desires of the other person and to the requirements of the situation. This means that one cannot remain in a fixed or taken attitude but must be flexible. Under such circumstances a shaking up will perhaps drive off the Typhonic oppression; as Plutarch says, nature, which has been bound, is released by the movement which Isis can bring.

In addition to the private mystery initiations, public rituals of Isis and Osiris were celebrated. The chief of these was a festival of fertility. It occurred in the month Hathor, November, the month of the Cow-Goddess. At that time "everywhere they exhibit a man-shaped image of Osiris, ithyphallic [that is with erect phallus], because of his generative and luxuriant nature." [20] The festival culminated in a procession at the head of which was carried the huge image of the phallus, representing the lost organ of Osiris. This was preceded by a vase of water, symbolizing the fertilizing moisture, the very power of the Moon, which is both Osiris and Isis. The bowl and the phallus are the eternal symbols of generation which recur again and again. We find them in primitive rites—the fire stick, which is called the man, and the cup in which it bores, called the woman; the fundus in the earth in the center of the camp into which each Roman soldier threw his spear; the chalice of the Holy Grail into which a spear, perpetually dripping blood, was thrust; the holy font of baptism fertilized by plunging in the lighted candle. The list could be indefinitely prolonged, for the spiritual meaning of such symbols can never be exhausted. We can only hope to understand them to the extent to which we have made their meaning our own through the spiritual experience of the regeneration or rebirth that they symbolize.

And so, year by year, the mysteries were exposed, the bowl,

[20] *Ibid.*, I, 331.

which is Isis, Mother, Vase of Life, and the Phallus, which is the fertilizing power of Osiris, lost and found again. As these inanimate objects were solemnly carried in procession, they silently proclaimed the eternal verities which might be read and understood by those who had eyes to see. Through the truth that was thus "shown forth," those who could understand might themselves partake in a new life which should be ever renewed like the life of the Ancient and Eternal Moon.

14

THE SACRIFICE OF THE SON

With the story of the mother goddesses, and especially of Isis, we pass to a new phase of the woman's emotional problem, requiring a further ordeal and deeper initiation. For here the sacred drama does not culminate in the marriage in the temple and stop there, but goes on to relate the story of the virgin-born child and the relation of his mother to him.

The child is, then, not only the hero, who has courage and power to conquer the enemy of the light, symbolizing for the woman her own renewal or rebirth, but also, his coming represents the actual relation between mother and child. The nature of her love is changed: no longer is it an expression of her instinctive need for satisfaction with a sexual partner; now it is maternal solicitude for her own offspring. She loves him and, in the myths, must always sacrifice him.

Generally speaking, in psychological and other interpretative writings, this relationship is taken from the point of view of the child where the myth of his sacrifice refers to the need of each individual to sacrifice his own childishness and dependence. The problem, for example, of the so-called Oedipus complex has become familiar to all. The longing of the child for the protection of the mother's womb, the incestuous back-turning of his libido, are matters of everyday comment. In *The Psychology of the Unconscious,* Jung wrote of this aspect of the relation to the mother, comparing it with the necessary longing all experience in time of crisis to return to the mother depths for renewal. For the mother is the source of all life, psychological as well as physical. In his chapter on the "Dual Mother Role" [1] Jung discusses the Attis myth and interprets it

---

[1] C. G. Jung, *Psychology of the Unconscious,* to appear in the Collected Works, Vol. 5, in a revised version as *Symbols of Transformation* (New York: Pantheon Books [Bollingen Series XX] and London: Routledge and Kegan Paul) .

in detail, showing what is the meaning, to the son, of castration and death on the tree, symbol of the mother. This aspect of the subject I shall not take up here. Jung has dealt with it far better than I could do. But the sacrifice of the son has another side which Jung did not develop in that study. He does not ask what the meaning of this act of sacrifice may be when it is looked at from the point of view of the mother.

The myth relates that when her son reaches manhood, he is sacrificed not in spite of her love and protective care but by the edict and consent of his mother. The young man is sometimes killed by an animal which represents the fierce and primitive aspect of the goddess herself, as Adonis was attacked by a bear, an earlier form of Aphrodite his mother. Attis castrated and killed himself because he was struck mad by his mother Cybele; Horus was wounded, perhaps even slain, by Set, whom Isis would not destroy but released after he had been brought to her in bonds.

In these myths the mother is not one, she is dual. She has two aspects: in her light aspect she is compassionate, filled with maternal love and pity, and in her dark aspect she is fierce and terrible and will not tolerate the childish dependence of the son. For his softness and clinging undermine her, just as her oversolicitude undermines him. His childish need appeals too intimately to her own desire to mother him. Her instinct is not only the instinct of sexuality. Intimate body contact is not only erotic to her, nor does it represent only her childish longing back to her own mother; it is also the maternal in herself which craves for the contact with her infant. Through such contacts she experiences her own maternity. Desirousness in her is not only the urge to make the man fulfill her sexual need, it may also take the form of a compulsion to make the object of her love serve her maternal instinct. Most women know the deep-seated longing for little clinging arms, for the warmth and softness of baby limbs. A physical delight lurks in the relation to an infant, offspring of her own body, which is not far in its intensity and lure from the delight of an erotic contact, although different in its nature.

This desirousness is not really love of the object as such, it is once more love of the object because it brings her personal satisfaction. Through the sacrifice of her sexual desirousness the woman, it seems, is not entirely released from the problem of her egotistic demands. She has moved one step towards release but in this second stage she may also fall a prey to her auto-erotic tendencies. She has become identified to the son. Her personal satisfaction is found through seeking his good. Instead now, of seeking her own way, her own advantage in an open egotism, as she did before her submission to instinct in the temple marriage, she seeks the good of her child. She is pleased if he is happy; her ambition is satisfied if he is recognized. She does not realize, as a rule, that this apparent altruism is in reality but a concealed egotism. And she does not suspect that her inability to say "no" to him is really because of her inability to say "no" to herself, or to deny on a deeper level her own softness and selfishness.

It is hard to recognize this attitude of indulgence to the son in all the viciousness of its true character, because society commends it as a virtue. Externally it looks so admirable for a woman to sink her interests in those of her child, and to sacrifice her own comfort and well-being at every point in order to further his interests. It is only later that the true nature of her course of action shows itself. Then, when the son's complete inability to face the hard realities of life, his total absence of self-discipline and his incapacity to take a responsible attitude, bear dolorous witness to the falseness of his upbringing, it is usually too late to remedy the situation. Even at this point society, and his mother herself, are apt to say, "How could he turn out so badly after all she did for him," not recognizing in the least that he remained childish just because she did so much for him, leaving nothing that he had to do for himself. Consequently it is very hard for a woman to realize the need to sacrifice the son. It seems such a wrong thing to do, so black an act. If she refused to do what he wanted she would feel as treacherous as the ancient mother goddess who yearly sacrificed her son and condemned him to death.

The problem of identification with the son does not stop, however, at the relation between a mother and her actual children. A woman who has not yet "sacrificed the son," that is sacrificed the instinctual maternal within herself, may have no actual children, but will nonetheless carry the maternal attitude into her relationships. She is under an inner compulsion to mother all for whom she cares. She cannot bear to see anyone unhappy or in difficulties. Motherliness dominates in her. She never realizes that her inability to accept hardness for her friends reflects her own inability to face the hard things of life for herself; still less does she appreciate the fact that her oversolicitous attitude towards them cultivates their worst weakness, throws them back into childishness and self-pity, by which indeed a man's very manhood is undermined. By this attitude she robs her son of his individuality. He is made soft, feminine. He is rendered impotent, all his virility is drained out of him. This is the false castration through the mother by which no redemption is achieved. Through this kind of maternal embrace, the son is killed, walled up in the tree like the coffin of Osiris.

When, however, a woman has the courage to say "no" as well as to say "yes," when the negative or black side of Eros has a place beside the light side, then the son as well as the mother may be redeemed by the sacrifice. For when he meets with her refusal to pamper and consider him and save him from hardship, he gains thereby the power to meet the real difficulties of the situation for himself, provided he accepts the reality of the situation and renounces his demand that she mother him and give him what he needs. So long as all his attention is directed towards persuading the "mother" to give him what he wants, he has no capacity to gain it for himself. His voluntary castration and death as *son* result in a rebirth as *man*.

It is no accident that the sacrifice of the son is represented by a castration, for the most fundamental demand for satisfaction that man makes upon woman is the demand for the satisfaction of his sexuality. It is in this realm that he feels himself most helpless to cope with his own need, except by demanding that the woman serve him. This childish demand on his part and the equally undeveloped maternal wish to give on hers, may serve on a low level of psychological development to produce an alliance between a man and a woman which passes for relationship. But when a necessity arises for something more mature in the situation between them this demand has to be replaced by a greater submission to the laws of Eros. The man may be compelled to recognize that the woman is something more than the reciprocal of his need, something other than the counterpart of his conscious personality. When she refuses any longer to mother him, no longer repressing her own needs in her determination to fulfill his, he will find himself faced with the necessity of meeting the reality of the situation, which shows itself as different from what he had thought it. This involves the sacrifice of his demand, a sacrifice which is not only symbolized by castration, but may indeed appear in reality as the need to renounce for the time being his desire for sexual satisfaction with this woman, whom he yet loves. It is a voluntary castration for the sake of Eros, corresponding to the initiation to Isis which Apuleius describes, when the postulant was compelled to experience all his unredeemed desire, the negative aspect of his own Eros libido; he was cast out from his fellows, made to feel alone and forsaken because of something in his own nature which was like Typhon, enemy of relatedness; he was beaten and illtreated, the prey of frustrated hunger and sex, the Typhonic aspect of the desirousness which blasts. For Typhon is not something entirely different from Eros. It is Eros in its unredeemed form, the under side, the opposite of relatedness. Only when the postulant had passed through this ordeal, only when he had fully experienced this aspect of life, and realized its hollowness and sterility, and was ready to sacrifice it forever—when he could accept self castration—then he found Isis the goddess, and on eating her roses was restored to the form of a man. The roses of Isis are the flowers of pure passion, symbolizing love redeemed from lust.

In like manner, in modern life, initiation to the goddess is achieved by the man who can sacrifice his sexuality, whether it occurs as simple physical desirousness or is aroused in him through the projection of his anima. In the latter case his task is far harder because it seemingly involves the heart as well as the sexuality. It does not, however, really involve the heart to any great extent, because love for a woman who carries the value of anima is not really love of the woman, herself. It is almost entirely love of her *as anima*. An involvement of this character does not permit her to be herself but makes her a function of the man's own psyche and involves the demand that she shall conform to his ideal and fulfill his desire. This demand has also to be sacrificed in the initiation to the goddess of love, for needless to say the initiation will not be fully accomplished by the sacrifice merely of physical desirousness, the harder sacrifice also has to be made. Until it is accomplished a man cannot even begin to understand the meaning of psychological relationship, gift of the Eros, or experience the psychological wholeness which results from serving his own inner truth, instead of seeking to be made whole through another. True love, true relationship, can only arise between two people who have each experienced such an initiation, or through their actual life together, come to realize it.

There is another aspect of this initiation which is quite practical in its implications. So long as a man is young the kind of emotion which results from an anima projection may well be the real expression of his relation to the Eros. Unconscious instinct carries for him the value and significance of psychological and spiritual relationship. In such a case a relation with a girl towards whom his anima has been aroused, with whom, as the saying is, he has fallen in love, may be entirely satisfactory. As the years go by, however, the time comes when he should have outgrown this adolescent phase and should be learning how to create a more mature relationship in which knowledge of the real character and personality of the partner play a larger and more conscious part. If, however, he fails to make this change in himself, if he remains in the relatively immature state where instead of taking up into his own psyche the emotional and feeling qualities which should be mediated to him through his anima, he persists in finding them outside himself in the projection to a woman, his relation to the feminine principle remains unconscious, and consequently he remains childish. His "love" still consists chiefly in "I want," and his sexuality in desirousness. But as the years go by a change comes over the situation, for while he may still want, or think that he wants, the old type of emotional involvement, he finds in actual experience that it no longer satisfies him. Search as he may for ever younger, more ideally beautiful girls, he still finds himself unsatisfied, perhaps even impotent. He is still seeking for emotional satisfaction in a form which he should have outgrown, he is clinging to a childish or immature pattern. His childishness is reflected in the expectation that the woman who, for the moment, carries the values of his anima should meet his need for emotional and sexual satisfaction. He expects her to give him the love he needs instead of realizing that mature love can only develop out of such an instinctual involvement as the result of long-continued and conscious effort. He expects life to give him what he wants, to act as mother to him. This very expectation, however, robs him of his manhood. It is, as the ancient myth

197

puts it, a castration to the mother. But this sacrifice is not the initiation ordeal voluntarily undertaken with a religious motive. It is an involuntary sacrifice to the mother, which brings no renewal. The sacrifice of desirousness is a late initiation which can only be attained by those who have already had experience of life and of their own natures. If it is undertaken prematurely, perhaps as a childish evasion of the risks and hardships of life, it can only result in disillusion, and loss of libido, —that is, of psychic energy and interest of whatever kind. This is again a false castration, a childish clinging to the mother by which all emotional development is forestalled or frustrated.

To follow blindly one anima projection after another is to be caught in this childish phase of emotional development. If the recognition of this fact is borne in upon a man involved in such a situation, so that he gains an insight into the true nature of his love and of his relation to the woman who attracts him, a new phase of psychological and emotional development may be ushered in. If, for instance, a man has become aware of the instability and unreality of the relation to a woman which is based simply on instinctive rapport, he may begin to seek for the reality behind the lure of his anima projection. Instead of giving himself up to the flow of instinct, he may voluntarily sacrifice his desire for immediate satisfaction by an act of inner withdrawal from the woman who attracts him in this compulsive way. Thus he renounces his own undisciplined "I want" and submits himself instead to the requirements of real relationship. In this way he serves the goddess, the Eros, and, as it were, sacrifices his sexuality, the unredeemed desire of the natural man, to her. This deliberate attempt on his part to change a situation which has been recognized as unreal, constitutes a kind of initiation. The change is brought about through a determined effort to become aware of the hidden motives, the actual reality behind the emotional illusion, no matter what the cost may be. It may be clearly recognized, even at the time, that the insight gained may dissipate his illusory happiness and show the emotion and glamour of his involvement to have had but the flimsiest of foundations. But only through accepting such a risk is it possible to find the truth behind the illusion. An attitude of this character requires the greatest courage, and devotion to values beyond those of personal satisfaction. The personal desirousness indeed has to be sacrificed before such an attitude can be attained. Where a man seeks for the Eros truth in this way the change in him takes place through an increase in his self-consciousness. It is a psychological change taking place in his inner life, even though it is also reflected or enacted in the outer happenings or events of his life.

Occasionally a similar transformation seems to take place in a more unconscious way. With some men the conflict is projected, concretized. What was, in the circumstances just described, emotional or psychological suffering becomes in these more unconscious situations physical pain; the symbolic castration and death of the first class becomes, in the second, an actual illness and threat of physical death.

In figure 32 is reproduced a picture drawn by a lad of seventeen, while he was in bed after a painful operation which had caused considerable shock, both physical and emotional. In the days immediately following the operation his relation to his mother was quite peculiar. It was almost as if he had become a little boy again. He could not get on without her and clung to her for support. Then one day he asked for pencils and paper and made the drawing which is reproduced. He was quite naïve about it.

Fig. 32. An imaginative drawing made by a boy of seventeen.

He did not know that it had any psychological meaning and at first declined to say anything about it, but later he gave the following explanation: "It is all inside a mountain," he said, "above is a temple. In the middle of the temple is the Holy Stone of the Highest. Around it are the inscriptions of ancient Priests who formerly sacrificed in the temple. A sacrifice has just taken place there. The bloodstained fleece of the sacrificial animal is stretched on the ground before the altar. Below is a dark cavern. Here is the bloodstained dagger with which the sacrifice was accomplished. It is the place where no one goes." Underneath this is a river which leads to a deeper, unknown underworld. After he had drawn this picture the boy's relation to his mother underwent a complete change. He came out of his regression and was himself again. From his explanation it is evident that the boy did not understand what he had drawn. The picture is an unconscious phantasy which shows the psychological significance of the external experience. The operation is represented in the unconscious as a sacrifice. The boy himself was the victim, who was slain. In the picture his skin is lying on the ground. Psychologically this means that he as his mother's "little lamb" has been slain. The experience of pain and suffering through which he was going is his initiation into manhood. For the future he may no longer hide behind his mother's skirts; she can no longer make excuses for him as for a little child; he may not shirk the responsibilities of manhood, for he is a man! During the period immediately following the operation, when psychologically speaking he had been sacrificed and was, as it were, dead, he entered again, metaphorically, into his mother's womb, so that he might be reborn. In consciousness, in the world of external facts, his retreat to the mother's womb shows itself as a regression to childlike dependence on his own mother. But, we ask, what will be born out of this ritual death? The answer to this question is given in the lower part of the picture. The symbol of the new life is to be seen in the depths of the mountain which he called "the place where no one goes," it is the deepest level of the unconscious. Here the crescent moon is seen arising, with a star between its horns.

In this imaginative drawing of a modern boy, we meet again the symbol whose significance we have been discussing. In this case the symbol foretells that out of his initiation-experience the young man will gain a new light in the sky, the light of the moon, of Eros. While he was a child his mother represented to him the values of Eros, but she can no longer be the only woman in the world for him. From this time on he must seek his feminine values for himself through his relations to women outside the family. Out of this experience woman was born for him. The coming of woman, or of his consciousness of woman, will bring with it the age-old problem of good and evil, the dark and the light. But the picture carries the situation a step further, for to him there comes from the depths a single star, symbol of unity, the star which is between the sun and the moon, a symbol of reconciliation, the promise of the solution for him of the problem of man's duality through the attainment of an individual human standpoint.

This is the modern equivalent of the ancient initiation to the goddess, which for the priests involved actual castration and for the ordinary initiant probably some form of ritual castration not involving physical mutilation. The outcome of the initiation was represented in the myths as bringing renewal or rebirth. The Son of the Mother, mutilated or killed, was the Moonman shorn of his powers at the time of the waning of the moon. There followed a period of darkness when the son was in the underworld from whence he emerged reborn, having obtained the power of immortality.

In the Egyptian account of the mutilation of the Moon God, the problem of his resurrection is gone into in much greater detail than in the Babylonian and Syrian myths, and a point of great importance for our modern interpretation is introduced. For we are told how Isis searched for the scattered parts of the body of Osiris and found them all except the phallus. As she could not find this vital organ, one especially necessary for a god of fertility, she made an image of it. Then through the power of her love and longing she enabled Osiris to become potent once more and conceived by him. Osiris had been killed by Set or Typhon who is lust, the negative aspect of fertility and of relatedness. This death has to do with the first stage of the initiation. The loss of the phallus refers to the necessity for the man to give up his demand that the woman satisfy his sexual and emotional needs as though she were his mother. As a general rule, awareness that he is making any such demand only comes to a man when he encounters reluctance or actual refusal on the part of the woman to play the role of mother to him. At that point he is confronted by the necessity of sacrificing his childish demand if a more real relationship is to be established between himself and the woman. The acceptance of this necessity to sacrifice his helpless wishing is the equivalent of the loss of the phallus, it is a self-castration. Through the voluntary sacrifice of his own childishness a new spiritual capacity arises within him. In the myth this is represented as the power to unite once more with the goddess. In the inner experience of the modern man it may manifest itself in a renewal of the power to love, but in a different way, for this new love will not be a demand for satisfaction but an emotion which recognizes the individuality of the other person. Or the new capacity born of the sacrifice of the childishness may show itself in the development of a new and independent personality. For Isis is not an individual woman, she is a goddess, and the power to love and unite with Isis means the renewal of the life force within, and not necessarily a love relationship with an actual woman.

In the story of Osiris the discrimination is clearly made between the drama of the gods and the part in which humans may participate. This distinction is especially clear in the account of the myth of Isis and Osiris which Plutarch gives, because he was primarily interested in the mystery initiation. Already in his day the drama of the gods was recognized as representing a spiritual or psychological drama in which man might take a part and so participate in the renewal of the gods. In Plutarch's story the human being seeking initiation is represented by the little boy, son of the king in whose palace rooftree the coffin of Osiris was walled up. It will be recalled that Isis tried to obtain immortality for this child by burning up his mortal parts but that the child's mother interfered and prevented the completion of the ritual. This episode corresponds to the first stage of the initiation. The burning up of the mortal parts is the destruction of carnality or lust. Isis, the goddess of love and relatedness, could have accomplished this completely were it not that the mother interfered. The child, the soul of man, is protected from experiencing the complete sacrifice of his desirousness by the mother who cannot bear to see him hurt. But the child goes with Isis when she leaves. He has been weaned from his mother by the experience of the goddess.

Then comes the next stage of the initiation. In order to attain redemption, he has to be able to stand the impact of the Eros in all its intensity. He must be able to be a witness to the emotion of Isis in her grief over the dead Osiris and, as the ancient story relates, to "stand the awe of her." This awe is of the goddess, not of a human woman, even though in the experience of many men the power of the Eros may be mediated through a human woman and her emotional experience. Men are almost proverbially afraid of emotion, their own or another's. Few, unless they are entirely callous, can stand the sight of a woman's tears. But the ability to stand the awe of the goddess does not refer to hardheartedness or lack of realization. It means, indeed, the capacity to understand fully the emotional depths which the woman's grief or joy express and to appreciate them, participate in them, and yet not to be undone by the experience. In some cases, however, this ordeal comes to a man apart from a relation to a woman who could in any way be considered the representative of the goddess Isis. Sometimes a man may have to experience the intensity of his own emotion in relation to a woman who is in herself a quite slender personality, perhaps even an insignificant one. If, however, the man has touched upon the depths of his own emotional intensity in relation to her, he can then experience the awe of the goddess through his own emotion. And, indeed, in recognizing the inadequacy of the woman in regard to whom these emotional currents have been set in motion, he is compelled to accept his experience as of inner moment, even while recognizing it as unimportant when viewed from an external standpoint.

Initiation to the goddess, then, requires that the man must explore the depths of emotional intensity within himself and be able to stand that revelation. This experience is the equivalent of the woman's ordeal in which she has to sacrifice the son. For the woman's impulse to protect and cherish another, to keep him a child and save him from the hardness of life, to mother him in short, is closely related to the self-protecting impulse which prevents her from facing life's reality and the intensity of her own emotions, for herself. For both man and woman, then, this second stage of the initiation implies the facing of emotional intensity.

This point is dramatically shown in Plutarch's story of the little boy whose name was both Diktys, the Fisher, and Maneros, Understanding of Love. Plutarch says he is a symbol for the soul of man, who because he was a witness to the grief of the goddess Isis and was not able to stand it, fell overboard and was drowned. The passage reads: "And they say that when first she [Isis] found solitude and was by herself, she opened the chest, and laying her face on his [Osiris'] face, she kissed him and shed tears. And that when the little one came up in silence from behind and understood, on sensing it she turned herself about, and passionately gave him an awe-ful look. And the little one could not hold himself up against the awe of her, and died. But some say it was not thus, but . . . that he fell out into the river." [2] The Fisher King of the Grail legends, who is either drowned or sick with a mortal illness, is the counterpart of this

2 G. R. S. Mead, *Thrice-Greatest Hermes* (London, 1906), I, 287.

same Diktys. He can only be restored to life by the hero who can face the ordeal in which he, the Fisher King, failed.

This legend forms the background theme for T. S. Eliot's poem, *The Waste Land*. The events which occur in the course of the poem have no logical sequence and yet have an underlying unity which seems in some curious way to be inevitable. One feels that the message of the poem came, not from the conscious intention of the writer, but from a much greater depth. The source of Eliot's poetic inspiration lies beyond the field of his conscious knowledge and his poem bears all the hallmarks of an unconscious product. Here the desolation and disruption of postwar Europe is described and is correlated with the Wasteland of the Grail legends. The two themes are so interwoven that they are hard to disentangle. When the hero comes at last to the chapel by the sea in which the Dead or ever-dying Fisher King lies, the dread revelation which shall break the spell is hinted at. The whole world pants waiting for rain. Then suddenly a flash of lightning, the rain falls,

> Then spoke the thunder
> DA
> *Datta:* What have we given?
> My friend, blood shaking my heart
> The awful daring of a moment's surrender
> Which an age of prudence can never retract
> By this, and this only, we have existed . . .

This "awful daring of a moment's surrender" is like the turning of the key in the prison door: "each in his prison thinking of the key." "I have heard the key turn in the door once and turn once only." They sail away

> The sea was calm, your heart would have responded
> Gaily, when invited, beating obedient
> To controlling hands
>   I sat upon the shore
> Fishing, with the arid plain behind me
> Shall I at least set my lands in order? [3]

[3] T. S. Eliot, *Poems 1909–1925* (London: Faber and Faber, and New York: Harcourt, Brace and Co., 1928).

We are left in doubt as to whether the moment's surrender was actually dared, for the poem ends with the Fisher still sitting by the sea with the arid plain behind him.

It is strange to find in this modern poem so close a correspondence to the ancient myths of the Moon Goddess. The drought of the Wastelands is to be cured by a miracle which is represented cosmically, by the release of tension in the thunderstorm and, emotionally, in the surrender of the ego-control and the acceptance of feeling. The heroic act is the ability to stand the awe of the goddess.

Acceptance of that which the Moon Goddess means is represented here as releasing the rain, bringing to the barren and arid earth the moisture which shall enable her to blossom once again. In Eliot's poem this miracle is sought not only on the personal plane. The barrenness does not only afflict the life of the individual man, his sterility is a symbol for the barrenness of the world. Eliot's poetry is conceived as an expression of the problems of the twentieth century. The misery and utter banality of Europe in the years between the two world wars form the background especially of *Waste Land* and *Ash Wednesday*, and it is out of his concern with these problems that his poetry arises. The voice of the thunder in *Waste Land* speaks not only of the emotional problems of modern man as an individual but also of world problems in a century where the almost exclusive concern with masculine and mechanical concepts of life had well-nigh choked the springs of living water which are gifts of the Moon Goddess, the feminine principle of Eros.

This heroic act by which he dares to accept feeling as a divine principle having equal rights with the masculine principle or Logos, is the correlate of the woman's no less heroic act in the sacrifice of the son. For her ability to say "no" to him means that she has to say "no" also to her own indulgent tendencies and face her emotions, no matter of what nature they may be, without being swamped. This is said to be the lesser sacrifice, but it is no easy one to make. It involves the breaking of her identification to her son and the relinquishing of her position of superiority as giver.

In any relationship the one who habitually gives seems to be the superior, but if this superiority depends on a compulsion to be giver it is only a relative superiority, for the recipient is a necessity. The woman related to a man in this maternal way is dependent on him, as he on her. She is identified to him and so is, in a certain sense, his counterpart, his syzygy. Only when she sacrifices her desire to mother him and by living true to her own emotions "sacrifices the son" can she, as a separate human entity, become virgin.

By facing her own emotion, love, fear, hate, whatever it may be, in stark reality, no longer camouflaged by the assumption of indulgence and maternal concern, she becomes once more one-in-herself, dependent only on the goddess, truly a Daughter of the Moon.

15

REBIRTH AND IMMORTALITY

In Eliot's poem *The Waste Land,* which was quoted in the preceding chapter, the ordeal or sacrifice demanded from the hero if the Fisher King was to be healed, or restored to life, is expressed in the words "a moment's surrender which an age of prudence can never retract." The meaning of this sacrifice at the Grail chapel, the dread of what may follow, only hinted at here, is given clearer focus by the prediction of the astrologer reported earlier in the poem. "Fear death by drowning." The surrender to feeling, "Your heart would have responded gaily," would have released the rain so sorely needed by the Waste Land. But immediately there arises a fear that once started the rain would not cease till all the world was drowned. A second deluge might be the outcome. Once more this poem shows itself to be a modern version of the moon mysteries.

Winds, floods, fire, these are symbols of emotion, which is essentially a movement of energy. If once let loose in the world these forces of nature may grow and spread, leading one knows not where. They may sweep aside all established rule and order and flood the known civilized world with a deluge which could break all bounds. The rise of instinct released from ancient taboos, the flood of emotion or of ecstasy rising from the unconscious depths of the psyche, the unleashed powers latent in the masses, where these things will stop if once let loose, we cannot tell.[1]

Civilization is characterized by the differentiation of values through which the individual has emerged from the herd and

[1] These words were written in 1933. I leave them in their original form in this second edition because their forecast proved to be so fatally correct. It is one little piece of evidence which demonstrates how insight can be gleaned from myths and the unconscious.

has also extricated himself from the purely collective and instinctive urges within his own nature. This is a selective process of enormous value, for it fosters the growth of the individual with all the advantages that result. In our culture, however, the differentiation has been limited far too much to the realm of intellect, with a consequent neglect of the emotional side of life. The Waste Land of Eliot's poem gives a true picture of a large proportion of individuals as well as of the Western nations in general. The rational attitude to life, with its attempt to control nature in the fullness of her creation and destruction, has resulted in a one-sidedness which threatens to fall over into its opposite. The disregarded emotional factors have accumulated in the unconscious while the conscious attitude has become dry and unsatisfactory on account of the absence of those very elements which have been so strictly eliminated.

The sterility of this arid life can only be cured by the life-giving waters of Eros, of the emotions which have been repressed. But the emotional energy, pent up in the unconscious, may erupt, violently, as Eliot's poem suggests, into our ordered and everyday life. If it does so it will break down the boundaries of the safe and the familiar built up by custom and convention. When such an eruption occurs in an individual life, instead of bringing renewal and fertility it may be a most destructive experience, leading to loss of orientation, to moral or mental dissolution or even to insanity. When such a flooding affects not just an individual here and there but whole communities, perhaps even whole nations, the deluge, instead of rejuvenating the national life, threatens to sweep away all man-made boundaries and to drag the world back into the original chaos out of which human civilizations have been built at so great a cost. Indications are not wanting in the present day that the tides are rising in the unconscious both of individuals and of nations. If these tides break forth violently, a deluge may once more sweep over the world obliterating the achievements of human civilization.

Western culture is threatened in this way because its basis has been too restricted. Large areas of the human psyche not included in the cultural differentiation, have remained relatively or completely unconscious and so have not been developed, nor have their limits been defined. Through the centuries these parts of the psyche have gradually become energized because of the repression of the human values which they represent, and now they are threatening to rise to the surface in a disastrous fashion. Obviously the present need is for differentiation in those realms which have been neglected, so that limits may be defined for the rising tide. To be effective against the uprush from the unconscious the limits imposed will have to be real. Arbitrary bounds, imposed by fear or by the ego and its demands, will be entirely powerless in these circumstances.

When instincts and chaotic images and urges arise from the unconscious in flood proportions they break up human or individual bounds. One thing only can stand against this power of the unconscious and this, paradoxical as it may sound, is the power of the individuality. The term individuality is here used in the sense in which Jung has defined it. It comprises the unconscious as well as the conscious parts of the psyche and so is not synonymous with the ego, which is the center of consciousness only. The ego represents just those human achievements which are being undermined by the flood from the unconscious and so cannot be appealed to for protection in the present danger. The individuality on the other hand takes in more than the conscious side of the psyche, it is indeed never fully conscious but remains a potentiality within the human being. Through inner experiences, such as we have been discussing in the preceding chapters, the individuality is progressively delimited. For these experiences bring to consciousness the lost values of the psyche, which lie so largely in the realm of Eros, and by this means the human being becomes more complete. In the terms of the ancient religions it would be said that through participating in the various stages of the mystery initiations man is born again and becomes a "twice-born" spirit. For when a man or woman submits to the laws or principles of his own being and gives up the personal orientation of the ego he gradually defines the limits of his own nature and the individuality crystallizes within him.

To find the limits or boundaries of one's own nature, however, and to come to know the impersonal principles which really rule in the depths of the psyche necessitates exploring one's own capacities to their uttermost. It is here that the initiation in the temple has its place. For in the service of the goddess, in the realm of the Eros, that is, the emotional experience is not hampered by the restrictions and considerations which must always be taken into account in a personal relationship. In the temple of the goddess the human being, whether man or woman, is face to face with himself, his own instinct, his own emotion. He must experience himself to the uttermost, as the women of ancient Greece or Babylon did in the *hieros gamos*, and the men of Egypt did in the initiation to Isis, where no mental reservation was permitted, no holding back either for fear of the partner's inability to stand the strain or on account of a dread that the initiant, himself, might not be able to face the ordeal. It is by no means unheard of for a postulant to die, in actual fact, or to become insane under the strain of the physical or psychological experience which some primitive religious initiations involve. Indeed initiation ordeals, all the world over, are designed to push the postulant to his limits and are aptly symbolized as a ritual of death and rebirth.

In an ordinary personal relationship, however, neither man nor woman dares as a rule to give himself up completely to the emotional experience. The woman must necessarily be on guard not to arouse the man's instinct beyond the place where she can remain mistress of the situation, for her human concern, as potential mother, is directed towards marriage and the establishment of a home. The man, on the other hand, fears to get caught by just this attitude of possessiveness on her part and, also, he fears to fall under the power of her fascination or, which is perhaps the same thing, to fall under the power of his own unexplored emotion. He dares not let himself go completely but seeks to keep the situation under control and, like the woman, to manage it, in a certain sense, by his conscious ego. And this is a very understandable and indeed wise attitude on the part of both. The possibility, however, of finding their own psychological and emotional limits is precluded by such an attitude for they are both determined to keep well within their limits. In the initiation to the Moon Goddess one of the essentials of the ordeal, in marked contrast to the requirements of a personal relationship, was that the initiant should be pushed right up to his limit. The man was compelled to experience his own Typhonic, or lustful, nature to the end, just as the woman must be prepared to experience her own instinct and desire in the *hieros gamos* without the justification of the man's love for her or involvement with her. Then in the second stage of the initiation the man had to "stand the awe" of the

Goddess in her abandonment of love and grief, so sacrificing his demand that the woman's love for him must be maternal, always considerate of him and his needs, moderated to his powers of endurance, and the woman had to sacrifice her own maternal softness in her sacrifice of the son. If the man is able to endure these ordeals and does not go to pieces, then he is given the Roses of Isis, he partakes of her nature. The power of the Goddess is born within him. He becomes a Moonman, as the woman, through her own ordeal of the *hieros gamos* and the sacrifice of the son, becomes Daughter of the Moon.

In the first stage of the initiation the human being entered the boat of the Goddess and journeyed with her over the floods to the region of the sun, where the cold-blooded desirousness of the watery region is replaced by the warmth and heat of his own emotions. In the second stage, having learned to face the intensity of the emotions which burn within him, by recognizing the nonpersonal character of that which often seems most personal, he is prepared for the next stage of the journey.

Another initiation, another sacrifice, however, is called for before he can take his place in the region of the full moon, ruled over by the Goddess of Perfect Intelligence, where, it is said, he will gain immortality by becoming Master of the Three Worlds. This further stage is only dimly hinted at in the most ancient and archaic religions. But in the Arthurian legends of the Christian centuries it is clearly portrayed in the search for the Holy Grail. There it is told how the seeker, who had found the Grail castle, had to pass a certain test. If he did so the Fisher King would be healed and the Wastelands made fertile again. The test was that, when the sacred objects were displayed before him, he must ask what the wonders he saw meant and whom the vessel of the Grail served. If he failed to ask the question the castle, the king, the Grail, all dissolved as a dream and the lands remained waste, until he or another should once more attain to it, when there was a second chance to ask the question. When Parsifal first reached the Grail castle he was so overwhelmed by awe and wonder at the mysterious procession of the Grail and the Spear and their attendants, that he failed to ask about them. Gawain, likewise, was overcome with sleep at the critical moment, so that he, too, failed to ask their meaning.

Here we see that it is understanding that releases from the paralysis of unconsciousness. To see the images of the unconscious is not enough. Unless we understand their meaning we remain spiritually children, subject to the spell of fate, caught in the net of Isis.

In Oriental texts regarding the soma, drink of the gods, which gives both immortality and inspiration, the same truth is expressed. In the Tantric texts, too, the evolution of consciousness is said to pass from the watery region by means of the crescent to the fiery region of the sun, and from there through the place of air to the full moon. In these texts it is said that he who reaches the full moon "sees the three periods . . . and is long lived," it is the gateway of "great liberation."

The three periods referred to are the past, the present, and the future. They correspond to the three worlds of the moon myths which are there called the underworld, the earth, and the heavens. The deities of the moon were believed to have dominion in each of these three realms, and, as we have seen, the moon god or goddess was often represented as having three aspects or forms corresponding to the three realms over which the deity ruled. Sinn, the triune moon god of Chaldea, was, at one and the same time, Anu, God of the Waters above the Earth, God of the Heavenly Sphere Enlil or Bel, Lord of the Heavenly Earth, Father of the Moon, King of Storms and Master of the Winds; and also Ea, the Primal Ocean, the Ancient Serpent, the Fish God or Leviathan.[2] In psychological terms, he who has attained to the realm of the full, or complete, moon has gained knowledge of the unconscious, as past, source, origin; he has power in this present world; and has insight into the realm of the future. He has become in a certain sense timeless, he transcends the limitations of time. He has gained immortality.

The immortality promised by the moon, however, is not an unending life in a golden city, where there is no night and where everything continues for ever and ever, changeless, completely revealed, bathed in unending light. The immortality promised by the moon is something of very different character. It is not a continuation in a state of perfection, but is an ever-renewed life like the moon's own, in which diminishing and dying are as essential as becoming.

In this world, at all events, the process of life consists in a

2 For further examples see Chapter 16, p. 218.

rhythmic increase followed by decrease, and not in a progress proceeding in one direction only. This principle of life is clearly recognized by the Orientals. To the Chinese it is symbolized by the Tai-gi-tu, the fish-bladder emblem, in which the light is as a seed in the dark, and the dark grows again and replaces the light. This is the basic principle embodied in their sacred Book of Changes, the *I Ching*, which represents their most ancient and profound religious philosophy. To the Hindus, too, the rhythmic alternation of life and death is a fundamental religious teaching. To them the Great Lord Shiva is manifested through his female counterpart, Shakti, in the phenomena of this world, which unfold themselves in all their multiplicity and are then indrawn into the godhead once more. Shakti, the mother, becomes Kali the Destroyer, and Shiva dances his world into destruction and nothingness as he had formerly danced it into being. In the myths of the moon, both primitive and ancient, the same rhythm of creation and destruction, which together form the life process, are accepted as the basis for immortality.

Here in the Occident we recognize too little the essential nature of this change. We rarely reflect how necessary it is that all things should wear out and decay. We forget that it is not in our creations, the things we make, the order we establish, but in our *functioning* that life is fulfilled in us. The important thing as far as we personally are concerned is that we should each create something which did not exist before, not in order that some new good thing should exist in the world, but that, by taking the raw material of life, which lies all about us, and by breathing our life into it and making of it a living creation, we should unfold the latent power of creator which slumbers within us, for this is our most godlike faculty. We realize this as the aim of our education, at least modern schools do so. There the teacher is not only the kind beneficent mother but the impersonator also of the destructive aspect of life, for she laboriously takes to pieces each night the created products of the children, restoring the sand of the child's mountain to the bin and the clay of his cups and bowls to the lump, in order that tomorrow he may again create. It would be no sort of an education to permit successive generations of children to use up all the sand, all the clay, fixing them permanently in created objects, so that subsequent students would have no room to exercise their own capacities but would be condemned, instead, to the contemplation of the works of their predecessors.

If death and decay had not been endowed with power as great as the forces of creation, our whole world would, by this time, have reached the pitiful state of stagnation and completeness pictured above in the hypothetical kindergarten, where the evil, the black, the destructive side of life was imagined to have been excluded. If everything remained forever as it was first made, all capabilities for "making" would have been exploited centuries ago. Life by now would have reached a standstill. And so, all unexpectedly, excess of good falls over into its opposite and becomes excess of evil. This condition of standstill corresponds to the stagnation pictured in the Assyrian poem relating how it was with the world when the Lady Ishtar was absent in the land of No-Return. It is also the condition of the world in the Grail legends where the sickness of the Fisher King is reflected in his country which has become the Wasteland.

It is relatively easy to see how necessary death and decay may be in the long sweep of the centuries. It is harder to admit the truth of the principle as applied to our own activities, and it is more difficult still to understand the meaning of this kind of immortality when it is applied to our individual lives in this world. We hate to see our work die. We tend to identify ourselves with our creation and feel that anything which threatens that strikes subtly at our being. But it is still harder to accept the fact that we ourselves must die, and we are apt to feel that a promise of immortality which carries with it the necessity of death is but a travesty and a mockery.

It is difficult to realize that the importance of a work is not comprised in the value of the finished product but in the psychological development which was achieved as gradually there came into being a real, an actual, entity, which formerly had no existence, and whose conception, whose birth, arose out of the hidden depths of the psyche. Similarly, it rarely occurs to us that our conscious personal life is but the creation, the work of some psychic "creator," actor, doer, whatever it may be called, functioning unknown to us in some hidden place of our being. Surely it was to this truth that St. Paul referred when he said "Not I live, but Christ liveth in me." A similar sense of "being lived" has been the experience not only of the religious, though many have borne witness to it in that realm, but also of others, men of genius or of outstanding personality, who testify to the inner sense of being directed by a voice or an inner presence which controls their actions and lives through them, subordinating their personal lives and personal concerns to its superior claims. Our works may die, while we live on, changed by the fact of having created. Is it not possible that this is a parable, an *analogy*, dimly hinting at a deeper and more important truth? The ego, the conscious personality dies, but we do not know and cannot even guess what happens to the "doer," the "creator," behind the scenes.

The inspiration or the germ, for a creative work, for a child of the imagination, comes, not from man's conscious thought, but arises from the hidden deeps of his being. The inspiration seems, indeed, to its so-called author to have an existence in its own right, to have pre-existed before he happened upon it. All truly creative impulses have this peculiar quality. The artist, the creative workman, or creative thinker, in whose work such an impulse is embodied, did not invent his idea. To him, it seems rather that he discovered it, that it arose in him often from depths which most men prefer not to explore. We have already spoken of modern art creations and their concern with the dark things of that *sinister*, "left," and of modern social movements, whose trend is towards the realms rejected and despised by our immediate predecessors. These things are instances of the stirring in this modern masculine, rational civilization of the dark, feminine principle symbolized by the moon.

It might be well to pause here and consider the attempts which early man made to represent this cyclic, changing character of the moon, so that we may glean, perhaps, a deeper understanding of the archetypal significance it embodied.

16

THE CHANGING MOON

From quite early times we find attempts to represent the cyclic changing character of the moon by the religious symbols that are used. The essential quality of the moon could not be represented by any single or static emblem. As we have repeatedly seen, the alternating bright and dark phases might be represented by portraying the moon god or goddess as alternately black and fair. But the moon cycle was not adequately expressed by this duality alone. The crescent moon was felt to be essentially different from the full moon as well as from the dark moon. These three aspects were sometimes represented by two crescents and a circle or disc. Again on a coin of Megara, three crescents are arranged in a sort of primitive swastika; similar crescents are seen on a coin from Mesopotamia, which represent "Hecate-Triformis." (Figure 33.) These coins form a link to many other representations of the moon goddess as threefold. Again and again the deity is represented not by one pillar, or one tree but by three. In the Phoenician stelae reproduced in figure 35 we see three pillars of unequal height, with the moon above them. This clearly represents the three aspects of the moon cycle. In another very beautiful picture the moon deity is represented by three pillars surmounted by crescents (figure 36). In the catacombs a symbolic drawing frequently appears which is entitled "The Kingdom of Heaven." It consists of three pillars, or three buds, with the crescent moon above them. (Figure 37.) In a picture taken from Lajard's collection (figure 38) are three little altars. On the first is a stone or cone marked with a cross and surmounted by a crescent. On the central one is a similar cross-marked stone but this is surmounted by bull's horns, while the third altar is occupied by a hound. These altars must represent the three phases of the moon. The cres-

Fig. 33   Fig. 34   Fig. 35

Fig. 36   Fig. 37

Fig. 38

Fig. 39

Fig. 33. Coin of Mesopotamia entitled "Hecate Triformis." *Fig. 34.* Coin of Megara. Three crescents represent the three aspects of the moon. (Figs. 33 and 34 from *The Migration of Symbols,* Goblet d'Alviella, 1894. By permission of Constable & Co., London. *Fig. 35.* Phœnician Stela, the Moon Deity represented in triune form. (From *Themis,* Jane Harrison, 1912. By permission of The Cambridge University Press and The Macmillan Company.) *Fig. 36.* Phœnician Moon Emblem. (From *A New System or Analysis of Ancient Mythology,* Jacob Bryant, 1774.) *Fig. 37.* A symbol found on the walls of the catacombs, entitled "The Kingdom of Heaven." *Fig. 38.* The Moon Deity in triune form. Three little altars are shown side by side. On the first, a cross-marked stone crowned with a crescent represents the waxing moon; in the centre, a similar cross-marked stone is surmounted by horns to represent the full moon; on the third, the dark or waning moon is represented by one of the "Hounds of Hecate." (From *Sur le Culte de Mithra,* Felix Lajard, 1847.) *Fig. 39.* "Hecate Triformis." (From *Religions de l'antiquité,* Georg Frederic Creuzer, 1825.)

217

cent is the waxing moon, the horns stand for the moon in its full power and the hound symbolizes the dark aspect.

The dog or hound is a frequent symbol for the moon. The connection between Isis and the Dog Star was mentioned in a former chapter. This dog of the moon is sometimes represented as three-headed. In Greek mythology, Hecate, the dark moon, is always accompanied by baying hounds. As Hecate Triformis she is represented as the three-headed dog, a reminder that in ages long past she, herself, was the dog of the moon. Her triune quality is represented also in later statues where she appears as a threefold woman. One of these statues is pictured in figure 39. Often she carried with her the dog which once she was, or she bears the torch which is emblematic of the moonlight which is her power of fertility and her special gift. In later times the Threefold Hecate took on a conventional form like a pillar, called a Hecaterion. (Frontispiece.) Often the statue of the moon goddess is crowned with a turretted headdress, which represents her threefold dominion, or she carries three emblems in her hands, "to signify," says Knight, "the triple extension of her power . . . in heaven, on earth, and under the earth." [1]

Sinn himself was triune (see figure 21), and the moon goddess who replaced him, was represented by the Three Holy Virgins. Islam has accepted these same three holy virgins and incorporated them into the religious system of the Prophet as the Three daughters of Allah, a device by which at least the appearance of monotheism is preserved.

These daughters of Allah retain the ancient names of the three aspects of the Arabian moon goddess. They are Al-Ilat; Al-Uzza; and Manat. These names are interesting. We have already spoken of Al-Uzza. She *was* the black stone which is still venerated at Mecca. The word Manat stands for "time" in the sense of "fate," it is equivalent to the Hindu concept of karma. The word "mana" which derives from it is commonly used by the Arabs in the sense of *luck*.[2] The threefold character of "luck" or fate is a common concept, it is parallel to "past, present, and future," or in mythological terms the rule of the underworld, the earth, and the heaven. Noldeke suggests that in this respect

[1] R. P. Knight, *The Symbolical Language of Ancient Art and Religion* (New York, 1892), p. 101.

[2] R. Briffault, *The Mothers* (New York and London, 1927), III, 81.

the threefold Arabian goddess is identical with the Greek Moirai, the Fates, and the Nordic Norns, all of whom being goddesses of fate or fortune are threefold in character.[3]

Other triune goddesses of the moon are to be found elsewhere. We would note here the Celtic Bridgets, representing three aspects of the Moon Goddess, Brigentis. These three Bridgets of Ireland are the same as the Three Ladies of Britain, who are phases of the great Celtic Mother Anu, or Annis, the moon, whose shrines are scattered all over Ireland, Wales, England, and France. In Southern France, Anu was known as The Shining One. She was patron of fertility, of fire, poetry, and medicine. But she had another side; she was also known as Black Anu,[4] who, in common folklore, devoured men or turned them into lunatics.

The correspondence between this Celtic moon goddess in all her attributes and the Magna Dea of the East is extraordinary, and would be completely inexplicable were we not beginning to realize that the facts of mythology, discredited as fiction by rational science, are today being re-established as *facts* of the unconscious, that is of the psyche.

When Christianity was introduced into countries where up to that time this threefold goddess had been revered, her worship was assimilated, as we have seen, into the Christian system. The idea of the threefold nature of the feminine divinity was present in the legends of the three Maries. So in Chartres Cathedral, the Virgin Mary is accompanied by Mary Magdalene and Mary the Gypsy. In Ireland the Three Bridgets are accepted by the Catholic Church and their shrines are considered to be wonder-working. But this assimilation did not take place entirely without protest. Saint Augustine in an attempt to bring discredit on the worship of Artemis writes, "How can a goddess be three persons and one at the same time?"—surely a strange question for a Christian Father to ask.

The triune aspect of the Greek moon goddess is discussed by Jane Harrison in its relation to the earliest divisions of time. Miss Harrison suggests that the month was formerly divided in

---

[3] T. Noldeke, "Arabia (Ancient)," Hastings' *Encyclopaedia of Religion and Ethics* (New York and Edinburgh, 1908), I, 659.

[4] J. A. MacCulloch, *The Religion of the Ancient Celts* (Edinburgh, 1911), pp. 41, 68, and "Celts," Hastings' *Encyclopaedia of Religion and Ethics* (New York and Edinburgh, 1908), III, 285.

Greece into three periods of ten days each, corresponding to the three phases of the moon and symbolized by Hecate Triformis, and that this arrangement preceded the division into four periods or weeks.[5] In Babylon and in the Semitic system which was developed from it, the weekly division of the moon month grew out of the observance of the Sabbaths, the taboo days which were kept first at new and full moon and later at each of the quarter phases of the moon.

The changes in the moon's cycle certainly constituted the first means by which primitive man took account of time. Time, for that matter, is still counted in many parts of the world by moons. "Many moons ago" or "a journey two moons long" are ordinary primitive expressions for the passing or the duration of time.

The original concept of the seasonal year was that of a period consisting of twelve moons or months. The months, unlike our present divisions, corresponded to the cycle of the moon; hence the first of the month fell on the day when the lunar crescent appeared. Duration of time was reckoned by nights, not by days. Caesar, for instance, records that the Celts calculated by moons and by nights. We have in our own language remnants of this mode of reckoning in the term fortnight and in the almost obsolete word "senight," meaning seven nights or a week. In one very significant connection we still use the word "moon" instead of "month"; that month which is dedicated to Aphrodite we still call a "honeymoon."

The Celtic calendar was, thus, reckoned by the moon and not by the sun. Even the summer and winter solstices—the time of the sun's change from the point furthest North or from the point furthest South—which we should say belong peculiarly to the sun calendar, were calculated by the Celts from the moon, and were called by the names of the lunar deities. Beltane was the summer, and Samhain the winter solstice. The festival in each case was considered to begin at the rising of the moon. In old France the same reckoning is evidenced by the fact that the solstice was called *la Lunade*. In the lunar calendar of the East the solstice was calculated from the conjunction and opposition of sun and moon, which gave a very accurate count.

In Aryan mythology the moon is the oldest measurer of

---

[5] J. Harrison, *Themis* (Cambridge, 1912), pp. 189–191.

time; in the Babylonian story of creation, also, the moon is the measurer. In the fifth of the "Five Tablets of Creation" it is said:

The moon god he caused to shine forth, to him confided the
  night.
He appointed him a being of the night to determine the days;
Every month, without ceasing, like a crown he made him, saying,
At the beginning of the month, when thou shinest on the land
Thou shalt show the horns, to determine six days,
And on the seventh day thou shalt divide the crown in two.
On the fourteenth day, thou shalt reach the half . . .[6]

In Egyptian mythology the god Thoth, the Measurer or Logos, won from the Moon God the five days which were necessary to change the Egyptian moon calendar into a sun reckoning. In China a moon calendar was still used until recent times and a watcher was appointed to determine by observation when the crescent first appeared. The officials were then notified that a new month had begun. In other countries where the secular calendar has been changed to sun reckoning, a moon calendar is still preserved for religious purposes. Jews, Mohammedans, and Christians calculate the dates of their chief festivals on the basis of a moon reckoning. Easter, for example, falls on the first Sunday following a particular full moon, and many other Church festivals are calculated from Easter.

In the early astronomical calendar of the Babylonians the twelve months were represented by the twelve signs of the zodiac, through which the Sumerians, as long as five or six thousand years ago, had traced the apparent course of the heavenly bodies. The Babylonians called these signs the Houses of the Moon and the whole zodiacal belt, known today as the Great Serpent of the Heavens, they named The Girdle of Ishtar. Month by month the signs of the zodiac pass across the heavens. To us moderns it is the sun who wings his course through them and it is his movement that is represented by the winged disc or by a solar swastika or gammadion. But to the ancients the zodiac was the Girdle of Ishtar, and they expressed the monthly changes in terms of the moon's position in the zodiacal circle. To them the moon was the Winged One, and

6 R. W. Rogers, *Religion of Babylonia and Assyria* (London, 1908), p. 128.

Fig. 40   Fig. 41

Fig. 42

Fig. 40. Moon Swastika from a Cretan coin. (From *The Migration of Symbols*, Goblet d'Alviella, 1894. By permission of Constable & Co., London.)

Fig. 41. Moon Swastikas from Sicilian coins. (From *Symbolical Language of Ancient Art and Mythology*, R. Payne Knight, 1892.)

Fig. 42. The Chariot of the Moon. The crescent moon is here shown being drawn in a chariot by goats. The Goddess Cybele in human form is often seen in a similar chariot replacing the lunar crescent. (From *Sur le Culte de Mithra*, Felix Lajard, 1847.)

Fig. 43

Fig. 43. The Egyptian Moon Boat, within which rests the moon, the crescent holding the full moon within its horns. It is said to be self-propelled, and is guarded in its journey by the two Eyes of Horus. (From *The Dawn of Civilization*, G. Maspero. By permission of The Appleton-Century Co.)

Fig. 44

Fig. 44. Moon Boat from Ur, ca. 2300-2100 B.C. The Moon God is seated in a crescent boat and is paddling himself across the sky. (British Museum, London.)

certain ancient swastikas have been found which have the lunar crescent instead of the solar disc in the center (figure 40). Goblet d'Alviella, who has collected several examples of moon swastikas, considers that they may have represented the revolution or even the phases of the moon, since the equilateral cross has been employed to represent lunar as well as solar radiation, and he states that the swastika has been attributed to the lunar goddesses, whose images they sometimes bear. [7] Among the Hindus the right-handed swastika represents the male principle—light, life, and glory; it is the sun in its daily course from east to west. The left-handed swastika is, on the contrary, the emblem of the goddess Kali; it is the female principle—darkness, death, and destruction. These are four-armed swastikas, based on the equilateral cross; in addition three-armed, or three-legged, swastikas called triskeles also occur, for example, in Sicily and the Celtic countries (figure 41). A three-legged swastika is the official emblem or arms of the Isle of Man, where the Celtic Moon Goddess, under the title of Anu or Annis, was formerly worshipped. The coin represented in figure 33 is inscribed *Hecate Triformis,* a title which at once established its connection with the three phases of the triune moon goddess. Thus these symbols represent the movement of the moon, both in its cyclic changes and also in its nightly journey over the heavens. They represent the journeyings of the moon goddess night by night and also through the twenty-eight days of her cycle.

In other pictures the moon is provided with a chariot in which to make her journey, or more characteristically with a boat, for her journey is a watery one. (See figures 42 and 43.) She is the moist principle, and her wanderings are represented as taking place over rivers or floods. Isis, for instance, travelled in a little boat, when searching for the body of Osiris, while Ishtar and the goddess Nuah who preceded her, built an ark, a crescent boat in which she could carry a few of her children, the seed of all living things, over the flood which she herself had made. The moon boat reproduced in figure 43 is Egyptian in origin. It is said to be self-propelled and it is guarded by the two eyes of Horus, which symbolized the light of the moon. There are also Assyrian pictures showing the moon god (probably Sinn) in a crescent boat, paddling across the sky. The one

[7] Goblet d'Alviella, *The Migration of Symbols* (London, 1894), p. 71.

reproduced in figure 44 comes from Ur and dates from 2300–2100 B.C.

Thus the movement of the moon across the sky was represented as a journey of the god, taken in a boat or chariot, while in other cases the moon itself was thought of as flying or rolling across the heavens. The movement was then represented by giving the moon wings, as in the Assyrian picture reproduced in figure 16, or legs as in the swastikas in figure 41.

Closely related to the swastika is the Buddhist wheel or chakra which represents the circling of the heavenly light. In the Brahmanical series the chakra is stated to be the moon, not the sun. An early Buddhist text reads: "The heavenly treasure of the Wheel . . . appeared to the king on the day of the full moon." That the wheel symbolizes the moon and not the sun presumably belongs to the thought of early Western antiquity, Assyria, and Egypt, which preceded the Indo-Iranian system. In that pristine cosmic myth of the evolution of light from the darkness of chaos, the moon was conceived as the luminary most closely associated with darkness and as traversing not only the sky but the waters of the deep under the earth.[8] In the *Vishnu Purana* a creation myth is recorded to this effect: Varuna caused the cosmic ocean to be churned, much as milk is churned. The solid coagulum which appeared as a result of the churning gave the Seven Gems of which the chakra or wheel with its thousand spokes, namely the Moon, was the first that arose. The soma, which is the *Spirit,* the drink of the gods which bestows immortality, was the last. Soma was so closely associated with the moon that in the *Rig-Veda* soma often means moon. Thus spirit comes from the moon as does also mind. In many languages the word for mind is cognate with the word for moon, showing that this association of mind and spirit with the moon is not confined to Indian thought. For instance, our own word mental is derived from the Latin *mens,* which means moon, while the root *men* is found as well in *mensura,* measure, and in *mensis,* month, and the word lunacy itself comes from the French lune which also means moon.

In Buddhist countries the wheel or chakra is twirled for divination and as a means of gaining inspiration. The practice

8 L. A. Waddell, "Jewel-Buddhist," Hastings' *Encyclopaedia of Religion and Ethics* (New York and Edinburgh, 1914), VII, 554.

recalls the original churning of the cosmic ocean which finally produced the soma or mind. It is also closely related to other methods of divination which belonged to the Moon Goddess. The sistrum of Isis it will be recalled was shaken or twirled as a magic means to drive off the enemies of Osiris during the resurrection rites. In certain of her statues, Diana carried the sistrum as her emblem. This musical instrument had a curved form which Knight asserts represents the lunar orbit.[9] Music which is itself associated with the moon, the word muse being cognate with moon, was always recognized as having magic qualities. "Music hath power to soothe the savage breast." Orpheus who possessed this power of music in the highest degree was called Museos, the Moonman.

In the worship of Hecate, the dark moon goddess, whose magic powers were thought to be so exceedingly potent, a similar instrument was used. This was called Hecate's circle. The "circle" consisted of a golden sphere with a sapphire concealed in its center. This was twirled with a thong of oxhide as a means to procure revelation of hidden things. In strange accord with this Greek emblem is the Buddhist saying that "the moon is silver without and a jewel within, cool in both its aspects, inner and outer."

The inspiration or understanding which the Moon Goddess gives is emphasized in many of her titles. The Chinese moon goddess, Shing Moo, is called Perfect Intelligence; Isis is Maat, the Ancient Wisdom; Ishtar sings "To give oracles do I appear, do I appear in Perfectness." In some of the Gnostic systems the Queen of Heaven is the Divine Sophia, the Wisdom. The Holy Ghost, the Spirit, is identical with her and was regarded as the Mother of Christ. The Spirit is represented by the dove—bird immemorial of the Great Goddess; Philo even regards the birds as identical with Sophia, the Wisdom. The moon thus represents the wisdom of nature, of instinct, while the sun signifies consciousness born of man's power to differentiate, to place in order, which is the function of the Measurer who is the Logos. "The effects of the moon," says Plutarch in his *Isis and Osiris*, "are similar to reason and wisdom [that is to say, to magic, knowledge, and art] whereas those of the sun appear to be brought about by physical force and violence."

9 Knight, *op. cit.*, p. 101.

There is, however, a dark side even to this aspect of the moon. For the Moon Goddess not only gives light, that is, understanding or intelligence, but her light may produce darkness, her intelligence may result in confusion. The ecstasy which comes from the soma drink may pass over into madness. She is the giver of knowledge, but this knowledge may be too strange for the man to bear, it may blast the human mind. To be illuminated by the moon (*mens*) produces mind (*mens*), to be struck by the moon (*lune*) produces lunacy.

So Hecate was called Antea, which means Giver of Visions, but she also could strike with madness. Cybele blasted her son Attis with an ecstasy resulting in madness when he fell in love with the king's daughter, and so it goes throughout the whole series of moon goddesses. For inspiration and the confusion of lunacy are not far apart. Genius lies not far from psychic abnormality. For the kind of understanding or inspiration which the moon gives is not rational thinking, it is more akin to the artistic intuition of the dreamer and the seer. An illustration of this point is given in the story of Isis' search for the lost coffin containing the body of Osiris. No one knew where it had gone. Isis got her first hint from the babbling of little children, who had seen the box float by. Her next clue came from the instinct of the dog Anubis, who led her to the place where it had gone ashore. But the box had already been taken away and there was no one to tell her who had taken it. Then she heard a daemon voice which told her what had happened. Childish babblings, the instinct of the animal, and the inner voice guided her in her search.

The inspiration of the moon is often conceived of as conveyed by the soma drink. In the myth cited above of the origin of the soma, it was said to have been formed from the churning of the cosmic ocean, it sprang, that is, from the primordial waters. In other myths the soma is said to come from the fruit of the moon tree. (Figures 20, 6, and 7. *See also* 13.) The moon tree was believed actually to grow on the moon, and to bear a fruit from which the gods brewed the soma drink. This is the divine draught to which they owed their wisdom and their immortality. But the moon tree also had its counterpart growing on earth, which is likewise called soma.[10] It is found in northwest India, and from it is prepared a sort of wine, having narcotic

10 The soma plant is probably Asclepias Acida, or Sarcostemna Viminale.

and intoxicating properties. It is used in a religious rite of communion with the divine spirit. E. Washburn Hopkins writes:

"Before the end of the Rigveda period the yellow soma plant (which was plucked by moonlight and bathed in water and milk and which also had the property of 'swelling' as it was thus 'purified') became esoterically identified with the yellow, swelling, and water-cleansed moon." [11]

The gods drank the soma of the heavenly tree and gained immortality thereby. In the Hindu soma-ritual, men drink of the earthly soma and gain thereby an ecstasy which identifies them with the gods; for they are filled with the spirit, the manas. A similar method of producing ecstasy by partaking of intoxicating drugs has been used in many religions; *hoama*, for instance, was used in the Zoroastrian rites; wine in the Dionysian mysteries; the peyotl drug in certain North American cults; and the intoxicant *Octli* in Mexico and Peru, while it must not be forgotten that wine is also used in the Christian sacrament. Of *hoama* it is said in the *Avesta*, the sacred book of the Zoroastrian religion, that it gives heaven, health, long life, and power against evils, and victory against enemies. *Hoama* is especially sought by young maidens in search of good husbands, by married women desirous of becoming mothers, and by students striving after knowledge. The *Avesta* states "I, Hoama, who am holy and keeper away of death, am not a protector of the sinful." In the *Satapatha-Brahamana* it is said that the cup of soma is no other than speech. "And indeed the Cup of Soma is also the mind." The Hindu women of Maharashtra perform the ceremony of soma-vati, which consists in circumambulating the sacred fig tree whenever the new moon falls on Somavara which is Monday, our own moon-day. In the Gnostic mysteries it is said that the Heavenly Horn of Men is the drinking vessel in which the king drinketh and divineth. Men, it will be recalled, was the Phrygian moon god.

The use of such drugs for religious purposes is remote from our conceptions of what constitutes religion, for religion to us has become almost synonymous with ethic. But under the influence of these intoxicants the worshipper, in these more

[11] E. Washburn Hopkins, "Soma," Hastings' *Encyclopaedia of Religion and Ethics*, XI, 686.

emotional rituals, gained a release from his everyday self. He experienced an exalted state of consciousness, which often mounted to ecstasy. He was filled with the god and lived for the time being in a spiritual union with the divine spirit. In this ecstatic state he experienced the "feeling of immortality."

Not only where the belief in the moon tree and the soma drink holds sway but among countless tribes and peoples of the earth, the moon is considered to have both immortal life and the power of conferring the boon on her worshippers. Prayers are addressed to her in such terms as the following: "As the moon dieth and cometh to life again, so we also having to die, will live again" (California Indians); "Even if people say to me, 'would that he die,' may I do just as thou doest, may I rise again like the moon" (Takelan Indians); "May the gods give me a life which, like the moon, is renewed every month" (ancient Babylonians); "May I renew my life as thou art renewed" (women of Loango); "He is risen! God has made thee rise again; God make all of us rise again" (Christian women of Abyssinia). Among the Bushmen there is a tradition that the moon herself sent a message to their people through the tortoise: "Go and give men this message from me. Tell them that as I dying live, so they dying will live again." Among the Tanala tribes of Madagascar there is a myth which tells how the first men were given the choice of dying like the moon, and, like the moon, living again; or of dying, like the banana tree, altogether, but with the opportunity of propagating their species, as the banana tree propagates by its roots. The first parents chose to propagate and die like the banana tree, and lost their opportunity to become immortal like the moon.[12]

Thus the moon is the giver of many gifts. She bestows inspiration, ecstasy, magical power, and immortality. In the Upanishads it is said that the moon *is* magical power, the mind, the manas.[13] And "When this manas [mind] was redeemed from death it became the moon." [14] In this text is expressed the connection between the magical power of the moon and immortality.

The two greatest miracles of life are gifts of the moon. She is the giver of fertility, that is, of rebirth through the offspring;

12 Briffault, *op. cit.*, II, 641–673.
13 Vedanta Upanishad.
14 Brihadaranyaka Upanishad, 1, 3, 16.

and beyond that she is considered also to be the giver of individual immortality. The Madagascan myth states that a choice is offered to man between immortality and propagation. An ancient Hindu text seems to agree with this idea. It reads: "Knowing this, the people of old did not wish for off-spring. What shall we do with offspring, they said, we who have this Self and this world (of Brahman) . . . This great unborn Self, undecaying, undying, immortal, fearless, is indeed Brahman." [15] And again: "All who part from this world or this body, go first to the moon, by their lives his waxing half is swelled and by virtue of his waning part he forwards their rebirth. But the moon is also the door to the heavenly world, and who can answer his questions, him he sends beyond." [16] In Persian, Hindu, and Egyptian literature the moon is represented as the place where the soul goes after death. On the moon the soul is judged and goes either to the upper world or back to the earth in a fresh incarnation. On the moon barge the dead travel to the underworld and await there their regeneration; thus Ishtar, the moon goddess, was known as the Ship of Life who bears the seed of all living things.

The moon is the *Place of Generation;* for she is Giver of Fertility; she is the *Place of the Dead,* for it is to the moon that they go when they leave the earth; and she is also the *Place of Regeneration,* for she gives both rebirth and immortality.

We cannot end our brief review of the symbolism of the moon more appropriately than by recalling the picture of the Indian mothers of Mexico holding up their babies to the new moon and beseeching Mother Moon to grant the children an ever-renewed life like her own. The renewal of the sacred fire symbol of the ever-renewed light of the moon, say the Hindus, assists in the renewal of life: "along with the renewal of his fires does the sacrificer renew himself; and beneficial to life, indeed, is that redemption of his own self." [17]

[15] Brihadaranyaka Upanishad, 4, 4, 22 and 25.
[16] Kaushitaki Upanishad, 1, 2. Translated from a German version.
[17] Satapatha-Brahamana.

17

INSPIRATION AND THE SELF

We have dealt at some length with the moon's gift of immortality. In the legend of the soma we find records of yet another gift, namely, inspiration or ecstasy, which leads on to the final initiation of the moon, that is into a higher stage of consciousness. This new condition comes, however, not from the Logos, the brightness of mind, or intellect, but from the unconscious.

For the inspiration of the moon comes, the myths relate, from the dark moon and from the soma drink brewed from the moon tree. It is not embodied in rational thought but in dark obscure movements, in thoughts and impulses of darkness, intoxicating like the soma drink, producing an enthusiasm which may even lead to madness. To eat the soma, or to drink the soma drink was to partake of the food of the gods, to become godlike and to share in those attributes which distinguish the gods from the mortals. These attributes are the power to transcend death, to be immortal, and the power to create, to make that which had not being before. These two gifts are bestowed by the soma drink.

In the Hindu teachings about the soma it is said: ". . . the moon. That is Soma, the king. They are food of the gods. The gods do eat it." [1] In another translation this text reads: "King Soma, he is the food of the Gods that Gods eat . . . But they who conquer the worlds (future states) by means of sacrifice, charity, and austerity, go to smoke, from smoke to night, from night to the decreasing half of the moon, from the decreasing half of the moon . . . to the world of the fathers, from the world of the fathers to the moon. Having reached the moon they become food, and then the Devas [the gods] feed on them there,

[1] Khandogya Upanishad 5, 10, 4.

as sacrificers feed on Soma, as it increases and decreases." [2] Another rendering reads: "Just as one eats the King Soma with the words 'swell and decrease' so they are eaten by the gods. . . . This moon is the honey [nectar] of all beings, and all beings are the honey of this moon. Likewise this bright immortal person in this moon, and that bright immortal person existing as mind in the body both are (madhu) [soul]. He is indeed the same as that Self, that Immortal, that Brahman, that All." [3] "The person or spirit that is in the moon on him I meditate. . . . I meditate on him as Soma, the king, the self [Atman] (source) of all food. Whoso meditates on him thus, becomes the self (source) of all food." [4] Or as another translation renders it, "becomes the Self of Nourishment."

The soma is nourishment of the gods, and man, too, can partake of it, thereby becoming part of the Self, the Atman. This is a mystical way of expressing the belief that through this ritual there develops within the worshipper a self which is not his personal ego, but is nonpersonal, partaking of the qualities of the divine self or Atman. This self is unique, it is said to be "free from all the pairs of opposites," "it never bends the head to anyone," "it is immovable and homeless." [5] Jung has called this nonpersonal, nonego, self the individuality, and I must refer the reader to his works for most illuminating discussions of the whole subject.

The ancient teachings about the moon state that this "self" develops in that individual who has undergone the required initiations to the moon deity, or, as we might say in psychological terms, who has related himself to the feminine principle. The "self" possesses those qualities which alone can stand against the inflooding of the chaotic unconscious. For it is said that the self is immovable, it is homeless, that is to say it is not dependent on being established or conditioned, its strength is in itself; one might also say its strength lies in its being itself. It is that which it is, and nothing else. "It never bends the head to anyone." The ritual of the soma drink was believed to have power to put the worshipper in touch with this aspect of his psyche, the eternal, immovable, reality of Self.

[2] Brihadaranyaka Upanishad 6, 2, 16.
[3] Brihadaranyaka Upanishad 2, 5, 7.
[4] Kaushitaki Upanishad 4, 4.
[5] Mahabharata, Anugita XLIII.

In drinking the soma the initiant gave himself up to be filled with the god. He knew that he would lose his personal, conscious control. He would become the prey of whatever thoughts or inspirations came to him out of the unknown. His mind would be the playground of strange thoughts, of inexplicable feelings and impulses. He would experience an intoxication, an ecstasy, which he believed to be a possession by god. Even those who think of God as all-good, a loving father, a beneficent spiritual being, might still hesitate before handing themselves over to His power in this way and renouncing their personal self-control through the influence of the soma drink. Even the boon of the renewal of life, which the soma is believed to give, might not be sufficient to induce them so to lay aside their personal autonomy. How much greater a sacrifice was demanded of those worshippers who believed that God, like the moon, was black as well as white, destructive as well as creative, cruel as well as kind. How great an act of devotion was needed can be sensed only when we contemplate giving ourselves up to the daemonic influence which arises within our own psyches. For in actual fact we find that the belief in the unity of the one good God is little more than an intellectual formula, counterbalanced by the theory that man is the victim of original sin which will arise spontaneously within him if he relaxes his control for a moment.

What it means, psychologically, to drink the soma and allow the inner voice of the daemon to speak within and take over the control for a space, Jung has discussed in his essay on the *Becoming of the Personality*. To dare to listen to that inspiration from within which voices the ultimate reality of one's own being requires an act of faith which is rare indeed. When the conviction is borne in upon one that anything which is put together, or made up, has no ultimate reality and so is certain to disintegrate, one turns to one's own final reality in the faith that it and it alone can have any virtue or any value. Jung has used the Greek word *pistis* to express the kind of faith that is needed. *Pistis* signifies a religious devotion, which has little in common with an intellectual credo or belief. It is faith in, or devotion to, the rightness, the wisdom of that inner spark which speaks and functions of itself, quite apart from our conscious control. This wisdom was called the Divine Sophia. The Greek word *sophos* means wisdom and Sophia is a personification of wisdom, the Lady Wisdom, or the Goddess Wisdom. She is the highest incarnation of the feminine principle, the Moon Goddess in her function of spirit, divine knowledge. The moon goddesses were, in the majority of cases, considered to be the source of knowledge and wisdom. The words used for mental activity are associated in many languages, it will be recalled, with the names of the moon or of the moon deities, while in many cases the name for the moon deity meant far more than mental activity. Plato, for instance, says that the ancients signified the Holy Lady by calling her Isia and also Mental Perception and Prudence, for the Greeks believed that the name Isis was cognate with *Isia* which means knowledge. The etymology is probably incorrect but the comment shows that to the Greeks of Plato's time the goddess Isis was goddess of knowledge. The robe of Isis, Goddess of Wisdom, concealed, it will be recalled, the deepest revelation, and Shing Moo, the Chinese moon goddess, is called Perfect Intelligence, while the Virgin Mary, Moon of our Church, is also the bearer of Perfect Wisdom. To the Gnostics of Greece and Egypt, Sophia was the Divine Wisdom, the female form of the Holy Spirit. Devotion to, or faith in, this wisdom is the one motive which can make it possible for a human being, whether man or woman, to listen to his inner voice, relinquishing his own autonomy and resigning himself to the inflow of the dark powers of the moon, through partaking of the drink of soma.

The ritual of the soma drink was, however, highly prized by the initiants and brought them the priceless gifts of which we have been speaking. Their confession was:

> We've quaffed the Soma bright,
> And have immortal grown;
> We've entered into light,
> And all the Gods have known.[6]

The soma drink was believed to bring not only immortality but also inspiration and wisdom. The wisdom it brought was not the outcome of wide knowledge, of great erudition, or of worldly experience, but was rather the wisdom of nature. It is the wisdom that knows without knowing how. A gull, for instance, can soar as no modern glider can. This unconscious

6 Rig-Veda, 8, 48, 3.

233

bird can utilize the winds with their varying currents and velocities, it knows all about areas of high pressure and areas of low pressure without, however, knowing anything about them at all. The bird's unknowing knowledge is a picture of the moon wisdom, which we human beings have so largely bartered for our conscious rationale and exact information. Our information is a priceless achievement but it is after all only a tool of the mind and not the real content of wisdom. Again, to quote from one of the sacred books of India, in the Mahabharata it is said: "The Supreme Lord creates all creatures . . . his mind is in the moon, his understanding dwells always in knowledge." "When the understanding, of its own motion, forms ideas within itself, it then comes to be called Mind." [7] This text agrees with primitive concepts that one of the chief characteristics of the moon is her ability to give men thoughts, ideas, and inspirations "of its own motion." For the moon, *mens*, is mind, not only in the language of many peoples, but in the underlying concept as well. In Hindu thought, moon is King Soma, and soma *is* manas, mind.

The ideas which the moon gives, however, are far from academic thinking, with its power to dissect, organize, and formulate. These aspects of thinking belong to the sun, while from the moon come phantasies, intuitions, and strange ideas, or so primitive men and the cultured people of antiquity as well, believed.

The moon, it was thought, insinuates into man's mind ideas and intuitions which are not at all in accordance with intellectual standards but are strange and bizarre, and, because of the profound truth hidden beneath their unusual form, they may be creatively new. These ideas are filled with a peculiar emotion or with intoxicating delight, like the ecstasy of the soma drink.

Thus the moon stands for that strange kind of thinking which comes and goes apparently with complete autonomy; man's rational laws have no more power to control it than his wishes control the moon's movements high in the heavens. A man can of his own will sit down and think logical thoughts. He can say: "Now I will work on this mathematical problem, or draw up a plan for this or that" and his thinking obeys him.

7 Mahabharata, Mokshadharma Parva cclxxx.

But "moon" thinking goes of itself. It is not under the sway of logic. It will not come when he bids it. It will not go at his command. It does not originate in his head. It rises rather from the lower depths of his being and befuddles his mind, like the intoxicating drink, soma.

Thinking of this kind is despised among us, but it has been highly esteemed in many ages and many civilizations. It is thought to be due to a possession by a divine power. Even in extreme form, as in the case of lunacy (lune is moon), primitives and the ancients thought that a god spoke through the man's delirium. Today in modern art we find again the cult of that which goes of itself. Our artists seek, painstakingly, to express that which is *not* rational and indeed unfolds of its own volition. There is to us, in this twentieth century, undoubtedly a value concealed in the irrational, in that which is not controlled by rational laws. It will be recalled that the wisdom of Isis, when searching for the lost body of the dead Osiris, was represented as coming to her in quite irrational ways. She was first guided by the babbling of little children, then by the instinct of the dog, and lastly by the word of her own daemon voice. These three stages represent ways through which men and women, today, may listen to the voice of the moon wisdom, much as Isis did. The babbling of little children represents, perhaps, taking note of the irresponsible phantasy which flits by beneath the contents to which conscious attention is directed; the instinct of the dog will represent those things that the body, the animal part of the human being, tells one. These intimations are also disregarded in large measure, by the average person, as being too trivial for serious consideration. And thirdly, the inner voice still speaks, although it is usually drowned out by the clamor of personal interests and the insistent demands of the world, during the daytime. It is more easily heard in the dreams and visions of the night.

To pay attention to these things is by no means easy, to do so requires the renouncing of personal autonomy over one's own thoughts for the time being and allowing dark, unknown ideas to take possession of one's mind. Usually a man in whom "moon thinking" arises feels that there is something inferior about the whole process, something uncanny, something not quite clean, by which he is besmirched. He feels that such thinking is not a masculine but a "womanish" sort of thinking; and he may add

235

that women think in that confused way most of the time. But certain women, if they were asked, would say that the thoughts and inspirations which come to them from the depths of their being are likely to be right, can be relied on, and can be acted on with confidence. When a woman thinks in her head as a man thinks, she is often wrong; she is very apt to be deceived by ready-made opinions, to spend her time on side issues; and her thinking, when of this kind, is usually unproductive and uncreative. Ideas formed under the moon, inferior though they may seem to be, yet have a power and compelling quality which ideas originating in the head rarely have. They are like the moon in that they grow of themselves. They demand an outlet; if a suitable one is not provided they may become obsessive and produce, as the primitives would say, "moon madness." For the children of the moon must come to birth just as surely as physical children. And furthermore as the Hindus have said, only when the Understanding of its own motion forms ideas within itself can it be called Mind. When written in this way with a capital letter the Mind refers to the Atman, supreme consciousness, the Self. In other words when one listens to the voice of that nonpersonal factor within one's own psyche one comes into touch with that unique factor within oneself, which the Hindus felt to be part of the Atman, the Self. Through such an experience it is said that the individual's life is renewed by partaking of the ever-renewed life of the moon.

What this may mean to us when the symbols are recognized as symbols and the whole is translated into psychological terms, is hard to say with any certainty. It surely does *not* mean that to give oneself over to the guidance of the unconscious, renouncing all the achievements of consciousness, will give one eternal life. Such a course of action could produce nothing but disintegration, the loss of individuality and, in extreme form, mental unbalance or insanity. To us the ravings of the lunatic certainly do not voice the oracles of divine wisdom. If the strange thoughts and images arising from the unconscious are to have any value at all for us, they have to be interpreted, made available for life, through the mediation of the human understanding. One must ask with the Knight of the Grail legends, "What does it mean?"

Here again, however, the teaching of the mystery religion must be understood in its own terms. For just as the prostitution in the temple was for the average woman a ritual initiation to be experienced once and once only, and was by no means to be a camouflage for a loose or licentious life, so the ritual of the soma drink was an initiation which did not imply that the worshipper was to give up his personal autonomy in matters of everyday life, nor did it justify a life of drunkenness and debauchery. When we translate this into terms of modern life, surely it means that just as every woman needs to experience, once in her life, that personal surrender by which she accepts her own emotion and her own instinct symbolized by the *hieros gamos,* the sacred marriage in the temple of the Goddess, in which the woman of olden times gave herself to her own instinct, sacrificing her demand to possess thereby the man's devotion, so also in a similar way, men and women must experience the voice of their inner daemon, allowing it to speak in them uncensored either by rational thinking or by conventional morality. Through such an experience an individual can become acquainted with the ultimate reality of his own nature. He learns to know his own depths and his own limits.

The religious texts say that such an experience confers the gift of immortality. We do not know, however, how that saying is to be understood today. We know nothing about a life beyond the grave; we do not know whether there is such a thing or not. But we do know that throughout the ages men have borne witness to the fact that initiation experiences, such as these we have been discussing, produce a feeling of immortality. To such people the considerations of this world are seen in a new perspective. They seem in some way, and this is a very real psychological experience, to be released from the absolute conditioning of here and now, as though, while still living in the world and being really in it, they yet see things *sub specie eternitatis,* as from the point of view of eternity. To attain such an attitude is at least a subjective experience of the state of being immortal, whether it implies an unending life after death or not.

There is a passage in one of the Hermetic texts, called Πέπλος, The Veil, which seems to express this point of view. There it is said that the veil "signified the Veil of the Universe, studded with stars, the many coloured Veil of Nature, the famous Veil or Robe of Isis, that no 'mortal' or 'dead man' has raised, for that veil was the spiritual nature of the man himself, and to raise it he had to transcend the limits of individuality, break the bonds of death, and so become consciously immortal." [8]

To raise the Veil of Isis must mean to see Nature as she really is, to understand what it is that underlies the manifestations of this world, and of the emotions which so move us, to see them in their ultimate reality, not veiled any longer by custom or convention, by rationalization or illusion. He who is able to do that and so to face reality, becomes consciously immortal, or perhaps it should read "conscious of immortality," for he has released his mind, himself, from the conditionings of time and space, and especially from the distortions of fact brought about by his own ego orientation. His center of consciousness has shifted from the personal "I" of his ego, to a more disinterested focal point, which embraces in its outlook a larger range and has in consequence a more detached attitude.

This change in psychic focus is so important and far-reaching in its consequences that it is symbolized in the religions of the moon as the attainment of immortality, or as giving birth to the immortal child, the savior. The child born of the initiation to the Moon Goddess is naturally not to be confused with the human child of the flesh. It is a psychic not a carnal child and is the symbol of the new individuality, which is brought to birth through inner experiences like those we have been discussing.

In *The Secret of the Golden Flower* the Chinese teaching in regard to this birth of the Holy Child has been rendered by Richard Wilhelm, while C. G. Jung has given an illuminating psychological commentary on it. There an Oriental method for turning the psychological energy within is described. If the energy is allowed to flow outwards, unchecked, it creates in the outer world, while if it is checked in its outward flowing and turned back towards the center it creates within the individual. The creations produced by the outflowing of the energy comprise all a person's outer activities, work, social relationships, children, a family and home, and so forth. The inner creation produced by the inflowing of the energy is the psychic child, which corresponds to Jung's concept of the individuality.

These ideas occur also in the teachings and hints of the moon religions. The bearing of actual physical children is set over against the power to develop the inner psychic child, who is

8 G. R. S. Mead, *Thrice-Greatest Hermes,* I, 62.

believed to be immortal, because he is beyond the conditioning of this world, existing, indeed, in a realm different from the external or visible universe.

The desire to have physical children is not unrelated to the almost universal desire for immortality. Among primitive peoples and also in the Orient, one of the chief reasons for desiring children is that there may be someone whose duty it is to perform the burial rites and continue the ancestor sacrifices which are believed to keep alive the spirit of the deceased and further it on its journey in the other land. Among many peoples, too, it is felt that the parents gain a certain kind of immortality through their children who carry on the family name and in whose lives the life of the parents is in a way continued.

In certain very early and primitive myths a distinction is made, however, between the partial, or quasi, immortality of a life lived in the person of the child, and a more direct immortality of the individual himself. The idea seems to be that the divine creative spark in man can either express itself in the creation of a human child or, alternatively, it can be assimilated into the individual himself, creating in him a spirit which is immortal. It is not only in primitive myths that this antithesis between immortality and the bearing of children is recognized. In the apocryphal *Gospel to the Egyptians* a conversation is recorded between Christ and a certain woman disciple named Salome as follows: "When Salome asked how long Death should prevail, the Lord said: So long as ye women bear children; for I am come to destroy the work of the Female. And Salome said to Him: Did I therefore well in having no children? The Lord answered and said: Eat every Herb, but eat not that which hath bitterness. When Salome asked when these things about which she questioned should be made known, the Lord said: When ye trample upon the garment of shame; when the Two become One, and Male with Female neither male nor female." [9]

The saying "When the Two become One, and Male with Female neither male nor female" suggests an inner marriage of the male and female parts of the psyche, through which the individual would become whole. If I am right in this reading of the text, the Lord's reply would mean that an inner marriage will give rise to that inner child whose birth brings release from

9 Mead, *Ibid.*, I, 153.

the power of death. This rendering accords with the Hindu saying "What need have we of children, we who have this Self?"

The Self is the fruit of psychic development, the child of the inner or sacred marriage. This idea should be compared with the Chaldean picture reproduced in figure 20. There the fruit of the sacred moon tree is shown to be Sinn, himself, the young or crescent moon, the hero who overcomes the enemy of his father. He is the fruit of the tree. The soma drink, pressed from this fruit, bestows upon the participant divine gifts which he, the divine fruit, possessed. This symbolism is very familiar to us. Adonis was the fruit of the tree, when in his death he was bound upon it; Dionysus was fruit of the vine, whose blood was the wine, drunk by his followers. Christ's death also showed forth the same mystery and the cup of his sacrament held the wine which represented his blood. It was the blood or juice of the fruit of the tree, that fruit which represented the highest development of the tree, which is the tree of life, and whose essence gives immortality. We find the same idea expressed in the symbolism of the rose and the cross, where the rose, Rose of Isis or of the Blessed Virgin, is the flowering of the cross or tree. In the initiation to Isis described by Apuleius, it will be recalled that the postulant by eating of the Roses of Isis, flower of the tree, was released from the bondage of his carnal nature.

This symbolism carries us beyond the point of development of *one* principle of man's being to the correlation of both principles, which in the Gnostic text quoted above was represented as the marriage of Male and Female. The Eros of the feminine principle is here united to the Logos or masculine principle and the fruit of the union, represented by the Moonman, the Hero Child, is the foreshadowing of that Self of which the Hindus speak with such certainty.

To us of the West, these things are mysteries only dimly sensed. We cannot speak of them with certainty, but at the same time we cannot ignore the fact that modern poetry and art and the dreams and phantasies of many people today agree with the myths and religious teachings of the past. The symbols, which appear today, and their development, show that a movement is taking place beneath the surface of consciousness, which resembles in a fundamental way the movements which have been immortalized in the teachings of the past. They tell of a path for renewal which is new in our day but old in actual fact, a path of redemption through the things that are lowest, which is the fundamental teaching of the moon religions, and of the worship of the feminine principle.

In the image of the Mother Goddess—ancient and powerful —women of olden times found the reflection of their own deepest feminine nature. Through the faithful performance of the ritual prescribed in her service those faraway women gained a relation to this very Eros. Today, the goddess is no longer worshipped. Her shrines are lost in the dust of ages while her statues line the walls of museums. But the law or power of which she was but the personification is unabated in its strength and lifegiving potency. It is we who have changed. We have given our allegiance too exclusively to masculine forces. Today, however, the ancient feminine principle is reasserting its power. Forced on by the suffering and unhappiness incurred through disregard of the Eros values, men and women are turning once again towards the Moon Mother, not, however, through a religious cult, not even with a conscious knowledge of what they are doing, but through a change in psychological attitude. For that principle, which in ancient and more naïve days was projected into the form of a goddess, is no longer seen in the guise of a religious tenet but is now sensed as a psychological force arising from the unconscious, having, as had the Magna Dea of old, power to mold the destinies of mankind.

INDEX